Race and Class in the American South Since 1890

Edited by

Melvyn Stokes
and
Rick Halpern

BERG
Oxford/Providence USA

First published in 1994 by
Berg Publishers
Editorial offices:
150 Cowley Road, Oxford, OX4 1JJ. UK
221 Waterman Street, Providence, RI 02906, USA

© Melvyn Stokes and Rick Halpern

All rights reserved.
No part of this publication may be reproduced in any form or by any means
without the written permission of Berg Publishers

Library of Congress Cataloging-in-Publication Data
A catalogue record for this book is available from the British Library

British Library Cataloguing in Publication Data
A catalogue record for this book is available from the British Library

ISBN 1 85973 031 0 (Cloth)
1 85973 036 1 (Paper)

Printed in the United Kingdom by Short Run Press, Exeter.

Contents

Contents

Introduction

Southern history, C. Vann Woodward declared in 1975, "has suddenly emerged in a position of central importance in national history, disclosed more relevance to the history of foreign peoples than any other American field, and attracted more than its share of first-rate talent."[1] Among the reasons for this development were the greatly increased interest in African American history brought about by the civil rights movement, the growing interest of northern historians in the origins of problems once considered exclusively "Southern" and the heritage of the Southern literary Renaissance. Another factor was the growing appreciation by historians of the usefulness of comparing the South not to the North but to other societies which had also undergone the experience of slavery, abolition and experimentation with various forms of tenancy, including sharecropping and peonage. Before the publication of Woodward's article, pioneering studies comparing southern slavery to slavery and race relations in the Caribbean and Brazil had appeared. Subsequently, other works documented comparisons between the American South and Russia or South Africa.[2] Finally, a number of northern cliometricians were attracted to southern themes, especially the history of slavery.[3]

Recent scholarship has undermined many of the traditional ideas and assumptions concerning Southern history. At least until the 1950s, there was a "Southern" interpretation of the history of the region which

1. C. Vann Woodward, *The Future of the Past*, New York, 1989, p. 58.
2. See Frank Tannenbaum, *Slave and Citizen, The Negro in the Americas*, New York, 1946; Herbert S. Klein, *Slavery in the Americas: A Comparative Study of Virginia and Cuba*, Chicago, 1967; Philip D. Curtin, *The Atlantic Slave Trade: A Census*, Madison, 1969; Carl N. Degler, *Neither Black Nor White: Slavery and Race Relations in Brazil and the United States*, New York, 1971; George M. Frederickson, *White Supremacy: A comparative study in American and South African History*, New York, 1981; John W. Cell, *The Highest Stage of White Supremacy: The Origins of Segregation in South Africa and the American South*, Cambridge, Mass., 1982; George Reid Adams, "Comparing the Comparers: White Supremacy in the United States and South Africa," *Journal of Social History*, vol. 20, 1986, pp. 585–99; Peter Kolchin, *Unfree Labor: American Slavery and Russian Serfdom*, Cambridge, Mass., 1987.
3. See Alfred H. Conrad and John R. Meyer, "The Economics of Slavery in the Ante Bellum South," *Journal of Political Economy*, vol. 66, 1958, pp. 95–130; Robert W. Fogel and Stanley L. Engerman, *Time on the Cross: The Economics of American Negro Slavery*, Boston, 1974. For a defense of this latter, much-criticized work by one of its authors, see Robert W. Fogel, *Without Consent or Contract: The Rise and Fall of American Slavery*, New York, 1989.

followed these broad outlines: slavery (a view advanced most notably by Ulrich B. Phillips) had been a benevolent institution that allowed the plantations to be run efficiently while, at the same time, it civilized the African. It had been overthrown in an unjust war.[4] At the end of the war, the victorious north imposed a period of "Black" or Radical Reconstruction on the south. Native whites were disfranchised and southern states humiliated under the corrupt rule of blacks, carpetbaggers, and scalawags. Eventually, the region was "redeemed" under the leadership of the old planter class. Having proved their incapacity both for politics and self-improvement, blacks were disfranchised and segregated. Whites, once divided, united in support of their leaders, who set out to create a "New South" of commerce and industry. With the South now in step with the North, a new pattern of sectional reconciliation arose. The South, in essence, became indistinct from the rest of the nation.[5]

This school of historians stressed continuity, white solidarity, African American contentment, and convergence between the sections. They legitimated, through their work, the aims and interests of the South's leaders, together with its existing social, economic, and political order. They blurred the picture, repudiating or denying the reality of conflict, in order not to spoil their case. Consequently, the first important critics of the "New South" idea sought to restore conflict to the history of the section. They focused particularly on struggles of class or race. An African American intellectual, W.E.B. DuBois, demolished the myth of black ignorance and failure during the course of Reconstruction, destroying in the process a major foundation of the white argument for the disfranchisement of blacks.[6] He also pointed out how racism had been used to prevent black and white workers from exploring their common needs.[7] In his biography of Tom Watson,

4. On the benign view of slavery and the way it developed, see Ulrich B. Phillips, *American Negro Slavery*, New York, 1913, and John David Smith, *An Old Creed for the New South: Proslavery Ideology and Historiography, 1865–1918*, Athens, Ga., 1991; on the war and nostalgia for the Confederacy, see, Douglas Southall Freeman, *R.E. Lee, A Biography*, 4 vols, New York, 1934, and Gaines M. Foster, *Ghosts of the Confederacy: Defeat, the Lost Cause, and the Emergence of the New South 1865 to 1913*, New York, 1987.

5. See John W. Burgess, *Reconstruction and the Constitution, 1866–1876*, New York, 1902; Philip A. Bruce, *The Rise of the New South*, Philadelphia, 1905; William A. Dunning, *Reconstruction, Political and Economic, 1865–1877*, New York, 1907; Claude G. Bowers, *The Tragic Era, The Revolution after Lincoln*, Cambridge, Mass., 1929; Paul H. Buck, *The Road to Reunion, 1865–1900*, New York, 1937; William B. Hesseltine, *Confederate Leaders in the New South*, Baton Rouge, 1950.

6. W. E. Burghardt Du Bois, *Black Reconstruction: An Essay Toward a History of the Part Which Black Folk Played in the Attempt to Reconstruct Democracy in America, 1860–1880*, Philadelphia, 1935, particularly pp. 711–29 on "The Propaganda of History."

7. Ibid., p. 680, 700–1; W.E.B. Du Bois, *The Negro*, New York, 1915, pp. 225–26,

published in 1938, C. Vann Woodward showed how the Populists of the 1890s had rejected white solidarity in order to take on the Redeemers, and cooperated with both African Americans and industrial labor in their crusade for economic justice. A year later, Roger W. Shugg traced the development of class conflict among the whites of Louisiana.[8]

Woodward was also the first to question seriously the idea that a "New South" had arisen from the ashes of the Reconstruction period following the Civil War. He argued that the region had not, in many ways, overcome those peculiar characteristics that had once set it apart and demanded separate treatment from historians. Economically, it continued to differ from the rest of the nation in indices of "per capita wealth, income, and living standards." In some ways, indeed, the South had become even more distinctive a region than had been the case in earlier periods.[9]

The principal causes of the South's distinctiveness were the region's economy, its class structure, and the divisiveness caused by race. A predominantly rural and agrarian society (only in the late 1940s did industrial workers come to outnumber farmers, and it was only in the following decade that most Southerners lived in cities and towns[10]), southern society differed from that in many northern states in the decades after Reconstruction through the nature of its political and economic elite, the relative absence of middle-class professionals, the comparatively small size of its industrial working class, and the presence of two differing underclasses – one black, one white, economically similar but racially distinct – who were mainly sharecroppers and tenant farmers.

Intense debate has centered around the question of the class structure of the postbellum South, with the issue of "planter persistence" being at the core. To what extent did antebellum planters retain their elite status and what new methods did they utilize to maintain economic and political control? C. Vann Woodward argued that the Civil War and Reconstruction had completely destroyed the South's old ruling elite. They were replaced with a new elite of bourgeois entrepreneurs intent

8. C. Vann Woodward, *Tom Watson, Agrarian Rebel*, New York, 1938; Roger W. Shugg, *Origins of Class Struggle in Louisiana: A Social History of White Farmers and Laborers during Slavery and After, 1840–1875*, Baton Rouge, 1939.

9. Woodward, *Origins of the New South, 1877–1913*, Baton Rouge, 1951, ix-x. Woodward later pointed out that the per capita wealth of the South in the 1900s was half the national average, with income forty per cent lower than the national average. C. Vann Woodward, *Thinking Back, The Perils of Writing History*, Baton Rouge, 1986, pp. 65–66. Woodward's work is complemented and extended in Edward L. Ayres, *The Promise of the New South: Life After Reconstruction*, New York, 1992.

10. Jack Temple Kirby, *Rural Worlds Lost: The American South 1920–1960*, Baton Rouge, 1987, xiv.

on modernization and industrial growth.[11] An opposing view, advanced most prominently by Jonathan Wiener, insists that the most powerful group in the South continued to be landowners who opposed industrialism and created a society based on tied agricultural labor. Alabama planters, according to Wiener, turned to sharecropping as a means of preventing a free market in land and labor. In a slight variation, Dwight Billings argues that the old planter elite in North Carolina led in embracing industrialization, seeing the textile industry – specifically the unique social relations of the mill town – as a variant of the old-time plantation and embracing the same tight paternalistic control. Developing the conceptual lead provided by Barrington Moore, Jr., both Wiener and Billings see the South following a "Prussian Road" to capitalism in which an alliance between the agrarian elite and an extremely weak bourgeoisie led to the development of an illiberal political economy.[12]

In the first essay in this book, Alex Lichtenstein refines this argument by pointing to the existence in the South of a genuine, politically potent, industrial bourgeoisie. Men like Henry F. DeBardeleben and J.W. Sloss developed the region's mineral resources without encountering significant opposition from the old planter class. They successfully mobilized the state on their behalf to secure convict labor for their enterprises. Indeed, Lichtenstein argues that coerced labor was a central and defining element in southern industrialization, guaranteeing entrepreneurs a disciplined work force and providing the edge that allowed them to compete with well-advanced northern producers. The "Prussian Road" thus had two forks – one led through the agricultural Black Belt, the other through the South's industrial districts.

Another important way in which the white elite, in both agriculture and industry, maintained and augmented its power was through the manipulation of race. Here, the very flexibility of racial categories, identities and ideologies provided the southern ruling class with a potent tool. Between 1850 and 1915, according to Joel Williamson, a major readjustment occurred in relationships among the three main elements of Southern society: the white elite, the black community, and the white masses. At the start of the period, the white elite had close links with the black population through slavery, and connections that were at best tenuous and uncertain with most whites. By the end, the white elite had

11. See Woodward, *Origins of the New South*, passim, and Sheldon Hackney, "Origins of the `New South' in Retrospect," *Journal of Southern History*, vol. 38, 1972, pp. 194–95.

12. Jonathan Wiener, *Social Origins of the New South: Alabama 1860–1895*, Baton Rouge, 1978, passim, and Wiener, "Class Structure and Economic Development in the South, 1865–1955," *American Historical Review*, vol. 84, 1979, pp. 970–92; Dwight B. Billings, Jr., *Planters and the Making of a `New South': Class, Politics, and Development, in North Carolina, 1865–1900*, Chapel Hill, 1979.

abandoned blacks, destroying their voting power and rendering them "invisible" through segregation, while bonding itself increasingly closely to lower class whites.[13]

Of course, at the same time as the ruling class attempted to buttress its political power through the manipulation of race, other groups in southern society set about fashioning an alternative – and at times oppositional – racial construction. Black tenants and croppers who joined with whites under the Populist banner, white coal miners in northern Alabama who put aside their received prejudices to organise UMWA locals, and longshoremen of both races in New Orleans who cooperated to share jobs and power at the turn of the century, all complicate the picture drawn by Williamson.[14] These examples, and numerous others, highlight the cogent point made by Barbara Fields that racial ideologies are not fixed, immutable phenomena but instead are the products of specific class actors functioning in historically defined contexts. Appreciating that race and class are historically linked and not alternative explanatory categories, historians can look to economic change and the process of class formation to provide clues to the emergence and salience of different conceptions of race.[15]

This viewpoint informs Rick Halpern's essay in this collection. Dealing with what might be called "industrialization from the ground up," he re-examines the attitudes of black and white southern workers towards race and unionism. Surveying recent scholarship, he finds an increasing tendency to reject the position that white

13. Joel Williamson, *The Crucible of Race, Black-White Relations in the American South Since Emancipation*, New York, 1984, p. 512 and passim.

14. Lawrence Goodwyn, *Democratic Promise, The Populist Movement in America*, New York, 1976, particularly pp. 276–306; Philip Taft, *Organizing Dixie: Alabama Workers in the Industrial Era*, Westport, Conn., 1981, particularly chapters 2, 5, and 7; Ronald L. Lewis, *Black Coal Miners in America: Race, Class, and Community Conflict, 1780–1890*, Lexington, 1987; Daniel Rosenberg, *New Orleans Dockworkers: Race, Labor, and Unionism, 1892–1923*, Albany, 1988; Eric Arnesen, *Waterfront Workers of New Orleans: Race, Class and Politics, 1863–1923*, New York, 1991.

15. Barbara J. Fields, "Ideology and Race in American History," in J. Morgan Kousser and James McPherson, eds., *Region, Race, and Reconstruction: Essays in Honor of C. Vann Woodward*, New York, 1982, pp. 143–77. Some scholars, including Richard King in his essay for this book, have criticised the tendency to see race relations "as a function of class relationships rather than as an autonomous form of human interaction." George M. Frederickson, "The Historiography of Postemancipation Southern Race Relations, Retrospect and Prospect," in *The Arrogance of Race, Historical Perspectives on Slavery, Racism, and Social Inequality*, Middletown, Conn., 1988, pp. 155–56. To regard class as real and race as not real, Frederickson argues in a forthcoming essay to be published in a volume by the University of Chicago Press, offers "a theory of social relationship that arbitrarily privileges one form of social inequality over others." If class as a concept arises from the fact that "all societies have economies," race is rooted in the further fact "that all human beings have a sense of family or kinship." Frederickson, "Reflections on the Comparative History and Sociology of Racism."

working class racism has been a constant in American labor history. Although conceding the existence of a strong tradition of exclusionary white craft unionism, he finds a vigorous counter-tradition of biracial – and at times genuinely interracial – organizing. As a result of this new conjunction between Labor and African American History, a more complex portrait of the region's race and class relationships is now emerging.[16]

If the southern working class was not as different from its northern counterpart as previously assumed, it is still beyond dispute that the terrain upon which it struggled was a world removed from the industrial valleys of Akron and Flint. The development of southern industry had not by the twentieth century produced the "diversified industry" Henry W. Grady and other proponents of the "New South" idea thought they could see around them in the 1880s.[17] In 1920, the South was still overwhelmingly rural. Much of it was semi-primitive. Poverty, malnutrition and illiteracy were appallingly widespread. The region was largely without electricity, proper roads or automobiles. Farms were unmechanized, using mules for power and transport; cotton and tobacco sharecropping was the dominant form of agricultural labor among both races.[18] In compensation for these material shortcomings, some historians have argued, the South was characterized by a folk culture of uncommon strength and persistence.[19]

The world of the sharecropper was undermined, and ultimately destroyed, by the processes of modernization, obliging croppers to abandon the land in search of alternative employment. These processes included structural changes wrought by mechanization, the growing use of chemical fertilizers and pesticides, and government intervention in

16. See, for example, Herbert Hill, "Race, Ethnicity and Organized Labor: The Opposition to Affirmative Action," *New Politics*, vol. 1, 1987, pp. 31–82; and Hill's "Myth-Making as Labor History: Herbert Gutman and the United Mine Workers of America," *International Journal of Politics, Culture and Society*, vol. 2, 1988, pp. 132–200.

17. On the supporters of "New South" idea, see Paul M. Gaston, *The New South Creed: A Study in Southern Mythmaking*, New York, 1970.

18. On the primitivism of the rural South, see Kirby, *Rural Worlds Lost*, particularly chapters 3, 4, 5, and 6, and J. Wayne Flynt, *Dixie's Forgotten People, The South's Poor Whites*, Bloomington, 1979, particularly chapter 4 ; on the role of mules in agriculture, see Robert Byron Lamb, *The Mule in Southern Agriculture*, Berkeley, 1963; on sharecropping, see Arthur F. Raper, *Preface to Peasantry: A Tale of Two Black Belt Counties*, Chapel Hill, 1936, and Theodore Rosengarten, *All God's Dangers: The Life of Nate Shaw*, New York, 1975.

19. See I.A. Newby, *Plain Folk in the New South: Social Change and Cultural Persistence, 1880–1915*, Baton Rouge, 1989; Flynt, *Dixie's Forgotten People*, chapter 2; Allen Tullos, *Habits of Industry: White Culture and the Transformation of the Carolina Piedmont*, Chapel Hill, 1989, passim.

the form of agricultural education and subsidies.[20] A little-studied aspect of this transformation has been the role of law. Pete Daniel, in his contribution to this book, maintains that, until the New Deal, courts in the southern states mediated class tensions within and across racial lines. The judicial process partially protected the property rights of sharecroppers of both races vis-a-vis white landowners. New Deal agricultural policy effectively destroyed this buffer, replacing state law with federal regulation and concentrating power in the hands of local AAA committees. White landlords used their control of these local committees to circumscribe the rights of tenants and sharecroppers, thus injecting their own ideas of race and class into federal policy. In alliance with federal bureaucrats in Washington, they discriminated against small farmers through the system of allotments and federal subsidies. Their racism showed itself in decisions affecting African American farmers, and the lack of African Americans on local committees and within the US Department of Agriculture itself. The destruction of sharecropping, as documented by Daniel and others, can thus be seen as a result of government policy rather than a consequence of an inexorable process of "modernization."[21] It was, moreover, a policy implemented without taking account of any local protest by black or white sharecroppers.

The two essays after Pete Daniel's are presented as commentary on his main thesis. Far from there being a change from legal decisions defending sharecroppers' rights to federal rules designed to undermine them, Martin Crawford argues, the white landlord-merchant elite consistently maintained its class control, only changing tactics once the New Deal began. Its dominance over the judicial process showed itself in the courts' determination to uphold contract labor and anti-enticement laws, and in the marked reluctance of sharecroppers and other tenants to seek legal remedy for their grievances. Crawford emphasises more than Daniel the racism of post-New Deal agricultural policy. African American cropping declined at a much faster rate to that of its white counterpart. While racial discrimination was in the process of being challenged by the civil rights movement, it survived in southern agriculture as a consequence of collusion between federal bureaucrats and the white landlords serving on agricultural committees.

William Beinart's essay belongs to a growing tradition of compari-

20. On the transformation of southern agriculture, see: Pete Daniel, *Breaking the Land: the Transformation of Cotton, Tobacco, and Rice Culture Since 1880*, Urbana, 1985; Gilbert S. Fite, *Cotton Fields No More, Southern Agriculture, 1865–1980*, Lexington, Kentucky, 1984; Kirby, *Rural Worlds Lost*, chapters 1 and 2.

21. Nicholas Lemann, for example, argues that it was the invention of the mechanical cotton-picker that destroyed the sharecropping system, forcing many blacks to migrate to northern cities. See Lemann, *The Promised Land: The Great Black Migration and How It Changed America*, New York, 1991, pp. 3–7.

son between the American South and rural society in South Africa. He maintains that South African sharecropping was a far more flexible phenomenon than in the United States. It was also easier to escape and, partly in consequence, less oppressive. Primarily a black phenomenon, cropping appealed mainly to Africans eager to accumulate wealth in the form of animals. Its decline, he argues, had less to do with such racially inspired legislation as the Native Land Act of 1913 than with economic depression and the consolidation of landholding, technological change and mechanization, and the growing mobility and collapse of authority within extended African families. Beinart raises questions that are of relevance to the American South about the changing nature of judicial appointments, the extent of technological change before the depression of the 1930s, and the manner in which the actions of sharecroppers themselves affected the institution.

The last essays in this volume deal with the consequences of, and responses to, the policy of segregation adopted by the white South. The early twentieth century saw the introduction of legal segregation. Before 1900, C. Vann Woodward points out, most Southern states had Jim Crow laws applying only to transportation on trains. Thereafter, states passed a variety of statutes segregating street cars, workplaces, hospitals, prisons, parks, and recreational facilities.[22] Starting with Mississippi in 1890, states also began – through a variety of legal strategems – to disfranchise African American voters.[23] The rationales advanced to justify these measures were primarily cultural. They revolved around the innate "inferiority" of African Americans, as "proven" by Darwinian ideas, science, and eugenic theory, and their political incapacity, demonstrated through the failure of "Black" Reconstruction.[24] The defenders of white supremacy advanced the supposed primitivism and wanton sexuality of African American males as the principal justifications for lynching and the use of racial violence.[25]

The acceptance of these cultural stereotypes, as Valeria Lerda argues in her essay, limited the content and diminished the scope of southern

22. C. Vann Woodward, *The Strange Career of Jim Crow*, 3rd rev. ed., New York, 1974, pp. 97–100. Segregation had a de facto existence in much of the South, Howard Rabinowitz argues, before it came to be formalized into law. See Rabinowitz, *Race Relations in the Urban South, 1865–1890*, New York, 1978.

23. On the process of disfranchisement, see J. Morgan Kousser, *The Shaping of Southern Politics: Suffrage Restriction and the Establishment of the One-Party South, 1880–1910*, New Haven, 1974.

24. I.A. Newby, *Jim Crow's Defense: Anti-Negro Thought in America, 1900–1930*, Baton Rouge, 1965; on Darwinism in general, see Richard Hofstadter, *Social Darwinism in American Thought*, New York, 1944, passim.

25. Forrest G. Wood, *Black Scare: The Racist Response to Emancipation and Reconstruction*, Berkeley, 1968; Williams, *The Crucible of Race*, chapters 4, 5, and 6.

white women's efforts at reform. Although challenging gender stereo-types to an extent, and fighting for more general rights for themselves, they largely failed to develop a sustained critique of patriarchy and the insistence on the need to "protect" white women by means of racial violence. Assumptions such as these underlay the campaigns of these women for temperance and the suffrage. Lerda draws attention to the failure of the first generation of southern female reformers to break with the conventions of white supremacy, as compared to the later participation of reformers such as Jessie Daniel Ames in the anti-lynching crusade of the 1930s.[26] Their racism also made it impossible for them to arrange gender coalitions across race lines and work with middle-class African American women who pioneered the assault on segregation and lynching – clubwomen like Mary Church Terrell or journalists such as Ida B. Wells.[27]

The African American middle class, indeed, took the lead in early attempts at resistance to discrimination. In opposition to the accommo-dationist approach of Booker T. Washington, a number of African Americans argued for a more direct attack on segregation. The most prominent of these was William Edward Burghardt DuBois, who advo-cated the need for a "Talented Tenth" of educated African Americans to lead the fight.[28] DuBois himself resolved to use the methods of science to fight the scientifically-backed racism which had developed in the early twentieth century.[29] David Turley, in his contribution to this book, traces the means by which DuBois developed his strategy, first as editor of the Atlanta University *Studies* and subsequently of *The Crisis*, the journal of the NAACP. Although the Atlanta University researches are usually thought of as concerned with the search for scientific truth, and *The Crisis* with demands for social reform, Turley demonstrates the consistency between the two types of discourse and the manner in which

26. See Jacquelyn Dowd Hall, *Revolt against Chivalry: Jessie Daniel Ames and the Women's Campaign against Lynching*, New York, 1979.

27. See Nancy Caraway, *Segregated Sisterhood, Racism and the Politics of American Feminism*, Knoxville, 1991, pp. 148–65; Jacqueline A. Rouse, "Atlanta's African American Women's Attack on Segregation, 1900–1920," and Rosalyn Terborg-Penn, "African American Women's Networks in the Anti-Lynching Crusade," both in Noralee Frankel and Nancy S. Dye, eds., *Gender, Class, Race, and Reform in the Progressive Era*, Lexington, 1991, pp. 10–23, 148–61.

28. On Washington, see Louis R. Harlan, *Booker T. Washington, The Making of a Black Leader 1856–1901*, New York, 1972, and *Booker T. Washington, The Wizard of Tuskegee 1900–1915*, New York, 1983; on DuBois, see Manning Marable, *W.E.B. DuBois: Black Radical Democrat*, Boston, 1986, and David Levering Lewis, *W.E.B. DuBois: Biography of a Race*, New York, 1993. On the "Talented Tenth," see W.E.B. Du Bois, *Dusk of Dawn, An Essay Toward an Autobiography of a Race Concept*, New York, 1940; new ed. 1968, p. 70.

29. Du Bois' main strategy, he later wrote, was "to put science into sociology through a study of the condition and problems of my own group." Ibid., p. 51.

DuBois successfully impugned the "scientific" view of African American inferiority with a critique of white southern barbarism.

Race and class in the South since the start of the modern civil rights movement are covered in two essays. Richard King, extending the point made by Barbara J. Fields, argues that "race" is an imaginative construct with a character which alters in accordance with the social context in which it is framed. If the context changes, so does the character. A major effect of the civil rights movement, King maintains, was the reconstruction of African American identity. This owed much to the experience of participation in a mass political struggle and the consequent redefinition of the meaning of "freedom" by African Americans. But, as demonstrated in the life of Martin Luther King, Jr.,[30] it was also a response to the thought of black and white intellectuals, and the "folk tradition" associated with the African American churches.

Brian Ward's essay utilizes the 1956 assault on singer Nat King Cole during a concert in Birmingham, Alabama, to show the way in which cultural differences sharpened conflicts of class and race. He places the assault within the context of the "massive resistance" to desegregation called for by Senator Harry F. Byrd in the wake of the landmark decision of the supreme court in the *Brown v. Board of Education* case (1954).[31] Ward examines class conflict within the white community, in particular amongst the citizens' councils, and the way in which cultural issues (rock and roll music in particular) became a major unifying factor in the fight against integration.

The publication of this book has been assisted by a grant from the Scouloudi Foundation in association with the Institute of Historical Research. The book itself is the result of many people's efforts. First and foremost, the editors would like to thank Pete Daniel, the Commonwealth Fund Lecturer of 1992, for his great encouragement and support. They are grateful to all the contributors for their diligence in getting the initial versions of these papers in on time and their subsequent good humor during the process of revision. They acknowledge their debt to the other organizers, including Martin Daunton and Christopher Abel, of the 1992 Commonwealth Fund Conference in London, where the papers were first presented. Without financial aid from the Commonwealth Fund of University College London, the

30. On King and the civil rights movement, see David Garrow, *Bearing the Cross: Martin Luther King, Jr., and the Southern Christian Leadership Conference*, New York, 1986; Adam Fairclough, *To Redeem the Soul of America: The Southern Christian Leadership Conference and Martin Luther King, Jr.*, Athens, Ga., 1987, p.16.

31. On "Massive Resistance," see Numan V. Bartley, *The Rise of Massive Resistance: Race and Politics in the South during the 1950s*, Baton Rouge, 1969; Neil R. McMillen, *The Citizen's Council: Origins of Resistance to the Second Reconstruction, 1954–64*, Urbana, 1971; Francis M. Wilhoit, *The Politics of Massive Resistance*, New York, 1973.

Economic and Social Research Council, the Royal Historical Society, the David Bruce Centre for American Studies at Keele University, the University of London Institute of United States Studies, and the History Department of Newcastle University, the conference itself could not have taken place. The editors would also like to thank those who chaired sessions at the conference, including Edward McBride, Tony Badger, and Martin Daunton. They are particularly grateful to participants at the conference for many comments and suggestions that have been incorporated into the published version of the papers. Finally, they would like to thank Haley Wilson, Nazneen Razwi, and Rachel Aucott for their help at various times in the preparation of the manuscript.

Part I
Race, Class and Industrialization

"Through the Rugged Gates of the Penitentiary": Convict Labor and Southern Coal, 1870–1900

Alex Lichtenstein

In a remarkable presentation before the National Prison Association in 1897, T.J. Hill, General Manager of the convict coal mines in east Tennessee, outlined for the NPA delegates the considerable contribution of prison labor to the development of the southern coal industry over the past two decades. Appropriately, Hill began by noting the compatibility of "industrial conditions" and the desired penal reform of "concentrat[ing] the convicts in large bodies at healthful locations about the coal mines." The permanent nature of the coal camps, Hill argued, were a vast improvement over the temporary and mobile convict camps that prevailed when convicts had been leased to railroads in the immediate aftermath of the Civil War. This penal "reform" was made possible by the fact that "a strong effort was ... being made to develop the iron and coal industries of [Alabama and Tennessee]," development then impeded by the difficulty of labor recruitment. Hill reminded his audience that during the 1870s "it was a practical impossibility to get our free native people, either white or black ... to work in the mines." As a result, the states agreed to lease convicts to the coal operators.[1]

Hill believed that much of the industrial development in east Tennessee and northeast Alabama could be traced to this decision to begin mining operations with forced labor. The use of convict miners "made possible the rapid development of the wonderful natural resources of the two states" and "gave an impetus to the manufacturing interests of the entire South, which could not otherwise have been possible, for at least many years." He left no doubt that "the enforced

---

1. T.J. Hill, "Experience in Mining Coal With Convicts," in National Prison Association, *Proceedings of the Annual Congress, 1897*, Pittsburgh, 1898, p. 389.

employment of so many laborers in the mines" led directly to the growth of "branches of manufacturing, dependent on the coal mines for fuel," thus providing employment to free workers, attracting capital, and providing a sturdy industrial infrastructure.[2]

Such structural benefits of forced labor extended to the creation of an entirely new industrial labor force as well. "The occupation of mining has been opened up to the negro," Hill proclaimed, "although his entry into the craft has been principally through the rugged gates of the penitentiary." The convict-lease thus served as a prime means of proletarianization for a black population "mostly from the agricultural districts [who] had not been taught trades." Hill claimed that convicts who worked in the mines frequently found employment as miners upon their release. For blacks this was a decided benefit, he said, since "the negro is practically barred from all higher branches of the mechanical arts," but "the released negro convict, if a skillful miner ... finds ready employment at fair and equal wages." Moreover, "to the ignorant negro ... a term in the penitentiary was without question the best lesson he could obtain in citizenship."[3]

Thus Hill argued that convict labor developed resources "impossible of development by free labor"; proletarianized a black labor force otherwise mired in agricultural labor and the legacy of slavery; and, far from competing with free labor, provided "employment to additional free labor" by stimulating industrial growth, especially in the iron industry that depended on cheap and readily accessible coal and coke for fuel.[4] No doubt all this can be read as an elaborate apologia for a penal system frequently condemned as economically backwards and corrupt, racially brutal and degrading, and destructively competitive with free labor. Indeed, its harshest contemporary critics insisted the convict-lease was a barbaric relic out of step with the genuine desire for progress and national acceptance that the most enlightened members of the New South sought for their region.[5] Most historians of the New South and of convict leasing have naturally embraced the perspective of the reformers, in one case going so far as to suggest that "southern penal practices ... left a trail of dishonor and death that could

2. Hill, "Experience in Mining Coal," p. 390.
3. Hill, "Experience in Mining Coal," pp. 390, 394–95.
4. Hill, "Experience in Mining Coal," pp. 396–97.
5. For critiques of the convict-lease system, see e.g. George Washington Cable, *The Silent South, together with the Freedman's Case in Equity and the Convict-Lease System*, NY, 1907; P.D. Sims, "The Lease System in Tennessee and Other Southern States," *Proceedings of the Annual Meeting of the National Prison Association, 1893*; *United Mine Workers Journal* (UMWJ), 25 October 1894; Rebecca Latimer Felton, *My Memories of Georgia Politics*, pp. 438–39, 463–66.

find a parallel only in ... the prisons of Nazi Germany."[6] The lease system is also commonly portrayed as a stain on the "honor" of the New South, which undermined the legitimacy of the ruling class and their "real" interest in progress or nostalgic attachment to paternalism.[7] While accurately portraying the viciousness of convict leasing, this approach tends to obscure the fundamental economic significance of southern penal labor. The problem is that the defenders and beneficiaries of the New South's peculiar penal system were hardly enemies of progress. To the contrary, some of the most prominent industrialists and financiers in the region leased convicts from Alabama, Georgia, and Tennessee in order to develop a coal and iron industry that they believed was essential to southern modernization. Certainly T.J. Hill flagrantly denied the obvious cruelties of a system that entirely subordinated penal function to the extraction of labor. Nevertheless, it is worth investigating the degree to which the rapid development of the Lower South's coal and iron industry during the last three decades of the nineteenth century rested on the ability of southern capitalists to use the penal system to recruit the core of their productive labor force.[8]

The convict-lease was a penal system unique to the postbellum South. Rather than house convicts in a penitentiary, the southern states leased them to the highest bidder, who was then responsible for feeding,

6. Fletcher Green, "Some Aspects of the Convict Lease System in the Southern States," in *Essays in Southern History*, Fletcher Green, ed., Chapel Hill, 1949, p. 122. Other important treatments of the history of convict leasing in the New South include J. Thorsten Sellin, *Slavery and the Penal System*, NY, 1976; Edward Ayers, *Vengeance and Justice: Crime and Punishment in the Nineteenth-Century South*, pp. 185–222; Matthew J. Mancini, "Race, Economics, and the Abandonment of Convict Leasing," *Journal of Negro History*, vol. 63, Fall 1978, pp. 339–52.

7. Fletcher Green, "Some Aspects of the Convict Lease System," p. 121; Ayers, *Vengeance and Justice*, pp. 208, 222; N. Gordon Carper, "The Convict-Lease System in Florida, 1866–1923," unpublished PhD. dissertation, Florida State University, 1964, pp. 218–65; E. Merton Coulter, *Georgia, A Short History*, Chapel Hill, 1960, pp. 414–16; E. Merton Coulter, *James Monroe Smith, Georgia Planter: Before Death and After*, Athens, 1961, pp. 64–92; Hilda Jane Zimmerman, "The Penal Reform Movement in the South During the Progressive Period, 1890–1917," *Journal of Southern History*, vol. 17, November 1951, pp. 462–92; A. Elizabeth Taylor, "The Origin and Development of the Convict Lease System in Georgia," *Georgia Historical Quarterly*, vol. 26, June 1942, pp. 113–28; A. Elizabeth Taylor, "The Abolition of the Convict Lease System in Georgia," *Georgia Historical Quarterly*, vol. 26, June 1942, pp. 273–87.

8. In my opinion, only Stanley Greenberg, *Race and State in Capitalist Development: Comparative Perspectives*, New Haven, 1980, pp. 209–26, attributes adequate significance to the role of convict labor in the industrialization of this region; Gerald Jaynes, *Branches Without Roots: Genesis of the Black Working Class in the American South, 1862–1882*, NY, 1986, p. 271, is suggestive however. Ronald L. Lewis, *Black Coal Miners in America: Race, Class and Community Conflict, 1780–1980*, Lexington, 1987, chap. 2, is a good survey of convict mine labor in all three states.

clothing, and restraining the convicts. In return, the lessee received the right to use the convicts' labor as he desired. This in itself was not unusual; nineteenth-century northern prisons had several systems of penal labor that often included contracting the prisoners' labor out to private entrepreneurs. Yet only in the South did the state entirely give up its control of the convict population to the contractor; and only in the South did the physical "penitentiary" become virtually synonymous with the various private enterprises in which convicts labored – including coal mines.[9]

Convict leasing is found at the nexus of the key elements in the ongoing debate over continuity and change in the political economy of the New South. Despite the undeniably massive transformation entailed by the destruction of slavery, there is little agreement about the degree to which the outcome of the Civil War effected a genuine revolution in the direction of the southern economy or the identity and ideology of its dominant class. In C. Vann Woodward's view – still the benchmark for studies of the New South – the Civil War and Reconstruction utterly destroyed the power, property, and pretensions of the antebellum planter elite, and replaced them with a class of ruthless capitalist entrepreneurs wedded to economic development, industrialization and growth, and thoroughly bourgeois values.[10] But historians have continued to argue about the identity, ideology, and economic interests of the New South's ruling class. Following Woodward, some have portrayed a New South dominated by bourgeois modernizers – merchants and capitalists who shaped social relations in ways that thoroughly transformed the region. Others, most notoriously Jonathan Wiener, have suggested that "anti-

9. The best description and summary of the various systems of nineteenth-century penal labor in the United States is found in U.S. Bureau of Labor, *Convict Labor, Second Annual Report of the Commissioner of Labor, 1886*, Washington, 1886, pp. 371–96; see also Glen A. Gildemeister, *Prison Labor and Convict Competition With Free Workers in Industrializing America, 1840–1890*, NY 1987, on the organization of convict labor in the North.

10. C. Vann Woodward, *Origins of the New South, 1877–1913*, Baton Rouge, 1951; Sheldon Hackney, "Origins of the New South in Retrospect," *Journal of Southern History*, vol. 38, May 1972, pp. 191–216; C. Vann Woodward, *Thinking Back: The Perils of Writing History*, Baton Rouge, 1986, pp. 59–79. On the continuity and change debate see Dan T. Carter, "From the Old South to the New: Another Look at the Theme of Change and Continuity," in *From the Old South to the New: Essays on the Transitional South*, Walter J. Fraser and Winfred B. Moore, eds., Westport, 1981, pp. 23–32; Lawrence Powell, "The Prussians are Coming," *Georgia Historical Quarterly*, vol. 71, Winter 1987, pp. 638–67; James C. Cobb, "Beyond Planters and Industrialists: A New Perspective on the New South," *Journal of Southern History*, vol. 54, February 1988, pp. 45–68; Michael Wayne, *The Reshaping of Plantation Society: The Natchez District*, Baton Rouge, 1984, pp. 202–10; Harold Woodman, "Sequel to Slavery: The New History Views the Postbellum South," *Journal of Southern History*, vol. 43, November 1977, pp. 523–33; Woodman, "How New Was the New South," *Agricultural History*, vol. 58, October 1984, pp. 429–545.

bourgeois agrarians" were hegemonic; in the not-so-New South they built a social order dependent on unfree agricultural labor and hostility to industrial development – what Wiener calls, following Barrington Moore, the "Prussian Road" to modernization.[11]

Contrary to Wiener's view, however, as originally formulated the "Prussian Road" consists of both "the preservation of the traditional agrarian social structure" *and* the economic empowerment of a nascent bourgeois-industrial class.[12] Since the agrarian elite retains social and political supremacy ("hegemony") in this coalition, the path to "modern society" is undemocratic at best, fully fascist at worst.[13] Actually, Eugene Genovese, not Barrington Moore, appears to be the first person to apply the Prussian analogy to the southern United States – but, ironically, with reference to the antebellum South. In the *Political Economy of Slavery*, Genovese argued that "the commitment of [southern industrialists] to slavery forced them to adjust their vision of an industrialized South to one dominated by a broadened slaveholders' regime" and that this "necessarily meant a Prussian road to industrialism, paved with authoritarianism, benevolent despotism, and aristocratic pretension." However, the war liquidated this possibility along with the slaveholders as a class.[14] Moore himself advances a similar thesis with the counter-factual proposition that a southern victory would certainly have led to "a latifundia economy, a dominant antidemocratic aristocracy, and a weak and dependent commercial and industrial class, unable and unwilling to push forward to political democracy." The outcome of the Civil War left a far more ambiguous legacy, in Moore's view, since "when Southern `Junkers' were no longer slaveholders and had acquired a larger tincture of urban business and when Northern capitalists faced radical rumblings, the classic conservative coalition was possible."[15]

On the one hand, this view seems in accord with Woodward's version of the bourgeoisification of the southern elite and their role as *compradors*

11. Jonathan Wiener, *Social Origins of the New South, Alabama 1860–1895*, Baton Rouge, 1978, pp. 3–4, 71–72; Jonathan Wiener, "Class Structure and Economic Development in the South, 1865–1955," *American Historical Review*, vol. 84, December 1979, pp. 970–92; Barrington Moore, Jr., *Social Origins of Dictatorship and Democracy: Lord and Peasant in the Making of the Modern World*, Boston, 1966.

12. Dwight B. Billings, Jr., *Planters and the Making of the "New South": Class, Politics and Development in North Carolina, 1865–1900*, Chapel Hill, 1979, p. 223.

13. Moore, *Social Origins*; Billings, *Planters and the Making of the "New South"*; Wiener, *Social Origins of the New South*; Wiener, "Class Structure and Economic Development," and Harold D. Woodman's comment that follows, p. 998; Jonathan Wiener, "Review of Reviews: Barrington Moore's Social Origins of Dictatorship and Democracy," *History and Theory*, vol. 15, 1976, pp. 146–75.

14. Eugene D. Genovese, *The Political Economy of Slavery: Studies in the Economy and Society of the Slave South*, NY, 1967, pp. 206–20.

15. Moore, *Social Origins of Dictatorship and Democracy*, p. 153.

in a "colonial" southern economy; on the other, Moore seems to imply that the new southern elite did in fact consist of old "Junkers" clothed in new garb. It is this latter implication that Woodward's radical critics – the "New Continuarians," in his words – seized upon more than twenty-five years after the publication of *Origins of the New South*. In Wiener's view, "planter persistence" led to a labor-repressive agrarian society, dominated by a planter class that used its political power to hamstring industrial development in Alabama. Sharecropping was the determining "relation of production" in Alabama's political economy. In this model of the Prussian Road, "Junker" hegemony in Alabama meant political authoritarianism, unfree black labor (at least in the agricultural sector) bound to the land by lien laws, vagrancy and anti-enticement statutes, debt peonage, racial custom, and the threat of extra-legal violence. The result was chronic underdevelopment of the state's resources. Above all, this is taken as an argument for the continuity of the "antibourgeois" South, unshaken by the destruction of slavery.[16]

Whatever the conclusion, the effort to distinguish continuity and change, to demonstrate the hegemony of agrarian or bourgeois, planter or industrialist in the New South, frequently relies on the faulty notion that unfree labor will be swept away by "modernization," and that, conversely, the perpetuation of "bound" labor will entail underdevelopment.[17] For Woodward's followers, the fall of the planter class entailed the liquidation of a political economy based on unfree plantation labor; alternatively, for his critics the persistence of "archaic" social structures – the plantation, forced labor, racial barriers to political or economic advancement – is linked to underdevelopment and the failure to industrialize.[18] In particular, the absence or presence of the defining feature of the Old South's economy, unfree labor, determines whether the New South was "capitalist" or not. But most analyses of the post-Civil War southern political economy have only considered the degree to which *agricultural* labor was free or unfree.[19]

16. C. Vann Woodward, *Thinking Back: The Perils of Writing History*, Baton Rouge, 1986, pp. 70–77; Wiener, *Social Origins of the New South*; Wiener, "Class Structure and Economic Development"; see Jay Mandle, *The Roots of Black Poverty*, Durham, 1978, for the underdevelopment argument.

17. Greenberg, *Race and State in Capitalist Development*, pp. 133–34, 395–96; Barbara J. Fields, "The Nineteenth-Century American South: History and Theory," *Plantation Society in the Americas*, vol. 1, April 1983, p. 7.

18. Powell, "The Prussians are Coming," pp. 640–41, for this observation; Mandle, *Roots of Black Poverty*, for a coherent exposition of the relationship between a plantation "mode of production" and underdevelopment.

19. For the relevant historiography see, e.g., Wiener, *Social Origins of the New South*; Mandle, *The Roots of Black Poverty*; Cobb, "Beyond Planters and Industrialists"; Gavin Wright, *Old South, New South: Revolutions in the Southern Economy Since the Civil War*, NY, 1986; Roger Ransom and Richard Sutch, *One Kind of Freedom: The Economic Consequences of Emancipation*, Cambridge MA, 1977; Woodman, "Sequel to Slavery."

As a result, the degree of freedom in New South labor relations generally has been measured by the status of laborers on plantations and farms, especially ex-slaves. From one point of view, if these labor relations were particularly coercive, the social order necessary to maintain this state of affairs hindered economic development. Hence the South remained "backwards." Alternatively, if plantation labor was relatively "free," then the social legacy of slavery was effectively abolished, and reasons for the region's persistent poverty would have to be sought elsewhere. On the one side are the believers in the almighty market, who argue that sharecropping and tenancy developed naturally, and were noncoercive "risk-sharing" mechanisms. On the other are historians who emphasize racism, lien laws, debt-peonage, the Klan, and a host of other "non-market" factors that "bound" croppers and tenants to the land, the landowner, and the merchant.[20] The focus of this debate serves to perpetuate the view that industrialization would threaten agrarian interests, since its reliance on free wage labor would undermine plantation labor control by creating an alternative labor market for blacks. Conversely, those who argue that free labor relations triumphed in the South after the Civil War point to the fact that "industries developed [and] railroads spread over the land," which they believe could only have occurred if labor relations were non-coercive in all sectors of the economy.[21]

The Prussian Road thesis forces us to examine whether or not the interests of planters and industrialists in the New South actually clashed. Much of the literature assumes this to be the case. If planters emerged hegemonic, then the ways of the Old South would be perpetuated; if the industrialists were the victors, then a New South – of rapacious or benevolent capitalism, depending on one's point of view – arose from the ashes. But the alleged incompatibility of labor-repressive agriculture and industrial development departs from historical reality as well as the theoretical Prussian Road, which after all

20. Joseph D. Reid, Jr., Robert Higgs, and Stephen J. DeCanio trumpet the hegemony of the free market; e.g., Reid, "Sharecropping as an Understandable Market Response: The Postbellum South," *Journal of Economic History*, vol. 33, March 1973, pp. 106–30; Higgs, *Competition and Coercion: Blacks in the American Economy, 1865–1914*, Cambridge MA, 1977; DeCanio, *Agriculture in the Postbellum South: The Economics of Production and Supply*, Cambridge MA, 1974; Woodman, "Sequel to Slavery," provides the best summary and critique of the work of these cliometric economic historians. Surprisingly, this approach has diminished during the 1980s. Jon Wiener and Jay Mandle emphasize non-market factors in the shaping of southern labor relations (some would say overemphasize); Wiener, *Social Origins*; Mandle, *Black Poverty*. Wayne, *Reshaping of Plantation Society,* Wright, *Old South, New South*; and Ransom and Sutch, *One Kind of Freedom* are three examples of balanced assessments that account for market and non-market (if one accepts such a distinction) forces.

21. Higgs, "Comment" on Wiener, "Class Structure," p. 997.

includes the development of modern industry. New South industrialists were able to use the state to recruit and discipline a convict labor force, and thus were able to develop the region's resources without undermining planters' control of black labor. Not only that, the penal system was used as a powerful sanction against blacks who challenged the racial order upon which agrarian labor control relied. The convict-lease was not the persistence of a "precapitalist" form of labor coercion, but a new forced labor system that was wholly compatible with a particular vision of economic development and the continuation of racial domination – a form of "modernization" acceptable to planter and industrialist alike.[22]

Indeed, much of Wiener's otherwise persuasive case rests on a major fallacy: the supposed stunted economic growth of Birmingham, Alabama. In truth, there was a Prussian Road to the modern south, but it did not run through the cotton fields of the black belt. Instead, it paved the way for dramatic industrial development in an arc sweeping southwestward from Knoxville to Birmingham, and its crucial relation of production was industrial penal labor, not sharecropping. The recruitment, control, and proletarianization of black labor for the regional development of the Deep South's coal and iron industries in the years from 1870 to 1900 was closely linked to the convict-lease system. The largest coal mines in the Deep South, at the base of the operations of the most successfully vertically integrated enterprises, relied on convicts as the core of their labor force.

Despite a shortage of capital, technological backwardness, weak markets, a poor labor supply, and competition with a predominant agricultural sector, a significant industrial complex did develop in isolated pockets of the New South. While the region always remained "underdeveloped" relative to northern states, and failed to keep pace particularly *after* the turn of the century, the period from 1870 to 1900 still showed incredibly rapid industrial development in several southern states. Considering that the South began the last three decades of the nineteenth century with a practically non-existent industrial base, the development of the southern coal and iron industry – always the structural key to industrial growth in any modern economy – was nothing less than extraordinary, even compared to the rapid industrial expansion north of the Mason-Dixon line during the same period. There is no need to dispute the "colonial economy" thesis – indeed, the corporations in the forefront of southern coal and iron development eventually found most of their

---

22. Cobb, "Beyond Planters and Industrialists," suggests that the interests of planters and industrialists in the New South coincided more often than they clashed. See also, Greenberg, *Race and State in Capitalist Development*; Fields, "The Nineteenth-Century American South."

capital in the hands of Yankees – to show that even without adequate home markets the industrial base of Georgia, Tennessee, and Alabama sustained significant growth between 1870 and 1900. Between 1880 and 1900 coal and coke production from these states multiplied five-fold, and pig iron output tripled. By the turn of the century, these states produced six percent of the nation's bituminous coal, thirteen percent of its coke, and eleven percent of its pig iron. The peak of this development, measured by production levels of coal, coke, and pig iron, occurred in the mid–1890s; in 1896 these three states produced nineteen percent of U.S. pig iron, and twice that percentage of open market pig iron not destined for steel production.[23]

In fact, the supposedly antibourgeois Redeemer regimes that came to power in the wake of Radical Reconstruction were often in the forefront of the successful attempts to build an industrial infra-structure. During the 1870s and 1880s numerous geologists, investors, politicians, boosters, and observers waxed eloquent over the enormous potential of the untapped resources lying under the southern tip of the Appalachian chain. Once this region was made accessible by rail lines, its advocates claimed, the proximity of bitu-minous coal fields, iron ore deposits, and limestone "flux" would make the mountain districts of Tennessee, Alabama, and Georgia "a region of coke-made iron on a scale grander than has ever been witnessed on the habitable globe." Noting the imminent arrival of the "iron horse, with his civilized shriek" in the rich iron ore beds and coal fields of east Tennessee, the State Commissioner of Agriculture and Mining had visions of "a chain of fiery [iron] furnaces ... that will illumine the whole eastern margin of the Cumberland Table-land" and heard "the eternal whir and buzz of machinery." Indeed, as railroads cut through the heart of the Alabama coal basins they "attracted the attention of capitalists, and in a few years the iron and coal industries on these great lines of rail-roads increased with astonishing rapidity," according to an observer in the mid–1880s. By 1886, when William "Pig iron" Kelley traveled to Tennessee, Alabama, and northwest Georgia, he reported that the

23. U.S. Geological Survey, *Mineral Resources of the United States*, 1883–84, 1889–90, 1891, 1900; Emory Q. Hawk, *Economic History of the South*, NY, 1934, p. 482, for the 1896 figure. On industrial growth in this region, and its dependence on northern capital, see Jaynes, *Branches Without Roots*, pp. 268–72; Gavin Wright, *Old South, New South*, chap. 6; Victor S. Clark, *History of Manufactures in the United States*, vol. 2, NY, 1929, pp. 211–20; and Woodward, *Origins of the New South*, chaps. 5, 11 for the classic account of the "colonial economy." For an excellent discussion of the various explana-tions for the relative weakness of southern industry see Robert J. Norrell, *James Bowron: The Autobiography of a New South Industrialist*, Chapel Hill, 1991.

burgeoning iron and mineral industries of the region were a great success, and held up this emerging industrial base as the best hope for the progress of the New South.[24]

In the early 1870s the coal and iron industries of the Appalachian escarpment remained practically undeveloped. For example, Alabama produced *no* coke-fueled pig iron until 1876, and only 20,818 tons of charcoal-fueled iron in that same year. In 1870, only 13,200 tons of coal were removed from Alabama's immense field, and this was for local consumption only; and coke production did not begin in the state until 1880. But in an astonishingly brief period of time Alabama built an integrated coal and iron complex of coke-fueled furnaces. By 1890 Alabama produced 4,090,409 tons of coal; 1,072,942 tons of coke; and 718,383 tons of pig iron. The U.S. Geological Survey for 1890 remarked that "in no other State have such rapid strides been made in the production of coal as in Alabama during the past decade," and that same year the U.S. Census Office enthusiastically reported that the growth of the Alabama coal industry since 1880 "has been almost phenomenal." This coal was transformed into fuel for iron production, and by 1895 Alabama had 20 iron furnaces "in blast," surpassed only by Ohio and Pennsylvania.[25] The story was no less dramatic in the mountains of east Tennessee. In 1870 the state produced only 133,418 tons of coal; by 1890 this figure had increased to 2,169,585 tons. And from 1872 to 1890 the production of pig iron in Tennessee multiplied over seven-fold, to 300,000 tons a year. By 1880 the state was ranked third in U.S. coke production. In one area of southeast Tennessee, in what the American Institute of Mining Engineers referred to as the "Chattanooga District," the number of blast furnaces using bituminous coal and coke

24. William G. Atkinson to Governor James M. Smith, 26 Sep. 1872, Box 82, Governor's Incoming Correspondence, Georgia Executive Department Records, Georgia Department of Archives and History (GDAH); Abram S. Hewitt, quoted in John T. Milner, *Alabama: As It Was, As It Is, and As It Will Be*, Montgomery, 1876, p. 192; Tennessee Bureau of Agriculture, Statistics and Mines, *Tennessee: Its Agricultural and Mineral Wealth*, Nashville, 1876, pp. 129–30; J.W. Burke, "The Coal Fields of Alabama," pamphlet, n.p., c, 1885, p. 5; American Iron and Steel Institute, Bulletin, vol. 20, 29 December 1886, pp. 346–47.

25. William B. Phillips, *Iron-Making in Alabama*, 2nd ed., Montgomery, 1898, p. 366; USGS, *Mineral Resources, 1889–1890*, p. 172; U.S. Census Office, *Report on the Mineral Industries of the United States at the Eleventh Census, 1890*, vol. 7, p. 355; USGS, *Mineral Resources*, 1890, p. 149; Phillips, *Iron-Making*, 1896, p. 25; Mable Mills, *The Coke Industry in Alabama*, Tuscaloosa, 1947, p. 2; Tennessee Division of Mines, *Fourth Annual Report of the Bureau of Labor, Statistics and Mines*, Nashville, 1895, p. 234; Woodward Iron Company, *Alabama Blast Furnaces*,, 1940, p. 19.

by 1884 was nineteen. There had been two such furnaces in the area in 1872.[26]

Yet the susceptibility of the south's iron furnaces to economic downturns revealed structural inadequacies in the region's evolving industrial base, and even enthusiasts expressed some reservations. The violent fluctuations in the business cycle that punctuated the 1870s, 1880s, and 1890s with depressions struck the pig iron industry – and thus the market for southern coal, coke, and ore – particularly hard.[27] From 1873 to 1878, eighty percent of southern iron furnaces did indeed shut down for a time, and the panic of the mid–1870s "almost swept the southern iron investments out of existence."[28] James Swank, President of the American Iron and Steel Association, believed that southern states had to meet at least two conditions in order to make the postwar iron industry a stable success. First, rolling mills and other home markets for pig iron would have to be established in the South. And second, production could be cheapened by further substituting mineral fuel – bituminous coal and coke – for charcoal, an anachronistic fuel still used in the South. Swank was greatly encouraged by the growth of the local coke industry, based on the opening of southern coal mines. Still, he questioned the quality of the fuel, and suspected that furnaces were sometimes built "in advance of the development of neighboring coke-producing coal deposits."[29] The poor quality of raw materials was also noted by southern mining engineer, William Phillips. "In Alabama," Phillips complained, "we have ores of a moderate content, and they must therefore be mined at a low cost." Thus, while the U.S. average productive ratio was 1.87 tons of raw ore for every ton of iron, in Tennessee, Alabama, Georgia, and North Carolina it was 2.31:1. In these same states 1.48 tons of coke were needed to charge a furnace for each ton of iron poured; the national average was 1.31 tons. In addition, efficient coal mining was made difficult by the thin and irregular seams in the southern fields. When added to the cost of shipping finished products such as rolled iron to

26. USGS, *Mineral Resources*, 1882, p. 7; 1889–1890, p. 271; Tennessee Division of Mines, *Second Annual Report of the Commissioner of Labor and Inspector of Mines*, Nashville, 1893, p. 314; Tennessee Division of Mines, *Fourth Annual Report of the Bureau of Labor, Statistics and Mines*, Nashville, 1895, pp. 223, 283; American Institute of Mining Engineers, *Transactions*, vol. 14, 1885, pp. 3–11.

27. American Iron and Steel Association, *Bulletin*, vol. 18, 21 May 1884, p. 133; on depressions see, e.g., Justin Fuller, "History of the Tennessee Coal, Iron and Railroad Company, 1852–1907," unpublished PhD. Dissertation, University of North Carolina, 1966, p. 54; Clark, *History of Manufactures*, vol. 2, pp. 286–303.

28. American Iron and Steel Association, *Bulletin*, no. 18, 20 August 1884, p. 210.

29. James M. Swank, "The American Iron Industry From Its Beginnings in 1619 to 1886," in USGS, *Mineral Resources*, 1886, pp. 33–38.

northern and western markets, these constraints could appear insurmountable.[30]

Nevertheless, the most militant advocates of industrialization in the South tended to overlook the fixed constraints on development and sang the praises of the contiguous mineral fields without hesitation. Not so the "labor problem," which for boosters and detractors alike served as the focus for explanations of the industrial South's economic problems. The same pessimist who produced the disheartening figures on ore to iron ratios admitted that labor was "abundant" but complained that "it is ignorant and unintelligent ...[and] constant and strict supervision is necessary." As late as 1903, in his survey of the U.S. iron and steel industry, Harry H. Campbell, General Manager of the Pennsylvania Steel Company, noted that "one of the great drawbacks [for this industry] in the South is the labor question." In the "absence of a white population trained to industrial pursuits" southern industrialists had to "depend upon the negro, and the colored man has had no education in this line of work." Campbell attributed the alleged deficiencies of black labor to the legacy of slavery, agricultural labor, and paternalism. In the prevailing racist view of the day, he believed that blacks were not "a saving provident, hard-working people," and complained that they "will work only long enough to get a little cash, whereupon they quit work and live in idleness upon their earnings." The result was both an appallingly high rate of labor turnover and a lack of labor discipline, since "a summary discharge has no terrors, as living [in the South] is cheap and their wants are few."[31]

Indeed, labor turnover and instability, rather than cost, were southern industrialists' greatest lament. When the U.S. Senate investigation of relations between labor and capital visited the Birmingham District in the 1880s, local businessmen put this forward as their primary complaint about the condition of industrial labor in the New South. J.W. Sloss, owner of the Sloss Iron Works in Birmingham (and a lessee of convicts) complained that to work his furnaces with free labor he needed 269 men but his monthly payroll averaged 569. "That is one of our troubles here. The irregularity of labor," he told the Committee. "We cannot do our work as effectively or thoroughly as if we had a regular force of

30. Phillips, *Iron-Making*, p. 4; American Institute of Mining Engineers, *Transactions*, vol. 14, 1885, pp. 7–11; Herman H. Chapman, *The Iron and Steel Industries of the South*, Tuscaloosa, 1953, pp. 47, 51, 155; and Peter Temin, *Iron and Steel in Nineteenth-Century America, An Economic Inquiry*, Cambridge MA, 1964, p. 200, on the low quality of southern ores. Also, see Chapman, *Iron and Steel Industries*, chap. 6, on the inconsistency of southern coal seams, esp. pp. 51–52, 60, 155, 176.

31. U.S. Congress, Senate Committee on Education and Labor, *Report of the Committee of the Senate Upon the Relations Between Labor and Capital*, 4 vols., 1885, vol. 4, p. 132; H.H. Campbell, *The Manufacture of Iron and Steel*, NY, 1903, pp. 674–75.

men." Sloss claimed to rely heavily on black labor for his furnace workers, drawn from all over the deep South; "a moving, restless, migratory
class," Sloss remarked, "quite different from the farm or plantation
negroes," who, he believed, tended to stay put. Of course he overlooked
the fact that his black workers had most likely been agricultural laborers
who had failed to do just that.[32]

This "migratory" class of black workers did not mind losing their
jobs, and would even behave badly in order to receive a dismissal before
pay day (the end of the month), collect their pay and depart. Moreover,
Sloss maintained, "they come and go as they please," attending burials,
holidays, and other events at their own discretion. Often the workers at
Sloss's furnace would leave on a Saturday without giving notice and fail
to return the following week. The consequences of this uncertainty
could be disastrous; if the company could not find replacements the
furnace might have to be shut down, potentially doing expensive
damage to the plant. Sloss calculated that the average time put in by
each of his employees was fourteen and a half days per month; "no
contract restrains them" from this fickle behavior, he bitterly concluded.
Similarly, the superintendent of the Euraka iron works in Alabama testified that the "class of colored people that have grown up to manhood
since emancipation we find the most unreliable of all."[33]

A steady supply of coal and coke was essential to predictable operations of iron furnaces, and some southern coal operators believed that in
the mines "convict labor [was] more reliable and productive than free
labor" and that "the convict accomplishes more work than the free
laborer." Convicts were "forced to work steadily [and] their output may
be depended upon," went the rationale. The coal operators' struggle to
obtain such steadiness from free labor continued into the twentieth
century. In 1903, in negotiations with the United Mine Workers, the
Birmingham coal operators insisted on their right to discharge any
miner who worked fewer than twenty days a month or was absent three
days running. "How [is] the operator or producer ... going to know how
much coal or coke he is going to produce in the year or in the month if
some of the miners work 10 days, some 15, some 12, and some 20 days
in the month," complained one operator. "In the Birmingham district,"
testified Shelby Harrison, an investigator for *The Survey*, "most of the
large companies have to keep from 50 to 75 percent larger number of

---

32. *Relations Between Labor and Capital*, vol. 4, pp. 286–90, for Sloss testimony.

33. *Relations Between Labor and Capital*, vol. 4, pp. 286–90, and 385–86. There were
also similar complaints about white workers in the "mountainous sections of [Alabama],"
p. 23; see also pp. 25–26. For complaints about coal miners see Alfred Brainerd, "Colored
Mining Labor," *Transactions of the American Iron and Steel Institute*, vol. 14,
1885–1886, p. 80.

negroes on the pay roll than they expect to be working from day to day."
On the other hand, when they used convicts, "300 men, for instance, go
to sleep at night, and 300 men get up the next day and are ready for
work," and this was for 310 days a year. "[Convict labor] is regular. I
was told by a number of employers that that was one of the greatest
things they liked about it," Harrison concluded. The assured labor of
convicts allowed select mines to achieve certainty of production levels,
making their contracts particularly secure.[34]

Certainly mine operators also looked to convicts because of the
cheapness of their labor and its effects on the cost of free labor. The
"mine owners [in Alabama] say they could not work at a profit without
the lowering effect in wages of convict-labor competition," the U.S.
Bureau of Labor reported in 1886. And naturally, in its attacks on
convict competition the United Mine Workers union pointed to the
comparative cheapness and lowering of wages as prime evils of the
lease. "Miners working near the mines where convict labor is
employed are working at lessor [*sic*] rates than they would if they had
no convicts around them," proclaimed the *UMW Journal*.[35] But
comparative costs were perhaps less significant to the New South
capitalists than the contrast between a fixed cost paid to the state for a
predetermined amount of long-term forced labor and an unpredictable
labor cost subject to the uncertain supply of reluctant proletarians or
wage negotiations with organized workers. Even when the cost of
leasing and maintaining convict labor approached the cost of free
labor, the problems of labor recruitment, training, discipline, turnover
and consistency were reason enough to use forced labor in the South's
coal fields.[36]

34. U.S. Bureau of Labor, *Convict Labor*, p. 301; U.S. Senate, *Reports of the
Immigration Commission, Immigrants in Industries*, 61st Cong., 2nd sess., Doc. No. 633,
pt. 1, vol. 2; *Bituminous Coal Mining*, Washington, 1911, p. 218; Joint Scale Convention
of the Alabama Coal Operators Association and the United Mine Workers of America,
Proceedings of the Board of Arbitration, Birmingham 1903, p. 7; U.S. Congress, House of
Representatives, *Hearings Before the Committee on Investigation of United States Steel
Corporation*, Washington, 1912, testimony of Shelby Harrison, p. 2982; see also John A.
Fitch, "Birmingham District: Labor Conservation," *The Survey*, vol. 27, 6 January 1912,
pp. 1527–40. On the need for a stable labor force see, e.g., Ronald D. Eller, *Miners,
Millhands and Mountaineers: Industrialization of the Appalachian South, 1880–1930*,
Knoxville, 1982, pp. 165–68, 193. On task labor see Keith Dix, *Work Relations in the
Coal Industry: The Hand-Loading Era, 1880–1930*, Morgantown, 1977; Alex
Lichtenstein, "The Political Economy of Convict Labor in the New South," unpublished
PhD. dissertation, University of Pennsylvania, 1990, chap. 6.

35. U.S. Bureau of Labor, *Convict Labor*, p. 301; *UMWJ*, 15 September 1892 and 26
Jan. 1899.

36. For comparative costs see, e.g., *Relations Between Labor and Capital*, vol. 4, pp.
438, 442; Alabama, *Second Biennial Report of the Inspector of Convicts*, Montgomery,
1888, p. 251; USGS, *Mineral Resources*, 1889–1890, pp. 170–71.

Keeping the cost of production down, competing successfully for labor with the agricultural sector, and maintaining stable labor relations were imperative because of the less readily removed shackles on the growth of the iron and coal industry. But reduction of labor costs and an increase in "reliability" had limits imposed by the workers themselves; it was precisely at this point in the productive process, particularly in its earliest stages and at its resource base – the coal mines – that convicts played an important role in the development of southern heavy industry. Reliance on a convict labor force leased from the state eliminated the problem of labor turnover and unpredictability, and the desire to limit uncertain operating costs in weakly established enterprises reinforced the tendency to seek bound labor. Convict labor resolved the problem of maintaining rapid industrial growth in the face of the extreme industrial vulnerability that plagued capitalist enterprises in the postbellum South.

Coal operators in particular, noting that "a miner is a like a bird ... here today and somewhere else tomorrow," relied on the lease system as a method of forced proletarianization.[37] In the coal fields of West Virginia, Illinois, and Kentucky a "judicious mixture" of migrant southern blacks, immigrants, and native whites, often helped coal operators dominate their labor force.[38] But in Alabama, Tennessee, and Georgia another layer was added to the segmented labor market. African American convict miners, particularly long-term prisoners, made up the core of an industrial working class that could not maintain agrarian work habits, could not quit before developing industrial skills, could be used as a reserve army of labor, and frequently filled the ranks of free miners after their release.

From its origins the convict-lease system's supposed ability to forge a black industrial working class from a peasantry was marshaled as a defense and justification for forced labor. "There can be no question that convicts produce more after than before conviction," the Alabama House Committee investigating the convict mines proclaimed. This "benefit" extended beyond the period of incarceration. As Tennessee debated the merits of convict coal mining in the early 1870s, the Nashville *Republican Banner* heartily endorsed the idea, maintaining that "when [the convicts] have served their time out, they are schooled miners, and may continue in that pursuit." Two decades later, T.J. Hill

---

37. Georgia General Assembly, *Proceedings of the Joint Committee of the Senate and House to Investigate the Convict Lease System of Georgia*, 1908, 5 ms. vols, on microfilm, GDAH, vol. 5, pp. 1562–63.

38. See Kenneth R. Bailey, "A Judicious Mixture: Negroes and Immigrants in the West Virginia Mines, 1880–1917," and the other essays in *Blacks in Appalachia*, William H. Turner and Edward J. Cabbell, eds., Lexington, 1985, esp. pts. 3, 4, and 5; Lewis, *Black Coal Miners in America*, esp. chaps. 7 and 8.

agreed that "with kind treatment and proper instruction a large percent-age of [black convicts] soon became excellent workmen." In the 1880s a convict at the Pratt mines in Alabama told the Senate committee on capital and labor that about 250 ex-convicts still worked for the company, and the prison warden defended convict leasing by pointing out that Alabama's black workers earned eight dollars a month on a plantation, but after being released from the convict mines an ex-pris-oner could earn up to three dollars a day as a free miner. "Of the men who have been discharged from [the penitentiary mines] with a good record for good conduct, nearly all have staid [*sic*] in the mine," claimed the warden.[39]

Even among the complaints about the unreliability of black labor some detractors could not help but remark that "the colored laborers here are making a good deal of money, especially our ex-convicts." This did not always result in labor docility, however. One group of ex-convicts struck for higher wages in 1882. "I do not know that they have [labor unions], but whether they have or not, they act in concert," a mine manager proclaimed. Alabama's inspector of convicts decried the fact that in the mines "the ex-convicts are most blatant about the rights of free labor [to be unhindered by convict competition], forget-ting that had they never been convicts, they would never have been miners."[40]

Free miners and other critics in Alabama also remarked on this process of state-sponsored forced proletarianization. "If you don't like common labor or farming you can go to the State warden of the prison and get a suit of striped clothes and be appointed a coal miner," "Dawson" wryly remarked in a letter to the *National Labor Tribune*. The dangerous conditions in Alabama's mines were at times attributed to the "ignorant" labor of the convicts, who were "gener-ally recruited from the cotton fields of South Alabama." This form of "recruitment" sprung from the "fee system," which perpetuated the "crying evil of convicting men for offenses in order that deputies and court officials ... may get their fees." Many of the prisoners at

39. Alabama General Assembly, *Journal of the House of Representatives, 1896–1897*, Montgomery, 1897, p. 638; *Nashville Republican Banner*, 20 December 1872; T.J. Hill, "Experience in Mining Coal With Convicts," p. 390; *Relations Between Labor and Capital*, vol. 4, pp. 434, 437, 442; Georgia Principal Keeper of the Penitentiary, *Report*, 1877–78, p. 10; *Investigation of Charges Against Penitentiary Companies One, Two and Three*, 2 vols., *Evidence for the State*, vol. 1, *Evidence for Julius Brown, Receiver*, vol. 2, 10–21 February 1896, Box 4, Julius L. Brown Papers, Atlanta Historical Society, vol. 1, pp. 120–25, vol. 2, p. 479.

40. *Relations Between Labor and Capital*, vol. 4, pp. 442, 446; Alabama, *First Biennial Report of the Inspector of Convicts, 1884–1886*, Montgomery, 1886, p. 21.

Coalburg mines in Alabama, for instance, were there for petty offenses, sent from every county in the state. "I do not wish it to be understood that I in any way approve of a man committing a wrong," cautioned black UMW organizer R.L. Davis after a trip to Birmingham, "but in Alabama they will for the most trivial offense give you a term at Coalburg or Pratt mines, and especially if it happens to be a dusky son of Ham."[41]

The criminal justice system provided a steady stream of blacks from the cotton belt to the Birmingham coal area. Many of these men, convicted of petty offenses that challenged the rigid racial proscriptions of agricultural districts, spent time in the mines for court costs long beyond their original sentence. In 1890, for instance, Hale County had twelve convicts at the coal mines, convicted of petty larceny, carrying a concealed weapon, failing to perform a contract, and poisoning a mule, among other crimes. Greene County, also in the heart of Alabama's black belt, sent ten convict miners to the Birmingham District that same year for assault and profanity, cruelty to animals, petty larceny, and "false pretenses and removing mortgaged property." This last crime brought a sentence of two years, and an additional year mining coal to pay the cost of prosecution.[42] Such convictions helped "antibourgeois agrarians" maintain control over agricultural labor, even while they provided a new source of labor for Alabama's industrial entrepreneurs. For these involuntary recruits to the mines often stayed in Birmingham.

Indeed, according to the mine managers in the Birmingham District up to one-half of the convicts who learned how to dig coal while incarcerated obtained jobs in the trade upon release. Given the steadily increasing percentage of free blacks in the coal mines from 1880 onwards – by 1898, Davis estimated, seventy percent of the miners in the Birmingham District were black – there may be some truth to this, since blacks made up over ninety per cent of the convict force in

41. Letter to *National Labor Tribune*, 4 January 1879, reprinted in Herbert Gutman, "Black Coal Miners and the Greenback-Labor Party in Redeemer Alabama: 1878–1879," *Labor History*, vol. 10, Summer 1969, p. 516; *Alabama Sentinel*, 13 June 1891; Thomas Parke Diary, 15 March 1895, 31 July 1895, BPL; *First Biennial Report of the Inspectors of Convicts, 1884–1886*, pp. 187–88; Alabama, *Second Biennial Report of the Inspectors of Convicts, 1886–1888*, lists of county convicts; *UMWJ*, 10 February 1898. For a later critique of the "fee system" see Shelby Harrison, "A Cash-Nexus for Crime," *The Survey*, 6 January 1912.

42. Alabama, *Third Biennial Report of the Inspectors of Convicts*, Montgomery, 1890, pp. 204, 206.

Alabama's mines.[43] In its investigation of the Birmingham District in 1910 the U.S. Immigration Commission attributed a "steadily increasing supply of efficient, steady and trained negro miners" over the last few decades to Alabama's convict-lease system:

> ... after the convict has worked in the coal mines for several years he has learned a trade thoroughly. Not only does he become a trained miner, but owing to the system of rigid discipline and enforced regularity of work, he becomes through habit a steady workman, accustomed to regular hours. When his term [in prison] ends he almost invariably ... continues to be a coal miner for the reason that he does not know how to do anything else, and because he has been taught to do one thing well and to earn a good wage.

The Commission estimated that fifty percent of the black coal miners in Birmingham were ex-convicts.[44] The convict camps thus may have proved to be a peculiar but effective training ground for a crucial component of the South's industrial labor force.

Men like R.L. Davis, and other UMW organizers, recognized that convict labor was "hurtful to the white and colored miner alike" in driving down wages and breaking strikes, and that forced labor was effective because it could not be organized. But another significant impact of forced proletarianization was the increase in labor supply and the creation of a reserve army of labor through the steady "unnatural" influx of ex-convicts into the coal fields. Thus the UMW *Journal* complained that "all of [the convicts] are coal diggers when set free, and sometimes take the place of honest, practical miners, and not one in every twenty ... saw a coal mine until convicted." "Jefferson County [Birmingham] seems to be the selected dumping ground of the state," complained "Observer," and convicts remained there after serving time, not only "bringing them into competition with free labor as convicts [but] filling up this county with ex-convicts from all over the state."

43. R.H. Dawson, President of Alabama Board of Inspectors of Convicts, in National Prison Association, *Proceedings*, 1888, p. 84; on percentage of black workers by the turn of the century see Paul B. Worthman, "Black Workers and Labor Unions in Birmingham, Alabama, 1897–1904," *Labor History*, vol. 10, Summer 1969, pp. 375–407. By 1920, seventy percent of Alabama miners were black according to one estimate; Alabama Coal Strike of 1920, File 170–1182, Federal Mediation Council Records, National Archives, Washington National Records Center, Suitland, MD; *UMWJ*, 10 February 1898; see also Lewis, *Black Coal Miners in America*, pp. 39, 191. On percentage of black convicts see Alabama, *Second Biennial Report of the Inspectors of Convicts, 1886–1888*, pp. 62–82; Alabama, *Second Biennial Report of the Board of Inspectors of Convicts, 1896–1898*, Montgomery, 1898, p. 19.

44. Reports of the Immigration Commission, *Immigrants in Industries, Bituminous Coal Mining*, p. 218.

Free miners objected to the "pouring loose on this community hordes of ex-convicts," which made it an undesirable place for free miners to live and work, and gave mining districts a bad reputation. The fact that this component of the labor force was black aided the coal operators in perpetuating the racial tensions so inimical to organization in the Birmingham District. If belied by occasional sympathy for the victims of the convict-lease, or rare attempts to organize them, the association of ex-convicts, cheap labor, and black strikebreakers, was a powerful one in the minds of white miners. Even in Kentucky, it was suggested, "nonunion camps are all black men, and they are constantly recruited from the convict camps of Tennessee and Alabama."[45]

Convict labor was not simply a wedge that was used to overcome what in the eyes of southern industrial boosters was an inefficient labor market; it also made a significant contribution to economic development of the region. The key factor in the successful operation of southern pig iron furnaces in the 1880s and 1890s was the use of locally produced coke as fuel; the crucial element in the production of southern coke was consistent access to cheap bituminous coal. The most successful coal and iron enterprises in the region were those that vertically integrated production of pig iron by stoking their furnaces with their own coke, which in turn had been produced with coal from their own captive mines. Coerced mine labor lay at the center of this productive process. Convicts appear in the first large-scale captive coal mines, in the most productive mines in each lessee's holdings – not to mention the region – and in the mines with the largest concentration of mine laborers in the Deep South. Finally, convicts labored for the most successful southern mineral companies, those that generally weathered the frequent depressions, swallowed up competitors, defeated challenges by organized labor, and moved into the vanguard of southern industrial growth.[46]

By the 1880s there were local observers who agreed that the coal and iron resources of Tennessee, Alabama, and Georgia were "destined to revolutionize the iron manufacture of the country" while admitting that "the important factor in the question of the cheap production of iron is prison labor."[47] Hoping for ever-increasing industrial growth the mine

45. *UMWJ*, 2 February 1898, 4 January 1894, 31 December 1891, 22 September 1904, 30 April 1891; *U.S. Steel Hearings*, p. 2984.

46. On integrated production see William T. Hogan, *Economic History of the Iron and Steel Industry in the United States*, 4 vols., Lexington, 1971, vol. 1, p. 74; Ethel Armes, *The Story of Coal and Iron in Alabama*, Birmingham, 1910, p. 275; Robert Gregg, *Origin and Development of of the Tennessee Coal, Iron and Railroad Company*, NY, 1948, pp. 13–14; Woodward Iron Co., *Alabama Blast Furnaces*; Tennessee Coal and Iron Division, *Biography of a Business*, 1960, p. 32.

47. Judge Milliken of Tennessee, quoted in American Iron and Steel Association, *Bulletin*, vol. 20, 29 December 1886, p. 347.

inspector of Tennessee pointed out in 1883 that "cheap coal and cheap coke are now the needs of our iron manufacturing enterprises," and that "from large operations doing a great business on a small margin of profit can only be expected [production of] cheap coal."[48] In the 1880s the largest coal mining and coke-smelting operations in the area were the Pratt mines in Birmingham, the TCI mines at Tracy City, Tennessee, the Knoxville Iron Co. mine in the Coal Creek District of Tennessee, and Joseph Brown's Dade Coal mines in northwest Georgia. Each of these enterprises used convicts for a significant portion of their labor force, both in the mines and at the coke ovens, and provided fuel for furnaces in Knoxville, Chattanooga, and Birmingham.[49]

Tennessee Coal, Iron and Railroad's Tracy City mines, for instance, were described in 1883 as "the largest single mining operation in the state," and two-thirds of the workers at these mines were leased convicts. In the early 1880s, the company operated four mines, 600 coke ovens, three iron furnaces, and twenty-three miles of rail line. It rested on three million dollars of capital – most of it held in New York.[50] By 1893 TCI, with its massive holdings in Tennessee and Alabama, was able to boast that it had become the "largest producer of bituminous coal and pig iron for the open market [i.e., non-steel production] of any company in America." And indeed TCI owned thirty percent of the mineral lands in Tennessee and Alabama, and produced sixty percent of the value of all coal and iron products in these two states.[51] In addition to its own integrated enterprise, TCI supplied fuel to railroads, cotton mills, oil mills, rolling mills, foundries, and cotton compresses all across the South. By 1898 a steel plant with a projected daily capacity of a

48. Tennessee Bureau of Agriculture, Statistics and Mines, *Coal: Report of Henry E. Colton, Geologist and Inspector of Mines*, Nashville, 1883, p. 51.

49. By 1882 the Pratt mines were the most productive in Alabama; Alabama, *Biennial Report of the Inspectors of the Alabama Penitentiary, 1880–1882*, Montgomery, 1882, pp. 82–84; Tennessee Bureau of Agriculture, Statistics and Mines, *Hand-Book of Tennessee*, Knoxville, 1883, p. 24; Tennessee Division of Mines, *Second Annual Report*, p. 303; U.S. Census Office, *Mineral Industries of the United States, 1880*, vol. 15, p. 926; Tennessee Bureau of Statistics and Mines, *Report of Henry E. Colton*, pp. 42, 80; USGS, *Mineral Resources*, 1882, p. 7; Tennessee Division of Mines, *Fourth Annual Report of the Bureau of Labor, Statistics and Mines*, Nashville, 1895, p. 222. Virtually all of Georgia's 150,000–300,000 tons were mined by convicts; on Joseph Brown's mines see Derrell C. Roberts, "Joseph E. Brown and his Georgia Mines" *Georgia Historical Quarterly*, vol. 52, September 1968, pp. 285–92; Lichtenstein, "The Political Economy of Convict Labor," pp. 150–81. Fuller, "History of TCI"; and Gregg, *Origin and Development of TCI*, pp. 8–14 for history of Tracy City; Armes, *Story of Coal and Iron*, p. 273ff., for history of Pratt mines.

50. *Report of Henry E. Colton*, p. 81; Tennessee Bureau of Agriculture, *Hand-Book of Tennessee*, p. 24.

51. TCI, *Annual Report*, 1893, pp. 3–4; TCI, *Annual Report*, 1898.

thousand tons was in the works – surpassed only by Carnegie's Homestead in Pennsylvania.[52]

The development of this vast southern industrial empire can be traced to the the first mines opened in Tennessee, which provided the raw material for the development of coke and then iron production in the 1870s and 1880s. Located about twenty-five miles northwest of the Tennessee, Alabama and Georgia border, the Tracy City mines were first sunk into 25,000 acres of the Sewanee coal seam of Grundy county in the 1850s.[53] Yet, immediately after the war, in 1866, the mines shipped only 9,240 tons of coal – a negligible amount. And as late as 1870 only 47,110 tons of coal and 668 tons of coke were shipped from Tracy City by TCI.[54] But the origins of large-scale corporate mining and coke production in the New South can be discovered the following year, in Colonel Arthur S. Colyar's decision to place convicts in the Tracy City mines.

In 1871 the company leased 100 convicts from the state and put them to work in the mines. Three years later these mines were producing nearly half of the state's coal output, and the Bureau of Agriculture stated that "the coal in [Grundy] county is now at the very foundation of commerce and manufacturing, and by means of the capital and enterprise which it has developed, many other industrial interests have taken a new start."[55] In eight months of 1869, working the mines with free labor, TCI had made a profit of $7,379.42; between May 1871 and May 1872, with a convict labor force in place, the same mines earned the company $58,456.66. By 1873, TCI was selling coal produced for 4.28 cents a bushel at the price of 9.24 cents.[56]

However, the convicts produced a very high proportion of "slack" coal (that is, fine or broken bits of coal as opposed to "lump" coal), suitable only for stoking coke ovens. One internal report on the Tennessee

52. Alabama, *Second Biennial Report of the Inspectors of Mines, 1898*, Birmingham, 1898, pp. 16, 18.

53. J.B. Killebrew, *Special Report on the Coal-Field of Little Sequatchee*, Nashville, 1876, map; Tennessee Department of Education, Division of Geology, *The Southern Tennessee Coal Field, Bulletin 33-A*, Nashville, 1925, pp. 4–5; Tennessee Bureau of Agriculture, Statistics and Mines, *Report of Henry E. Colton*, p. 80; Fuller, "History of TCI," p. 280; Armes, *Story of Coal and Iron*, pp. 362–68. On the antebellum and Civil War history of TCI see TCI Division, *Biography of a Business*, pp. 3–8.

54. Tennessee Bureau of Agriculture, Statistics and Mines, *Report of Henry E. Colton*, p. 80.

55. Fuller, "History of TCI," pp. 176, 289; Tennessee Bureau of Agriculture, Statistics and Mines, *Report of Henry E. Colton*, p. 80; *Nashville Republican Banner*, 18 December 1872; Tennessee Bureau of Agriculture, *Introduction to the Resources of Tennessee*, Nashville, 1874, p. 746; Tennessee Bureau of Agriculture, Statistics, and Mines, *Tennessee: Its Agricultural and Mineral Wealth*, Nashville, 1876, pp. 90–117.

56. Sewanee Mining and Tennessee Coal, Iron and Railroad Company Records, Birmingham Public Library, microfilm, p. 6.

mines suggested that the proportion of slack in convict mines was as high as forty-six percent, twice that common in free mines.[57] In general, the more dependent a mine operation was on convict labor, the more likely it was to coke a high proportion of its own coal in subsidiary ovens.[58] Indeed, one of the reasons TCI built 120 coke ovens in 1873 was to provide an outlet for its convict-mined slack coal, which was difficult to sell on the open market. The company then expanded to pig iron production which would rely on the Tracy City coke for fuel.[59] By 1876 the state geologist claimed that Sewanee coal had been "mined more extensively than any other in the state.... It makes excellent coke, which is used extensively in the manufacture of pig iron, and in rolling mills," he boasted.[60]

The success of these mines should come as no surprise, for Col. Colyar, President of TCI in the early 1870s, was quite explicit about the distinct advantages he saw in forced labor. In June of 1870 the Nashville *Republican Banner* had suggested that the state purchase the then struggling Sewanee coal mines from Colyar and work its convicts there, in order to provide cheap fuel for other industrial enterprises in the area. With a steady supply of inexpensive coal, the *Banner* believed, "manufacturing enterprise and capital will flow into the state." Furthermore, "if the scarcity of fuel is attributable to the scarcity of labor" in east Tennessee, convict labor provided the ideal solution. Rather than competing with free (white) labor, convict workers in the mines would stimulate manufacturing and increase the opportunities for employment, drawing the state's population into the industrial sector.[61]

But Colyar himself did the paper one better, by suggesting that the state provide him with the convicts while he maintained ownership of the mines. Iron and coal production in Tennessee were "in their incipiency," but "having absolute control of the [convict] labor ... [will]

---

57. USGS, *Mineral Resources*, 1886, p. 252; Tennessee Division of Mines, *Fifth Annual Report of the Commissioner of Labor and Inspector of Mines*, Nashville, 1896, pp. 210–11; Tennessee Division of Mines, *Third Annual Report of the Commissioner of Labor and Inspector of Mines*, Nashville, 1894, p. 93; Report by L.E. Bryant, Chief Engineer of Tennessee State Mines, in USGS, *Mineral Resources*, 1894, p. 189; "Report on Tracy City Division of TCI, April 1, 1895," pp. 5–6, Erskine Ramsey papers, BPL.

58. USGS, *Mineral Resources*, 1883–1884, p. 160; Georgia Penitentiary, Principal Physician, *Report*, 1884–1886, p. 109; USGS, *Mineral Resources*, 1900, p. 372; USGS, *Mineral Resources*, 1901, pp. 358, 430, 443; Charles W. Hayes, "The Southern Appalachian Coal Field," in USGS, *Twenty-Second Annual Report*, pt. 3, p. 260.

59. Sewanee Mining and Tennessee Coal, Iron and Railroad Company Records, BPL, microfilm,, pp. 7, 10–11.

60. Killebrew, *Special Report*, pp. 9, 17–20. Also, see Gregg, *Origins and Development of TCI*, pp. 13–14.

61. *Nashville Republican Banner*, 10 and 11 June 1870.

make it a certainty that the labor can be profitably used," Colyar insisted. Best of all, he argued, with convict labor "you remove all danger and cost of strikes, which is a big [cost] item in the production of coal in this state." The cheaper and steadier labor of convicts would provide cheaper coal for all the state's people, including its free workers, Colyar concluded.[62] By the end of 1872 Colyar again wrote to the paper, unabashedly proclaiming that "this noticeable speck of enterprise ... is especially due to the convict labor system adopted by the company," and the success of the Tennessee coal trade was the "result of a steady and uniform system of labor" made possible by coercion.[63]

During the 1880s, TCI continued to expand its operations in Tennessee, purchasing an iron furnace in South Pittsburgh from a failing British company in 1882, and then preceding to open up the nearby Inman ore mines with a convict labor force. With the security of convict-produced coke from Tracy City and the iron ore from the Inman mines, TCI erected two additional furnaces at South Pittsburgh; these three furnaces, with a daily capacity of 125 tons of pig iron each, were the largest in Tennessee.[64] TCI became Tennessee's dominant coal company, operating thirteen of the state's sixty-six coal mines by 1891, and was responsible for over twenty percent of the state's coal output even within a vastly expanded industry. Tracy City's coke ovens alone in 1892 produced 132,541 tons of the state's total of 334,508 tons of coke, far surpassing all competitors; the company's furnaces produced nearly one-third of the state's pig iron. Convicts continued to lie at the heart of this integrated production of coal, coke, and iron.[65] TCI's success in Tennessee was surpassed in the 1890s when the company's position of strength allowed it to cross the border and buy up some of the most promising companies in Alabama's coal field, especially in the Birmingham District. Thus, in 1896, when the state of Tennessee reclaimed its convicts and placed them in a state-owned mine, coal production at Tracy City declined twenty-five

---

62. *Nashville Republican Banner*, 14 August 1870.

63. *Nashville Republican Banner*, 12 and 13 December 1872.

64. Tennessee Division of Mines, *Second Annual Report*, pp. 314, 341; Armes, *Story of Coal and Iron*, pp. 390–91; Fuller, "History of TCI," p. 49.

65. Tennessee Division of Mines, *Second Annual Report*, pp. 52, 48, 62–63, 303, 50, 342; Tennessee Division of Mines, *Fourth Annual Report of the Bureau of Labor, Statistics and Mines*, January 1895, p. 283; USGS, *Mineral Resources*, 1891, p. 320; "Report on Tracy City Division of TCI, April 1, 1895," pp. 4, 7, Erskine Ramsey papers, BPL; TCI, *Annual Report for the fiscal year ending January 31, 1892*, p. 3; Tennessee Division of Mines, *Second Annual Report*, p. 314.

percent, but TCI had already shifted the bulk of its operations to Birmingham, where the convict-lease was secure.[66]

Coal and iron development in Alabama closely paralleled that of east Tennessee and northwest Georgia; the original mines, the most productive mines, and the mines most central to industrial integration were the ones that successfully concentrated, monopolized, and exploited convict labor. In 1874 Alabama's Commissioner of Industrial Resources could still complain that "coal mining in this state ... can only be considered at this time in the merest dawn of its infancy," only 40,000 tons in 1873 – easily surpassed in the 1880s by a single convict mine. By 1885, the year before TCI bought into the Alabama field, the state mined 2,225,000 tons of coal, 401,000 tons of which were dug by convicts.[67] In large measure this "new era in the coal business of Alabama" could be attributed to the Pratt Coal and Coke Company, which opened mines six miles from Birmingham in 1879. By 1886, Pratt's four mines produced 622,940 tons of coal. Two of these four mines were worked entirely by 506 convicts; indeed, the Pratt Co. was the primary lessee of both state and county convicts in Alabama. Essentially, its coal mines were the penitentiary.[68]

The Pratt Coal and Coke Co., later to be made TCI's Alabama division, was the creation of one of the postbellum South's most notorious capitalist entrepreneurs, Henry F. DeBardeleben. Contemporaries described the ruthless DeBardeleben as "the most successful organizer of great industries who, probably, ever lived in Alabama," as well as "one of the wealthiest men in the South." Even the United Mine Workers acknowledged "King Henry" as "the great `developer' of the coal and iron industry of Alabama," but pointed out that "he is also well known ... to be among the first employers of convict labor in the

66. For TCI's move to Alabama see Fuller, `History of TCI," p. 177; Gregg, *Origins and Development*, pp. 15–16; TCI Division, *Biography of a Business*, pp. 22–24; for production figures for the company's divisions see TCI, *Annual Report, 1892*, pp. 3–4. On the transfer of convicts to state-owned mines see Tennessee, *Report of the Board of Prison Commissioners, December 15, 1896*, n.p. n.d, pp. 12, 33; "Report on Tracy City Division," 1 April 1895, pp. 2–3, Erskine Ramsey papers, BPL; Tennessee Division of Mines, *Sixth Annual Report* Nashville, 1896, pp. 158–59.

67. Alabama Bureau of Industrial Resources, *Report of the Commissioner of Industrial Relations of Alabama*, Montgomery, 1875, p. 9; Geological Survey of Alabama, *On the Warrior Coal Field*, Montgomery, 1886, p. 13; Alabama, *First Biennial Report of the Inspector of Convicts, 1884–1886*, Montgomery, 1886, p. 21; USGS, *Mineral Resources*, 1886, p. 237.

68. USGS, *Mineral Resources*, 1886, p. 237; USGS, *Mineral Resources*, 1882, p. 36. For figures on convicts see Alabama, *Biennial Report of the Inspectors of the Alabama Penitentiary, 1882–1884*, Montgomery, pp. 104–110; Alabama, *First Biennial Report of the Inspectors of Convicts, 1884–1886*, Montgomery, 1886, pp. 113, 119, 187–88.

mines."[69] This New South entrepreneur brought together the crucial elements of outside investors, cheap coal from captive mines, coke ovens, iron furnaces dependent on his own fuel, and forced labor. This combination lay at the heart of Birmingham's industrial growth, and the "Magic City" became in turn the most significant example of industrial development in the Lower South. By 1898, with conversion to steel production on the horizon, Alabama's inspector of mines and industry looked back over two decades of rapid industrial development and concluded that "the Birmingham district owes more to the Pratt mines for its existence than any other agency," mines that continued to work nearly a thousand convicts.[70]

The most dramatic leaps in the levels of coal production – and consequent investment in blast furnaces – in Alabama appear to coincide with the large-scale use of convict labor in the 1880s by the Pratt Company and its main competitor in the Birmingham District, the Sloss Company mines at Coalburg. These two companies together monopolized Alabama's convict lease by the end of the 1880s, and consequently established the region's most sophisticated integrated coal, coke, and iron facilities.[71] Above all it was DeBardeleben's initial demonstration that cheap coal for coking purposes was available in the Birmingham District that in turn "induced other capitalists to invest at Birmingham in blast furnaces and rolling mills."[72] A coke-fueled iron furnace had been put in blast during the war, but "the experiment was not continued" because of the absence of a steady supply of coal; convict labor had solved this problem.[73]

69. John W. DuBose, ed., *The Mineral Wealth of Alabama and Birmingham Illustrated*, Birmingham, 1886, p. 145; American Iron and Steel Association, *Bulletin*, no. 17, 4 July 1883, p. 179; *UMWJ*, 26 April 1894. The best secondary sources on DeBardeleben are Armes, *Story of Coal and Iron*; Fuller, "History of TCI"; Justin Fuller, "Henry F. DeBardeleben, Industrialist of the New South," *Alabama Review*, vol. 39, January 1986, pp. 3–18; and Marjorie L. White, *The Birmingham District: An Industrial History and Guide*, Birmingham, 1981. See also Worthman, "Black Workers and Labor Unions in Birmingham," pp. 376–79.

70. Alabama, *Second Biennial Report of the Inspectors of Mines, 1898*, pp. 16, 19, 21; Armes, *Story of Coal and Iron*, pp. 273, 275; Clark, *History of Manufactures*, vol. 2, p. 215.

71. Alabama, *Annual Report of the Alabama Penitentiary, From October 1, 1873 to September 30, 1874*, p. 5; U.S. Census Office, *Minerals*, 1880, vol. 15, p. 866; USGS, *Mineral Resources*, 1886, p. 237; *Biennial Report of the Inspectors of the Alabama Penitentiary, 1880–1882*, p. 4; *First Biennial Report of the Inspectors of Convicts, 1884–1886*, pp. 187–88.

72. American Iron and Steel Association, *Bulletin*, vol. 17, 4 July 1883, p. 179.

73. DuBose, *Mineral Wealth of Alabama*, p. 145; White, *The Birmingham District: An Industrial History*, p. 44; Armes, *Story of Coal and Iron*, p. 261; Fuller, "History of TCI," p. 236; *Annual Report of the Inspectors of the Alabama Penitentiary, 1875–1876, 1876–1877*; for the importance of the shift to coke-fueled furnaces see J. Allen Tower, "The Industrial Development of the Birmingham Region," *Bulletin of Birmingham-Southern College*, vol. 46, December 1953, pp. 11–12,

Recognizing the potential for cheap iron production, DeBardeleben and his original partner James W. Sloss purchased 30,000 acres of the Warrior coal field, adjacent to the fledgling city of Birmingham, in 1878.[74] The Pratt Company opened its first two mines in 1880 and 1881 with approximately 110 convict miners leased from the state.[75] On 23 November 1880, DeBardeleben put into blast the city's first iron furnace, "Alice No. 1," fueled steadily by coked coal from his convict mines. This furnace supplied pig iron to the Birmingham Rolling Mills, which by 1888 was the city's largest employer in manufacturing, with 900 workers.[76]

With an assured, virtually limitless, and adjacent source of mineral fuel, Birmingham industry boomed from 1880 onwards.[77] In the four years after the Pratt mines began to ship coal, eight new major industrial concerns were founded, bringing rolling mills, furnaces, and additional mining companies to the district. Many of these industries relied directly on convict-mined coal, and in fact were founded or encouraged by DeBardeleben and Sloss themselves, as outlets for their product. The Pratt Coal and Coke Co. grew apace, as did the related pig iron industry in the area. By 1886 developed industry in Birmingham included over five million dollars of "active capital engaged in the manufacture of pig iron," and between 1880 and 1890 the amount of capital invested in Alabama blast furnaces rocketed from 2.7 to 15.7 million dollars.[78]

When Pratt Coal and Iron was subsequently absorbed by TCI in 1886 it was "the largest coal company in the South," and half of the company's daily coal output was maintained by its force of convicts.[79] Consequently, one of the first steps TCI took on its accession to power in the Birmingham District in the late 1880s was to secure a guaranteed force of 600 convicts for ten years, paying $18.50 a month for a "first class" miner, who was required to produce four tons of coal daily. Given that in 1889 free coal miners in Alabama earned on average $2.15 per

74. Armes, *Story of Coal and Iron*, p. 273; Fuller, "History of TCI," pp. 183–84. For the best history of Birmingham see Carl V. Harris, *Political Power in Birmingham, 1871–1921*, Knoxville, 1977.

75. Alabama, *Second Biennial Report of the Inspectors of Mines, 1898*, pp. 23, 28; *Biennial Report of the Inspectors of the Alabama Penitentiary, 1880–1882*, Montgomery, 1882, p. 4.

76. DuBose, *Mineral Wealth of Alabama*, p. 67; White, *The Birmingham District: An Industrial History*, p. 46.

77. White, *The Birmingham District: An Industrial History*, p. 46.

78. Armes, *Story of Coal and Iron*, pp. 283–84, 290–93; DuBose, *Mineral Wealth of Alabama*, pp. 173–74; Clark, *History of Manufactures*, vol. 2, p. 215.

79. Fuller, "History of TCI," p. 69; DuBose, *Mineral Wealth of Alabama*, pp. 169, 173; Alabama, *First Biennial Report of the Inspectors of Convicts, 1884–1886*, pp. 113, 119, 187–88; Gregg, *Origins and Development*, pp. 15–16; TCI Division, *Biography of a Business*, pp. 22–24.

day, and worked about sixty days fewer than convicts during the course of a year, TCI obtained from the state a steady labor force at a good savings, even with the cost of maintaining the convicts.[80]

Despite its efforts at monopolization, the Pratt/TCI nexus of coal and iron production was not the only industrial concern in Alabama able to place convicts at the base of its productive process. During the 1880s the Sloss company underwent a similar trajectory. In 1881, DeBardeleben encouraged his partner, James W. Sloss, to start his own furnace company in order to widen the local market for the rapidly expanding production of Pratt coal and coke. With "the promise of cheap coal from the Pratt mines" Sloss established the Sloss Furnace Company and erected two blast furnaces and some coke ovens ten miles north of the city. Then, in 1886/87, Sloss sold out to northern capitalists, and a consolidation capitalized at three million dollars was effected, creating the Sloss Iron and Steel Co. Significantly, in this reorganization the company acquired its own captive convict mines in the district, severing its dependence on coal from its main competitor, TCI.[81]

These were the mines at Coalburg, owned since 1882 by the Coalburg Coal and Coke Co., Alabama's second largest lessee of convicts. In its first two years the Coalburg Co. went from a production level of 125 to 4,000 tons a day. The Pratt Co., and then TCI, leased the majority of the *state* convicts. But the Coalburg Coal Co. – and consequently Sloss Iron and Steel – were able to recruit their miners from the pool of convicts sentenced in Alabama's county courts, in surrounding Jefferson county and across the state in nine other counties. Often these convicts were sentenced for court "costs" or fines they were unable to pay. Before the consolidation, in 1886, Coalburg worked 192 convicts in two of its four mines, which overall produced 186,000 tons of coal – second only to the Pratt mines.[82] By 1889, having acquired additional county convicts, the Sloss Co. worked 320 convicts at its Coalburg

---

80. Alabama, *Second Biennial Report of the Inspectors of Convicts, 1886–1888*, pp. 2–3, 251; USGS, *Mineral Resources*, 1889–1890, pp. 170–71, for free wages; R.M. Cunningham, "The Convict System of Alabama in Its Relation to Health and Disease," in National Prison Association, *Proceedings*, 1889, pp. 108–41; for labor in the Alabama mines see also Alabama General Assembly, *Journal of the House of Representatives, 1896–97*, pp. 627–29.

81. White, *The Birmingham District: An Industrial History*, pp. 46, 145–46; Alabama, *Second Biennial Report of the Inspectors of Mines, 1898*, pp. 11, 13; DuBose, *Mineral Wealth of Alabama*, pp. 172–73; Armes, *Story of Coal and Iron*, pp. 288–89, 347–53; Woodward Iron Co., *Alabama Blast Furnaces*, pp. 128–29.

82. Armes, *Story of Coal and Iron*, pp. 438–39; Alabama, *First Biennial Report of the Inspectors of Convicts, 1884–1886*, pp. 187–88; USGS, *Mineral Resources*, 1886, p. 237.

mines, and production expanded as the number of prisoners continued to grow.[83]

By 1892 the Sloss Iron and Steel Co. furnaces, fueled by the Coalburg coal and coke, produced 175,000 tons of pig and foundry iron annually – again, second only to TCI.[84] And much as TCI was built upon the conglomeration of numerous coal mines, coke ovens, and blast furnaces, so too did the Sloss Co. form the nucleus of ever larger concentrations of capital by absorbing smaller competitors and, in turn, merging with others itself. In great measure these corporations' strength can be attributed to the steady access to the cheap fuel that lay at the base of their industrial pyramid. As the scale of production swelled, convict labor guaranteed "a certain supply of a definite amount of coal."[85] Thus, in Alabama's mineral district by the turn of the century, TCI was only seriously rivaled by the recently consolidated Sloss-Sheffield Steel and Iron Company, which operated seven blast furnaces, 1,500 coke ovens, and five coal mines – including the original two convict mines at Coalburg, now working over 500 convicts at hard labor.[86]

Clearly convict-mined coal provided the necessary fuel for the exploitation of the Deep South's iron ore and the creation of a significant pig iron industry. By the mid–1890s, in fact, after a special investigation, Canadian Customs barred the importation of pig iron from twenty-three furnaces in Alabama and Tennessee because it was produced "under the taint of prison labour" by reliance on convict-produced coal and coke.[87] In the lower Appalachian coal field convicts were located in the mines that lay at the heart of the largest companies' ability to integrate and consolidate their operations on a massive scale. Indeed, in the southern states, as elsewhere, conglomerations of industrial enterprises into ever-larger and dominant corporations marked the period from 1880 to 1900.[88] Unlike the rest of the

83. Alabama, *Third Biennial Report of the Inspectors of Convicts, 1888–1890*, pp. 51, 97; Alabama, *Fourth Biennial Report of the Inspectors of Convicts, 1890–1892*; Alabama, *Mine Inspector, First Biennial Report of the State Inspector of Mines, 1892–1894*, p. 56.

84. White, *The Birmingham District: An Industrial History*, pp. 145–46.

85. Alabama, *House Journal, 1896–97*, p. 651. For mergers and acquisitions in Alabama's iron industry see Chapman, *Iron and Steel Industries*, p. 141; Tower, "Industrial Development of Birmingham Region," pp. 13–16; Gregg, *Origins and Development of TCI*, pp. 16–19; Woodward Iron Co., *Alabama Blast Furnaces*, p. 31.

86. Alabama, *Second Biennial Report of the Board of Inspectors of Convicts, 1896–1898*, p. 19; Barbara J. Mitchell, "Steel Workers in a Boom Town: Birmingham 1900," *Southern Exposure*, vol. 12, November/December 1984, pp. 56–60; White, *The Birmingham District: An Industrial History*, pp. 145–46; Wayne Flynt, *Mine, Mill and Microchip: A Chronicle of Alabama Enterprise*, Northridge CA, 1987, p. 115.

87. "The `Prison-Made' Pig Iron in Canada," *Ironmonger*, n.d., James Bowron Scrapbooks, 1895–1902, BPL.

88. Clark, *History of Manufactures*, vol. 2, pp. 239–42, 280–85.

nation however, this process was closely tied to the availability of forced labor.

Corporate consolidation was closely related to another characteristic of the Deep South's coal field during the 1880s and 1890s, also similar to national trends. Nationwide, the coal industry was noted for labor strife, strikes, and violence; as the U.S. Geological Survey complained in its 1889 report, "strikes are of almost constant occurrence [in the coal industry] in one part of the country or another," due to the miners' refusal to accept wage cuts when "the state of the market renders a curtailment of mining expenses necessary." Alabama and Tennessee were no exception. During the 1890s industrial development, rural dislocation, urbanization, and economic depression both swelled the available free labor pool in the South and exacerbated conflict between labor and capital in the region. Even while in sheer numbers convict labor declined in significance as southern industry expanded its free labor operations, it remained crucial to the patterns of labor strife and industrial integration in the New South even into the twentieth century.[89] Rapid industrial development in a poorly developed and capital-scarce region was dependent on stable labor relations; disputes between labor and capital threatened to impede production or scare away desperately needed capital investment. Thus convict labor was placed at a key point in the industrial process in order to insure a predictable supply of coal, and to keep iron furnaces in blast during strikes or labor unrest.

Despite T.J. Hill's suggestion that convict labor "was a benefit instead of a detriment to the larger class of free labor," in the South over twenty recorded coal strikes between 1881 and 1900 were in opposition to convict labor in the mines. Where convicts and free miners worked in the same vicinity, they "[did] not come in contact without friction," TCI reported. The pages of the *United Mine Workers Journal*, which began publication in 1891, are filled with denunciations of convict leasing in the mines: the miners recognized that prisoners were used "to prevent the spread of organization and as an `effectual preventative' during a strike." "Free men cannot contend and strike in a state that the largest coal output is worked by convict labor,"

89. USGS, *Mineral Resources*, 1889–1890, p. 169; Anna Rochester, *Labor and Coal*, NY, 1931, p. 179; *Engineering and Mining Journal*, no. 86, 15 August 1908, pp. 335–36; Richard A. Straw, "The Collapse of Biracial Unionism: The Alabama Coal Strike of 1908," in *Blacks in Appalachia*, pp. 183–98; Lewis, *Black Coal Miners*, pp. 45–58; Robert David Ward and William Warren Rogers, *Convicts, Coal and the Banner Mine Tragedy*, Tuscaloosa, 1987, pp. 49–50.

complained a UMW district organizer in Alabama in 1895, in the wake of the failed strike of 1894.[90]

The union's antagonists were hardly reticent in agreeing with this observation. DeBardeleben himself told the Alabama General Assembly that "convict labor competing with free labor is advantageous to the mine owner. If all were free miners they could combine and strike and thereby put up the price of coal," he pointed out, "but where convict labor exists the mine owner can sell coal cheaper." He also noted that in the absence of labor troubles, the operator – and presumably the state's industries that relied on cheap coal – benefited from "the certainty of filling his contracts." As late as 1911, TCI's new president readily admitted in a letter to the Board of Convict Inspectors that "the chief inducement for the hiring of convicts was the certainty of a supply of coal for our manufacturing operations in the contingency of labor troubles." One investigator of Progressive Era industrial conditions in the Birmingham District told the U.S. Congress that "one peculiar advantage [of convict labor] which the employers admit is that it gives them a club over organized labor. Whenever there is a strike, the convict mines go on turning out coal regularly," he noted. "So long as coal is mined here by convicts the mine workers will never close this district," industrialist James Bowron proclaimed in 1923, more than three decades after the UMW's first attempts to organize the Alabama field.[91]

From the beginning the most successful coal operators had recognized the potential for labor control embodied in convict labor. As Arthur S. Colyar of TCI remarked in 1872, "to put on foot successful mining operations in Tennessee with two strikes a year was impossible.... This has been remedied by convict labor."[92] With forced labor, a supply of cheap fuel was secure and delivery was certain. "Those dependent on coal have no such security anywhere [else]," he boasted. The convict mines in Tennessee were the "only mines in the United States free from strikes," and this fact would certainly attract capital and manufacturing enterprises to the region. In this respect the Tennessee mines would prove a sharp contrast to the Pennsylvania coal fields, which were wracked by class conflict. "The reason given for the high price of coal in all northern cities is the uncertainty of labor to mine it," the Colonel proclaimed. "Using our convict labor in the very commence-

90. T.J. Hill, "Experience in Mining Coal With Convicts," p. 396; Hilda J. Zimmerman, "Penal Systems and Penal Reforms in the South since the Civil War," unpublished PhD. dissertation, University of North Carolina, 1947, p. 220; TCI, *Annual Report*, 1890, p. 7; *UMWJ*, 30 April 1891, 28 March 1895.

91. *UMWJ*, 26 April 1894; George Crawford to J.G. Oakley, 24 November 1911, reproduced in *U.S. Steel Hearings*, p. 3112; *U.S. Steel Hearings*, testimony of John A. Fitch, p. 2940; Norrell, *Autobiography of a New South Industrialist*, p. 241.

92. Arthur Colyar, letter to the *Nashville Republican Banner*, 27 December 1872.

ment of our mining operations ... we may avoid the conflict between labor and capital which has made the immense mines of Pennsylvania a boiling cauldron under the commerce of the nation," he concluded.[93] Other observers also favorably contrasted southern coal mining with the northern industry. "The condition of the coal trade in the North has been clearly portrayed by the almost constant strikes and disputes between employers and employed ... while here [in Alabama] there has been no interruption in the production of coal," remarked the editor of a Philadelphia paper during a trip to the South in the 1880s, pointing to the successful use of convicts as one of the reasons for labor peace.[94]

Such peace was shortlived. The great coal and iron boom of the 1880s was followed by new challenges to the industry in the 1890s: increased competition, a deep depression, and a sharp drop in the price of coal and iron; the pressing necessity to convert iron production to steel; and labor conflict on a massive scale, particularly as the Knights of Labor and then the UMW made inroads in the Alabama field and corporations attempted to cope with the drop in prices.[95] Access to convict labor proved a crucial asset for the corporations that weathered these crises, by providing flexibility during economic downturns, helping to defeat labor's challenge, and allowing TCI and Sloss to consolidate power in the Birmingham District and convert to steel production.

Convicts proved significant to labor conflicts in several ways during the 1890s. First, rather than cut tonnage rates to cope with diminishing coal markets, a company might curtail production by laying off its free workers, and maintaining its convict mines at full production levels. One of the main grievances miners in Tennessee voiced about convict labor was that "in dull times, when orders [for coal] were slack, free labor was made idle, while convicts were compelled to perform their tasks." The *UMWJ* concurred that "when trade is slack, the convict works and the free miner stays at home. When cars run slow in the mine, the convict gets his usual quota while the free miner remains a looker on."[96] Second, in the event of a strike a company with convicts could continue to produce coal, which in turn could be used to meet contracts

93. *Nashville Republican Banner*, 17, 19, and 27 December 1872.

94. Reprint of letter by A.K. McClure, *Philadelphia Times*, 28 January 1885, in J.W. Burke, "The Coal Fields of Alabama," pamphlet, c. 1885, p. 39.

95. Norrell, *Autobiography of a New South Industrialist*, introduction; Ward and Rogers, *Labor Revolt in Alabama*; Clark, *History of Manufactures*, vol. 2, pp. 302–3; Alfred M. Shook to Arthur S. Colyar, 30 September 1892; G.B. McCormack to Nat Baxter, 1 April 1892; and Alfred M. Shook to Benjamin Talbot, c. 1894, all in A.M. Shook Papers, BPL.

96. Fuller, "History of TCI," pp. 293–94; see also letters to the *National Labor Tribune*, 4 January and 2 August, 1879, reprinted in Gutman, "Black Coal Miners and the Greenback-Labor Party," pp. 516, 526; and USGS, *Mineral Resources*, 1896, p. 607;

or stoke their own furnaces – avoiding the costliest damage of a strike to integrated coal and iron production, the taking of a furnace out of blast. "In case of strikes," TCI assured its stockholders in the annual report for 1890, "[the convicts] can furnish us enough coal to keep at least three of the Ensley furnaces running."[97] In frequent instances convicts actually entered mine labor in direct response to a strike, effectively replacing the free labor force in a particular mine for good or opening a new mine altogether.[98]

A shift from dependence on free to convict labor might also occur as a lockout, in order to enforce a wage cut or a speed-up, or to break an *anticipated* strike. Fearing that free miners were planning a walkout at the end of 1890 in order to renegotiate their wage scale and join the newly formed UMW, TCI president Alfred Shook advised his General Manager G.B. McCormack to prepare to break the strike. "Bank *every* furnace you can," he told "Mac," and "seal up the [coke] ovens." During the lockout the company should "put all convicts on coal, in whatever mines are best," and then sell the coal to "railroads, rolling mills, [and] other large customers." Moreover, if "there is any trouble between the [free] miners and the convicts" then "the state of Alabama should protect you with the strong arm of the law." The other danger was that of miners "working on the convicts to induce them not to do extra work during the strike," but the Warden could guard against that. "By this means you can certainly whip the strike in 45 days," Shook assured McCormack, and within two weeks the strike indeed appeared to be "whipped" and a ten to fifteen per cent wage cut was anticipated. "This strike has done more to put off the day when convicts will be taken out of Jefferson County than anything," presciently remarked one of Alabama's convict inspectors at the close of 1890.[99]

A similar strategy used the following year in Tennessee had far less beneficial results, however, when miners took militant action to insure that "they would no longer be forced to compete ... with men who had by their criminal acts forfeited the right to liberty."[100] In fact, the notorious "convict war" of east Tennessee in 1891/92 was a direct result of attempts

97. Tennessee Division of Mines, *Second Annual Report*, pp. 141–42; Tennessee Coal, Iron and Railroad Company, *Annual Report for the Fiscal Year Ending January 31, 1890*, p. 13; TCI, *Annual Report*, 1891, p. 9; TCI, *Annual Report*, 1892, p. 9.

98. Tennessee Division of Mines, *Second Annual Report*, pp. 141–42, 193; Erskine Ramsey to G.B. McCormack, 13 February 1896, ER Papers, BPL.

99. A.M. Shook to G.B. McCormack, 24 November 1890, 4 December 1890, 9 December 1890, and 16 December 1890, Shook Papers, BPL; Ward and Rogers, *Labor Revolt in Alabama*, pp. 32–33. A.T. Henley to R.H. Dawson, 19 December 1890, Reports from Inspectors and Other Officers, Incoming Correspondence, vol. 4, Department of Corrections Records, Alabama Department of Archives and History (ADAH), Montgomery.

100. *UMWJ*, 25 August 1892.

by mine operators to replace free workers with convicts, a shift induced both by layoffs and strikes.[101] In the first instance, with a glutted coal market, some operators curtailed production by shutting down their free labor mines and maintaining their convict mines, where labor was a predetermined cost, fixed by the state. Alternatively, following disputes over wage rates or the weighing of coal (a notorious means of extracting surplus from miners), miners would stage a walkout and then find themselves replaced by convicts and locked out.[102] "Not content with using convicts in their own mines," the *UMWJ* complained, the lessees "have adopted a hiring-out system, so that when miners sought to improve their position convicts would be supplied to the operators for the purpose of further crushing their workmen" in the Tennessee field.[103]

Within the space of thirteen months, Tennessee's coal miners attacked five convict camps, including TCI's Inman ore mines and the Tracy City coal mines, on three different occasions. Miners first struck the Tennessee Mining Company mines at Briceville in mid-July when their request to have a worker weigh the coal (a "checkweighman") was rejected. "Convicts from Coal Creek were sent to fill the places of the striking miners," the *UMWJ* reported, and the miners responded by driving the convicts from the mines by force.[104] When the legislature subsequently failed to abolish convict leasing the miners planned and executed "the final attack on the convict camps and the release of the prisoners." TCI's mines were spared until August 1892, when the convict camp at Tracy City was finally burned to the ground by free miners, and the convicts were set free. "There has been much dissatisfaction among the miners of Tracy City because of the lease system, which allows the bulk of the labor to be done in the mines by convicts," the *UMWJ* somewhat drily remarked. In fact, as the miners' paper had pointed out before, in Tennessee the convict question had ultimately "resolved itself into a contest of labor against capital."[105]

101. For descriptions of East Tennessee's "convict war" of 1891–92 see Tennessee Division of Mines, *Second Annual Report*, pp. 63, 142–43, 228–29, 341; USGS, *Mineral Resources*, 1893, pp. 377–83; and Friedrich A. Sorge, *The Labor Movement in the United States: A History of the American Working Class from 1890 to 1896*, Westport, 1987, pp. 13–24; Zimmerman, "Penal Systems," pp. 220–30; Pete Daniel, "The Tennessee Convict War," *Tennessee Historical Quarterly*, vol. 34, Fall 1975, pp. 273–92; and Archie Green, *Only a Miner: Studies in Recorded Coal-Mining Songs*, Urbana, pp. 155–91, for good secondary treatments.

102. Fuller, "History of TCI," pp. 126–27; USGS, *Mineral Resources*, 1896, p. 607; P.D. Sims, "The Lease System in Tennessee and Other Southern States," in National Prison Association, *Proceedings*, 1893, pp. 123–24, 126–27.

103. *UMWJ*, 23 July 1891.

104. *UMWJ*, 16 and 23 July 1891.

105. *UMWJ*, 24 September 1891, 5 November 1891, 18 August 1892; "Report of Assistant General Manager, Tennessee Divisions, TCI, Jan. 31st 1893," Shook Papers, BPL, pp. 3, 8; *UMWJ*, 5 November 1891.

The anti-convict insurrections in the Tennessee coal field were so severe that in 1892 the upheaval was held responsible for the fifteen percent reduction in coal output suffered by the state that year. Arthur Colyar himself publicly proclaimed – prematurely – that "when the Tennessee Coal and Iron Company gives up its lease it will never again employ convict labor." In an internal report the company noted that

> .... we have sustained the most serious losses by reason of the "Convict troubles" ... which resulted in the actual destruction of much valuable property, the temporary stoppage of our works, the increased cost of the material produced by convict labor, and the general demoralization [i.e., assertiveness] of all our labor.

This alone was a powerful admission of how central forced labor was to TCI's operations. "We have not been able to `reestablish' the standard of labor or the quality of coal and coke," since the convicts were released the report claimed, and the company's iron furnaces "suffered from the use of inferior coke," the report concluded. Despite the turmoil, the state returned the convicts to TCI only two weeks after they were released in 1892; by 1893, on the eve of a general strike by free miners, TCI operated two large new convict mines to supplement the Lone Rock mine at Tracy City, with an additional 185 convicts. By 1896, on the eve of the abolition of convict leasing in Tennessee, convicts working in two mines continued to produce seventy-three percent of Tracy City's coal, while convict coke oven workers made ninety percent of the division's coke. Tennessee did abolish the convict lease, but the miners' violence and suppression by the militia severely weakened the fledgling UMW in the Tennessee field, by the union's own admission.[106]

The same economic forces that generated the violent opposition to convict labor led to "a strike of unusual dimensions" in the spring of 1894, one that affected the entire Appalachian bituminous field, from Pennsylvania to Alabama. In response to unilateral wage cuts instituted by the coal operators one hundred and fifty thousand coal miners were called out of the mines by the national UMW on 26 April 1894, and the strike lasted most of the summer. But in Tennessee and Alabama the convict mines continued to produce coal – and turn a healthy profit, as

---

106. Tennessee, Division of Mines, *Fourth Annual Report of the Bureau of Labor, Statistics and Mines*, p. 282; USGS, *Mineral Resources*, 1892, pp. 491–92; *UMWJ*, 25 August 1892; "Report of Asst. GM, TN Divisions, TCI, Jan. 31st 1893," Shook Papers, BPL, pp. 1, 3, 5, 8; Tennessee Division of Mines, *Second Annual Report*, pp. 141–42, 77; Tennessee Division of Mines, *Third Annual Report of the Commissioner of Labor and Inspector of Mines*, Nashville, 1894, pp. 90–92; *UMWJ*, 21 September 1899.

coal became scarce and prices began to rise while the labor costs in convict mines remained fixed.[107] In Tennessee, for example, all the miners in the Coal Creek District went out on strike, but "the striking miners dislike very much the idea of the convicts turning out from twelve to eighteen cars of coal a day while they are on strike." In Tennessee the strike was short-lived; the most productive companies relied on their convicts, and held out.[108] In Alabama, convict labor in key productive sectors during this period of intense class conflict also proved essential to the survival and renewed dominance of the industry by the Birmingham District's most powerful corporations.

"Me thinks I hear the bugle sound ... and the Tennessee war is being tried at Pratt City and Coalburg and every man is on his way and soon the convicts are loose and the stockade is burning," wrote "Cromwell" in the *UMWJ* at the commencement of the 1894 upheaval.[109] Despite this call to arms, the Birmingham District did not experience a direct attack on convict mines as Tennessee had two years earlier, even though the 1894 walkout in Alabama led to an increased reliance on convicts.[110] Claiming that the two thousand daily tons produced by convicts at the Pratt mines were "not sufficient to keep the larger industries in the immediate district running" during the strike, TCI proposed to open a third convict mine. The company noted that such a step would be "an unprofitable transaction for us except for the advantage we may indirectly gain in the settlement of the labor troubles."[111] With this third mine TCI increased the number of convicts under its control to 1,138. The Sloss Company maintained its convict force at nearly 600 workers.[112]

Furthermore, production at the convict mines increased in 1894 by over thirty percent, while as a result of the strike the state's overall production dropped to 4,361,312 tons, a decrease of nearly one million tons (17.2 percent) from 1893. Thus, during the year in which Alabama coal operators faced their greatest challenge since the opening of the field, forced labor mined twenty-four percent of the state's coal, a substantial increase over the 14.4 percent of the previous year.[113] As the

107. USGS, *Mineral Resources*, 1894, pp. 9–10, 22; USGS, *Mineral Resources*, 1893, pp. 203–4. Also see *The Tradesman*, vol. 31, 1 May 1894, p. 50 on the strike in Alabama.

108. Tennessee Division of Mines, *Fourth Annual Report*, pp. 49–52, 66–67.

109. *UMWJ*, 19 April 1894.

110. On the 1894 strike in Alabama see Ward and Rogers, *Labor Revolt in Alabama*; USGS, *Mineral Resources*, 1894, pp. 9–10, 22–23.

111. Minutes of the Board of Managers of Convicts, 21 April 1894, pp. 49–50, Minutes 1893–1895, Department of Corrections Records, ADAH.

112. Alabama, *First Biennial Report of the Board of Inspectors of Convicts, 1894–1896*, pp. ii–xiii; Alabama, *First Biennial Report of the State Inspector of Mines, 1892–1894*, pp. 65–66.

113. These calculations are made from figures in Alabama's *First Biennial Report of the State Inspector of Mines*, pp. 56–57, 65–66.

U.S. Geological Survey reported at the end of 1894, in the Alabama mines "where convict labor is employed, the convicts continued to work while the free labor was out [on strike]." Thus, while the Pratt mines lost 1,500 workers to the strike, TCI could continue to supply coal to its coke ovens and fuel to the furnaces it intended to keep in blast. Similarly, the Coalburg mines reported that their convict force worked 310 days of 1894 – the most in the state – but their free labor worked only 170 days that year.[114]

The Tradesman, a southern industrial trade journal, noted in the early weeks of the strike that "the fact that there are about 1,000 convicts at the Pratt mines and 600 at Coalburg who mine coal has been the main factor in preventing a stoppage of production," since only 735 free miners remained at work in Alabama's mines. In fact, the journal hinted that the strike could be interpreted as a lockout. Due to the depression the operators preferred to idle most of their mines and furnaces, and keep only their convict force at work at a fixed labor cost so low they could afford it, even as coal and iron prices plummeted. As the Alabama House of Representatives reported, "when coal is short in sales the convicts continue their usual output, while the free miners are stopped."[115] Evidence from company records also suggests that what was a strike nationally was a lockout in Alabama, made possible by convict labor. A full month before the UMW's strike call one of TCI's director's advocated a lockout in order to institute a twenty-five percent wage cut. Henry F. DeBardeleben suggested that all the convicts be moved to the company's Blue Creek mine, "mining coal enough there for all the furnaces and closing down the other mines." Another group of convicts could be moved from Pratt to Blocton mines, and "the men thrown out of work there [Blocton] would be told they could get work at Pratt at a reduction of about 25%." By June Alabama's miners recognized that "the miners of Alabama came on strike one week prior to [the UMW]... because we were forced to it by trickery on the part of our employers," and that their strike was threatened "because of the hundreds of convicts we have that fill two of the largest and best mines in this section of the country."[116]

114. USGS, *Mineral Resources*, 1894, p. 67; Alabama, *First Biennial Report of the Inspector of Mines*, p. 66. On the effects of the strike on production see also J.J. Ormsbee, "The Coal Interests of the South," *The Tradesman*, vol. 34, 1 Jan. 1896, p. 111; see Ward and Rogers, *Labor Revolt*, pp. 89, 116, for the importance of convict labor in eventually breaking the strike.

115. *The Tradesman*, vol. 30, 15 May 1894, pp. 61–62; *The Tradesman*, vol. 30, 1 May 1894, p. 50; Alabama, *House Journal*, 1896–1897, p. 639.

116. A.M. Shook to G.B. McCormack, 10 March 1894, pp. 2–3, Shook Papers, BPL; *UMWJ*, 7 June 1894.

By the end of the summer the strike was broken, and TCI and Sloss emerged from the period of labor turmoil and economic depression in a stronger position than ever to dominate the market. With the state takeover of convict mining in Tennessee at the end of 1895, TCI continued to pour resources into its Alabama holdings where the lease was secure. In 1897 TCI's eighteen mines produced 47.4 percent of Alabama coal – and their three convict mines provided one-fourth of the company's total output. Convicts still made up 40.1 percent of TCI's labor force at the Pratt mines, and thirty-six percent of the Sloss Company's total coal mining force. And at this time, when Alabama produced thirty-five percent of all pig iron used in the country's foundries, mills, and pipe-works (production uses excluding steel plants), TCI's 2,250 ton *daily* output represented half of the state's production of this crucial industrial product.[117]

After 1898 TCI began the long-overdue conversion to accommodate the production of steel, fulfilling Alfred Shook's prediction that "as soon as the labor troubles are settled in the South, an active start looking to the manufacture of steel will be made at or near Birmingham."[118] Indeed, before the onset of the economic crisis and subsequent labor conflict, Shook had written to Arthur Colyar, extolling the past two decades of development while warning that it would be for naught without advancing to steel production. From the Tennessee and Cumberland watersheds, through north Georgia, down into Birmingham, coal, and pig iron had lain at the heart of the plateau's successful growth, Shook observed. "Without this development," he insisted, "the whole country from Roanoke Va[sic]... down to Chattanooga and Birmingham ... would today be practically what it was when the war closed. It has given employment ... compelled railroad systems to extend their lines," provided a market for timber and farm produce, and built schools, churches, villages, towns, and cities. Yet, Shook maintained, the future was in steel, and unless the South entered this market, its economy would be left behind. "If we are forced to stop the development of our yet practically untouched mineral fields for want of a [local] market, then the growth of our iron industry must stop," Shook concluded.[119]

117. Alabama, *Second Biennial Report of the Inspectors of Mines, 1898*, Birmingham, 1898, pp. 16, 19–20, chart; "Report on Tracy City Division," 1 April 1895, Erskine Ramsey Papers, BPL; Alabama, *Second Biennial Report of the Board of Inspectors of Convicts, 1896–1898*, pp. 9–10, 19; TCI, *Annual Report for the Fiscal Year Ending December 31st, 1897*, p. 6; Phillips, *Iron-Making*, 2nd ed., 1898, pp. 21, 4.

118. See TCI, *Annual Report for the Fiscal Year Ending December 31st, 1898*, p. 5; TCI Division, *Biography of a Business*, pp. 26–28; AMS to Benjamin Talbot, c. 1894, Shook Papers, BPL; source 100, 30 Nov. 1899, p. 39.

119. AMS to ASC, 30 Sept. 1892, Shook Papers, BPL; on the late conversion to steel, see Norrell, *Autobiography of a New South Industrialist*, pp. xxvi–xxxii; Wright, *Old South, New South*, pp. 164–70.

The corporations in the forefront of the south's coal and iron industry relied on convicts to recruit a reliable labor force, to build their enterprises, to integrate production, to consolidate corporate control, and to crush the labor organization that was the inevitable result of the creation of a southern industrial proletariat; these same powerful corporations were in the vanguard of the twentieth-century southern steel and cast-iron products industries as well. In 1902 the Sloss-Sheffield Steel and Iron Co. moved all of the convicts from Coalburg to its new Flat Top mines with a projected capacity of over 1,000 tons of coal per day, and 200 coke ovens that would provide "ample supply" for the company's seven furnaces. This improvement was "absolutely necessary both from an economic standpoint and in order to guarantee operations in face of bad weather, railway disasters, strikes, or other contingencies," the company's annual report confided. "The idea is to make the company independent in the matter of raw materials." With such independence, Sloss-Sheffield became a major supplier of pig iron to the region's pipe foundries.[120] TCI, the corporation that first opened a small convict mine at Tracy City in 1871 and brought steel to Birmingham at century's end, could boast that "the company is entirely self-contained, producing from its own land its iron ores ... and the coal, converting [it] into coke in its own ovens, producing its pig iron in its own blast furnaces, and converting the same into steel in its open hearth furnaces." TCI sold its twenty-three coal mines, eighteen ore mines, 3,000 coke ovens, sixteen blast furnaces, and eight open-hearth steel furnaces to U.S. Steel in 1907 for forty-nine million dollars; the conglomerate continued to use convicts to mine its coal.[121]

Convicts worked in Alabama's mines until 1928, longer than they were kept in comparable work in any southern state. Elsewhere – in Georgia, North Carolina, and Tennessee for example – during the first decades of the twentieth century southern convicts began to be placed on the roads, where their labor contributed to the development of a commercial infrastructure rather than extractive industry. In these states a new class of southern entrepreneurs and boosters advocated forced black labor for public rather than private benefit, for agricultural as well as industrial modernization, and conjoined the chain gang to the Progressive Era movement to improve the South's backward road-

120. Minutes, Stockholders and Board of Directors, 1899–1919, p. 87, Sloss-Sheffield Steel & Iron Co. Records, BPL; *Second Annual Report of the Sloss-Sheffield Steel and Iron Co., 30 November 1901*, pp. 10, 13; George Stocking, *Basing Point Pricing and Regional Development*, Chapel Hill, 1954, pp. 99, 103.

121. Prospectus," circa 1901, Bowron Scrapbooks, 1895–1902, BPL; TCI Records, microfilm, BPL, p. 57; Alabama, Governor, *Convict Department and Its Management*, Montgomery, 1913, pp. 50–51.

ways.[122] It was a testament to the power of Birmingham's coal barons that they were able to resist this new use of penal labor for so much longer than their counterparts in neighboring states.

U.S. Steel's southern division corporate hagiography, published in 1960, was dedicated to these nineteenth-century progenitors of TCI and the south's steel industry. The company recognized that Tennessee Coal and Iron's "earlier years, and in fact its first half century, marked a period of adversity which many times threatened its collapse."[123] Clearly the New South's capitalists did face several political, technological, financial, and structural checks on the growth of an industrial infrastructure. The lack of available capital, high transport costs to distant markets, and the problems of converting flawed mineral resources into high grade products all hampered regional industrial development. Furthermore, the southern coal and iron industry proved vulnerable to economic fluctuation because it already faced these impediments to its growth. Indeed, the sensitivity of southern industry to larger market trends was one of the compelling factors in southern industrialists' turning to convict labor in the first place. As in all societies undergoing rapid industrial transformation, the question of labor supply and control loomed large in the basic industries of the New South.[124] The scarcity of experienced labor, the unsteady and undisciplined nature of the pool of recently proletarianized southern workers, and competition for labor with the agricultural sector thus led southern capitalists to call on the state to intervene in the labor market with the penal system.

Barbara Fields has suggested that the political economy of the postbellum South be considered a "transition period between one dominant mode of production [slavery] and another [capitalism]," in which all southerners "found themselves drawn into the orbit of the capitalist market: but on the basis neither of the old social relations nor of mature capitalist ones." This particular model of underdevelopment reframes the question of continuity and discontinuity, and casts new light on the issue of whether the social relations of the New South traveled the "Prussian Road" or not. From this vantage point industrialization and unfree labor did not preclude one another. For in this "transitional"

122. On the good roads movement and convict labor see Alex Lichtenstein, "Good Roads and Chain Gangs in the Progressive South: `The Negro Convict is a Slave,'" *Journal of Southern History*, vol. 58, February 1993.

123. Tennessee Coal and Iron Division, *Biography of a Business*, n.p., 1960, frontispiece.

124. Steven Hahn and Jonathan Prude, eds, *The Countryside in the Age of Capitalist Transformation*, Chapel Hill, 1985, pp. 10–15; David M. Gordon, Richard Edwards, and Michael Reich, eds., *Segmented Work, Divided Workers*, Cambridge, 1982, chap. 3; Ira Katznelson and Aristide Zolberg, eds., *Working-Class Formation: Nineteenth-Century Patterns in Western Europe and the United States*, Princeton, 1986.

period, "hybrid forms [of capitalist social relations] made up of relics of slavery grafted onto developing new labor relations" defined the organization of production.[125] In the agricultural sector of the postbellum South the most notorious "hybrid form" was sharecropping, and its lever was the crop-lien. Outside of agriculture, convict labor exemplified a "hybrid form" linked to the classic symptoms of underdevelopment, including coercive labor relations. When the available free labor force was reluctant to enter the wage labor market on a steady basis, or attempted to collectively defend its interests within that labor market, the New South's industrialists turned to forced labor. What anti-enticement laws, crop-liens, and vagrancy statutes were to the planters, the convict-lease was to the emerging class of industrial entrepreneurs. TCI's corporate hagiography proudly noted the fact "that TCI survived to become the South's major steel producer is tribute enough to those daring pioneer businessmen who time and again risked their capital and their standing as industrialists to pull it back from the brink of disaster." True, economic "modernization" did occur in the New South, and a new class of southern entrepreneurs and industrialists did help promote this development that "typically represented the American spirit of free enterprise and business venture." But they did not hesitate to rely on penal slavery to make it possible.[126]

125. This theoretical approach is derived from Barbara J. Fields, "The Nineteenth-Century American South: History and Theory," esp. pp. 8, 22, 24–25. Fields, in turn, draws heavily on dependency theory and Marxist analyses of the transition from feudalism to capitalism.

126. Tennessee Coal and Iron Division, *Biography of a Business*.

Organized Labor, Black Workers, and the Twentieth Century South: The Emerging Revision[1]

Rick Halpern

Scarcely a decade ago, the history of black workers and organized labor in the twentieth-century South was straightforward and relatively free of contention. With its deeply held traditions of white paternalism and racial hierarchy, the South, historians maintained, remained a vast open shop thorn in the side of the labor movement. From the collapse of the IWW in the early twentieth century, through the failure of the CIO's post World War II southern organizing drive, the history of organized labor in the South has been depicted as one of frustration and defeat.[2]

An explanation of this dismal record is assumed to lie in the behavior of southern workers. Both black and white laborers, historians have long argued, have acted in ways that reflect their racial rather than class identities. While important instances of interracial working-class cooperation punctuate the history of the late nineteenth century, the institutionalization of Jim Crow brought this trend to a definitive end.[3]

According to the traditional view, supremacist ideology prevented southern white workers from understanding that their true economic interests paralleled those of blacks. Where southern unions have gained a foothold, whites have used them to insulate themselves against job competition from blacks, excluding African Americans from membership or denying them access to skilled jobs. White racism thus drove blacks away from trade unionism and towards the pro-employer, anti-

---

1. The author wishes to thank Robert Gregg, Ron Mendel, Edward Johanningsmeier, and Robert Zieger for helpful comments and criticism on earlier drafts of this essay.

2. Classic accounts that stress how paternalistic elements within southern culture mitigated against unionism include W.J. Cash, *The Mind of the South*, NY, 1941; and Liston Pope, *Millhands and Preachers: A Study of Gastonia*, New Haven, 1942.

3. For nineteenth-century interracialism, see Peter Rachleff, *Black Labor in Richmond, 1865–1890*, Urbana, 1988; and Melton McLaurin, *The Knights of Labor in the South*, Westport, 1978.

union polices of Booker T. Washington. Remaining aloof from the "white man's union," blacks pragmatically chose to ally themselves with southern capital and provide reserve labor during times of strife in order to seize valuable job opportunities. Thus, reviewing the history of black workers and the labor movement in 1982, William H. Harris saw little of significance besides racial exclusion and discrimination. "The critical issue," he wrote, "was not so much how blacks got along on their jobs but whether they got jobs at all."[4]

This, at least, is the conventional wisdom. Recent scholarship is calling into question the main features and core assumptions of this historiographic portrait. The convergence of two fertile fields – Labor History and African American History – has produced a number of detailed local studies that suggest an alternative and less monolithic view of southern blacks' relationship to organized labor.[5] While accepting the dominance for most of the twentieth century of exclusionary craft unionism, the new scholarship has uncovered a vigorous tradition of biracial unionism in a number of industries and locales. Although achieving fullest expression in the CIO's campaigns in mass production industries such as tobacco and food processing, this tradition had important antecedents in the Mine Workers attempts to organize Alabama's coalfields at the turn of the century, and in the efforts of Gulf port waterfront workers to construct durable institutions in the progressive era. Mindful of the limits of interracial cooperation, and rejecting the tendency to romanticize labor-based racial progress that befuddled an earlier generation of scholars, the new history is forcing a re-evaluation of organized labor's racial record.

The most significant features of the ongoing revision concern three broad subject areas: the racial policies and practices of the AFL; the role played by black rank-and-file workers in the industrial union movement of the 1930s; and the relationship between organized labor and the struggle for civil rights in the South. In each of these areas older interpretations are under assault. Whereas it was once agreed that the southern affiliates of the American Federation of Labor pursued a uniform policy of black exclusion, recent studies have found important instances of inclusive organizing activity and the wielding of genuine power by black unionists.

Similarly, as recently as 1985 David Brody reflected the prevailing orthodoxy when he wrote that black workers played a minimal part in

4. William H. Harris, *The Harder We Run: Black Workers Since the Civil War*, NY, 1982, p. 3.

5. For general discussion of the progress made during the last decade by labor and social historians in documenting the experiences of southern workers, see Robert Zieger's introduction in his edited volume *Organized Labor in the Twentieth Century South*, Knoxville, 1991, pp. 3–12.

the CIO upsurge, seeing the establishment of industrial unions as "less a hopeful event than a threat to their precarious place in American industry."[6] Fresh research has turned this generalization on its head: it is now apparent that due to blacks' central role in many mass-production processes, their support was often the critical ingredient to CIO success. Rather than regarding the new unions as threats to their security, black workers eagerly joined industrial unions, motivated not just by traditional economic concerns but also by the desire to use these organizations as vehicles with which to advance the struggle for social and political equality.

Traditionally, historians have treated the labor and civil rights movements independently of each other. Indeed, it is widely assumed that the black freedom struggle emerged in the mid–1950s, just as the labor movement lost its momentum. While recognizing that the financial support of liberal unions such as the United Automobile Workers helped establish organizations such as the SCLC and SNCC, and that individuals such as A. Philip Randolph simultaneously occupied leadership positions in both spheres, scholars have not identified grass roots connections between the two movements. At best, there has been a vague acknowledgement that the headway made by the CIO in certain southern regions "laid the groundwork" for the civil rights movement of the 1950s in some sort of Whiggish way.[7] The new writing on southern labor history suggests not only a different chronology, but an important and concrete relationship between the unionization of southern industry and the early civil rights movement.

Recent studies of Memphis, Winston-Salem, and other southern cities reveal that black workers who joined CIO unions were in the vanguard of efforts to transform race relations. As might be expected, much of this activity was workplace-oriented, as workers used the seniority and grievance provisions of union contracts to combat long-standing discriminatory practices. But militancy also extended beyond the factory gate: bypassing established groups such as the NAACP and Urban League, black unionists led a host of local initiatives, including voter registration and desegregation campaigns, rallying other sections of the community behind them. Attuned to the boundaries of this early stage in the struggle for equality, the new scholarship has also suggested reasons for the limited nature of its achievements, most notably the way in which postwar anti-communism split the black community along

6. David Brody, "The CIO After 50 Years: A Historical Reckoning," *Dissent*, Fall 1985, p. 467.

7. The title of one recent book neatly illustrates this point: Merl E. Reed, *Seedtime for the Modern Civil Rights Movement: The President's Committee on Fair Employment Practices, 1941–46*, Baton Rouge, 1991.

class lines, isolated activists from white unionists, and eroded support from white liberals.

The emerging revision of the history of black workers and organized labor in the South is not free of controversy or debate – indeed, it is animated by sharp differences of interpretation and opinion in several key areas. At the same time, much of the new scholarship can be criticized for failing to take into account the interplay between community dynamics and the character of local labor movements. Many of the better studies are uncomfortably reminiscent of the "old labor history" with its near-exclusive focus on the trade union and the workplace. Other works maintain a conspicuous silence on issues of gender, declining to explore the important connections between the sexual division of labor, the specific form of workplace struggles, and the construction of racial identities. Both of these shortcomings are surprising given the influence of social history upon the writing of working-class history over the past twenty years and the more recent challenge posed by women's history to the gender-blind categories traditionally employed in labor studies.[8] This essay traces the major contours of this new wave of scholarship, showing how and where it extends, challenges, and breaks with traditional views. In reviewing these findings, in making critical observations, and by identifying topics where further historical scrutiny is neccesary, it aims to interest other scholars in the new history and to suggest some fresh ways of viewing the political economy of the twentieth-century South.

It is hardly surprising that the mine workers continue to be the subject of historical writing on race and the labor movement. From its establishment in the last decade of the nineteenth century until the collapse of the coal industry in the mid–1950s, the United Mine Workers of America (UMWA) formed the backbone of the labor movement in the United States. One of the largest affiliates of the AFL, and later the CIO, the UMWA exerted a powerful influence on the policies of the national labor federations. One of the first unions to organize on an industrial basis, the mine workers developed early on a unique relationship with unskilled, immigrant, and black workers. In 1902, 20,000 black miners carried UMWA cards, a figure that represented more than half of all black workers within the AFL; ten years later this figure had

8. For the influence of social history, see the piece on the new labor history in Eric Foner's edited collection, *The New American History*, Philadelphia, 1990; for the challenges posed by women's history see Ava Baron's introductory essay in *Work Engendered: Toward a New History of American Labor*, Ithaca, 1991; and the recent review essay by Eileen Boris, "Beyond Dichotomy: Recent Books in North American Women's Labor History," *Journal of Women's History*, vol. 4, no. 3, 1993. A more polemical and wide ranging critique of labor historians' failure to utilize gendered categories of analysis is found in Joan W. Scott, *Gender and the Politics of History*, NY, 1988.

doubled, and African American miners comprised more than seventy percent of all organized black workers.[9] Moreover, the chaotic competitiveness of the coal industry, and the growing importance of the rich bituminous fields of northern Alabama compelled the UMWA to launch full-scale southern organizing drives in each of the first three decades of the twentieth century.

Historians have long recognized that the racial practices of the mine workers marked a break from the rest of the organized labor movement.[10] But they have portrayed the motivations behind this departure in a way that downplays or denies any egalitarian impulse. Only because an unorganized mass of black miners threatened the privileged position of whites, they argue, did the union pursue an industrial strategy. Thus, expediency rather than a genuine commitment to multiracialism explained the UMWA's deviation from the norm. Race relations between black and white rank-and-file miners, they further argued, were little different from those prevailing elsewhere. Scholars as different as W.E.B. DuBois and Herbert Northrup documented instances of white "hate strikes," unequal treatment and uneven job distribution to buttress the pessimistic conclusion that while the *policies* of the union were egalitarian, their implementation on the local level left much to be desired. Commenting on the UMWA leadership's "inability or unwillingness to draw any distinction between the absence of racial discrimination in constitutional principle and the appearance of it in everyday fact," Sterling Spero and Abram Harris expressed the skepticism that characterizes the traditional literature on the mine workers.[11]

The first real challenge to this interpretation came in 1968 with the publication of Herbert Gutman's "The Negro and the United Mine Workers," an article that traced the career of a black miner and union official, Richard Davis, active in Ohio's Hocking Valley at the close of the nineteenth century. Basing his case on Davis' printed letters and references to him in the *United Mine Workers Journal*, Gutman argued

9. W.E.B. DuBois, *The Negro Artisan*, Atlanta University Publications, No. 7, Atlanta, 1902, pp. 169–70; Frank Wolfe, *Admission to Trade Unions*, Baltimore, 1912, pp. 122–24.

10. See, for instance, DuBois, *The Negro Artisan*; W.E.B. DuBois, *The Negro American Artisan*, Atlanta University Publications, No. 17, Atlanta, 1912; Sterling Spero and Abram Harris, *The Black Worker: The Negro and the Labor Movement*, NY, 1931, pp. 352–84; Horace Cayton and George Mitchell, *Black Workers and the New Unions*, Chapel Hill, 1939.

11. See DuBois, *Negro Artisan*, p. 161; Lorenzo Greene and Carter Woodson, *The Negro Wage Earner*, Washington DC, 1930, pp. 186–97; Spero and Harris, *The Black Worker*, pp. 355–57; Herbert Northrup, *Organized Labor and the Negro*, NY, 1944, pp. 160, 170. Quotation from Spero and Harris, *The Black Worker*, p. 357. Elsewhere, Harris decried the "Ku Klux Klan spirit" within the UMWA that kept blacks from entering the union fold; see *Opportunity*, July 1925, quoted in Philip Foner, *Organized Labor & The Black Worker, 1619–1981*, NY, 1982, p. 170.

that, to a very large extent, the union's inclusive membership policy resulted not only from the need to control the labor market but from an alternative set of values and a vision of community based upon class rather than ethnic or racial loyalty. Moreover, Gutman maintained that egalitarian sentiment penetrated through all levels of the miner's organization. The UMWA, he stated, "functioned as a viable, integrated trade union and quite possibly ranked as the most thoroughly integrated voluntary association in the United States."[12]

Despite its bold conclusions, Gutman's article had a tentative, provisional feel. Lamenting the "absence of detailed knowledge of the `local world' inhabited by white and Negro workers," Gutman noted the difficulties in generalizing from the experience of a single individual. Unwilling to assess the typicality of the case of Richard Davis, he instead called for more research into working-class race relations, especially on the local level, and for the need to bridge the divide between labor and African American history. Over the course of the next decade, as the so-called "New Labor History" came into its own, younger scholars heeded this programmatic note. Stephen Brier extended Gutman's findings back in time to the era of the Knights of Labor; and David Corbin explored the experience of the southern West Virginia miners, writing precisely the kind of community study that Gutman had desired.[13]

These contributions notwithstanding, the New Labor History failed to produce a study of black mine workers that looked beyond a single locale or offered a fresh way of viewing the interactions between blacks, whites, and the union apparatus.[14] The "Gutman revision" also provoked considerable controversy. In a fierce polemic, former NAACP Labor Secretary Herbert Hill attacked Gutman's writing on Davis as a shoddy piece of research and dismissed the scholarship he inspired as little more than "romanticized popular front leftism" that denied the central role of

12. Herbert Gutman, "The Negro and the United Mine Workers of America: The Career and Letters of Richard L. Davis and Something of Their Meaning, 1890–1900," in *The Negro and the American Labor Movement*, Julius Jacobson, ed., Garden City, 1968, pp. 114–15. The article was reprinted in Gutman's *Work, Culture & Society in Industrializing America*, NY, 1976.

13. Gutman, "The Negro and the United Mine Workers," pp. 117, 125–6. Stephen Brier, "Interracial Organizing in the West Virginia Coal Industry: The Participation of Black Workers in the Knights of Labor and the United Mine Workers, 1880–1894," in *Essays in Southern Labor History*, Gary Fink and Merl Reed, eds., Westport, 1977; David Alan Corbin, *Life, Work, and Rebellion in the Coal Fields: The Southern West Virginia Miners, 1880–1922*, Urbana, 1981.

14. Summing up the progress made by the New Labor History in rewriting the history of black workers, Eric Arnesen observes that while Gutman's 1968 article pointed the way forward, "the project that he proposed – to shift attention from the policies of racial exclusion and discrimination by union internationals to the practices of local unions and communities – remains ... largely unaccomplished." Eric Arnesen, *Waterfront Workers of New Orleans: Race, Class and Politics, 1863–1923*, NY, 1991, p. viii.

race in working-class history. Although Hill's vicious tone is regrettable, and his stubborn insistence that race and class are similar analytic categories is misguided, he assembles substantial evidence that must be taken seriously. Employing the same sources as Gutman, Hill demonstrates that discrimination against black miners was pervasive and widespread, and that the UMWA repeatedly bowed to the racism of its members by excluding blacks from work and from union office. Allowing that the mine workers' racial practices "were different from those of other labor organizations," Hill castigates Gutman and his followers for succumbing to the temptation to "place the UMW on a pedestal" and propagate a historically inaccurate and politically dangerous myth.[15]

There is much of merit and validity in Hill's case. It is clear that Gutman ignored contrary data, including material from pages of the *United Mine Workers Journal* that could not have escaped his eye. Davis' letters to the journal alone point to the existence of tremendous racial tension within the union; and Hill convincingly demonstrates that such unity as it did possess was far more fragile than Gutman believed.[16] Hill also makes a number of sound criticisms regarding Gutman's overly fluid chronological benchmarks, his errors concerning the mineworkers membership and power in the early twentieth century, and his failure to fully acknowledge the under representation of African Americans in policy making positions within the union. Similarly, Hill's critique of the New Labor History, when shorn of its overblown rhetoric, is a trenchant one. The field *does* have what Nell Painter dubbed "a race problem" – that is, it fails to include race in its analysis, consistently downplays the strength of working-class racism, and shrinks from exploring the ways in which racial consciousness shaped the class identity of both black and white workers. The impassioned outrage occasioned by Hill's article testifies to the accuracy of these critical arrows.[17]

15. Herbert Hill, "Myth-Making as Labor History: Herbert Gutman and the United Mine Workers of America," *International Journal of Politics, Culture and Society*, vol. 2, no. 2, 1988, pp. 133, 137.

16. In addition to evidence about the wholesale exclusion of black miners from unionized areas and a number of remarkable racist statements on the part of high union officials, these omissions include Davis' alienation from the UMWA and his bitterness about the organization's willingess to ignore racist practices within its ranks and elsewhere in the labor movement. "Myth Making as Labor History," pp. 158, 160–63, 164–68, 188–92.

17. Nell Irvin Painter, "The New Labor History and the Historical Moment," *International Review of Politics, Culture and Society* vol. 2, no. 3, 1989. For an outraged rejoinder to Hill's assault, see Stephen Brier, "In Defense of Gutman: the Union's Case," ibid. Other critiques of the New Labor History that make similar points, albeit in a less impassioned manner, include Lawrence McDonnell, "'You Are Too Sentimental': Problems and Suggestions for a New Labor History," *Journal of Social History*, vol. 17, 1984; and David Roediger, "'Labor in White Skin': Race and Working-class History," in *Reshaping the US Left*, Davis and Sprinker, eds., London, 1987.

Yet on another level Hill's broadside misses the mark. Although demolishing a good portion of Gutman's argument, it does not advance our understanding of black workers' relationship to organized labor. Instead, it simply restates the traditional view of unions as white job trusts whose primary function is the protection of their members against competition from black workers. This analysis not only overlooks the role played by the state and capital in perpetuating racial discrimination and working-class fragmentation (especially in the South), it allows no room for the kinds of social and cultural change that result from collective struggle that transcends – even if only episodically – racial and ethnic divisions.[18] Moreover, Hill chooses to remain oblivious or indifferent to the strengths of Gutman's essay, especially the way in which Davis and other black UMW activists are allowed to speak for themselves and, thus, appear as agents and not simply as victims of racism or unambiguous symbols of biracial unionism.

The framework to which Hill would have us return is as flawed as Gutman's romanticism. The key questions for students of black labor concern not the absence or presence of racism in a given situation, but the ways and circumstances in which workers either subordinate their prejudice to the project of building an alliance with "others" or capitulate to those feelings and confine their efforts to the ethnic/religious/racial enclave. Despite the mine workers' shortcomings, it left a powerful legacy of interracial organizing that CIO activists drew upon in the 1930s. The "UMW formula" of splitting local union election slates between blacks and whites was not an ideal arrangement – as Herbert Hill has noted. What is more important, though, is that this compromise afforded fledgling unions in the South and other racially conservative locales a solution to a vexing and potentially destructive problem. Similarly, backgrounds in the mine workers gave many CIO activists in other industries the conviction and commitment to challenge local customs and racial mores. These historically significant examples cannot fit into Hill's socially static model.[19]

18. Responding to an early piece by Hill, a number of commentators developed this first point. "Employment patterns are presented as if they were created by workers or unions," Martin Glaberman complained, while both David Brody and Nelson Lichtenstein observed that Hill ignores the way in which the evolution of American capitalism generates and sustains ethnic hierachies independent of the labor movement. See Herbert Hill, "Race, Ethnicity and Organized Labor: The Opposition to Affirmative Action," *New Politics*, vol. 1, no. 2, 1987; and the symposium on the piece that appeared in *New Politics*, vol. 1, no. 3, 1987. Hill has dismissed as "sheer nonsense" the idea that workers can shed racist attitudes as they participate in interracial movements; see his rejoinder in *International Journal of Politics, Culture and Society*, vol. 2, no. 3, 1989.

19. For the "UMW formula" see Foner, *Organized Labor & The Black Worker*, p. 218; and Michael Honey, "Labor and Civil Rights in the South: The Industrial Labor Movement and Black Workers in Memphis, 1929–1945," unpublished PhD dissertation, Northern Illinois University, 1987, pp. 127–28. Honey's book, *Southern Labor and Black Civil Rights: Organizing Memphis Workers*, Urbana, 1993, appeared too late for inclusion in this essay; all references are to his dissertation.

While the Gutman-Hill controversy generated more smoke then fire, a more promising line of inquiry has recently been opened by Ronald Lewis and Joe Trotter. Attentive to regional variations and the influence of both mine operators and the state upon employment practices, Lewis has written the broadest study to date of black miners. Trotter's examination of southern West Virginia complements Lewis' national perspective by offering a detailed portrait of class and racial inequality in a single locale. Striking a balance between Hill's all-consuming focus on discrimination and Gutman's overly sanguine view of race relations, Trotter shows how black miners simultaneously fought on two fronts: against the exploitative practices of employers and the discriminatory behavior of white workers. Situated upon a middle ground between hostile forces, blacks pursued both class-based and racial strategies. Taken together, the two books provide a wealth of new empirical information. Equally significant, by refusing to privilege either race or class, they point the way out of a debilitating conceptual cul-de-sac.[20]

"Black miners did not share a monolithic experience," Lewis cautions in his opening pages. "There was neither a uniform black presence nor a common pattern of race relations but, rather, several unique regional histories." Although Lewis identifies five distinctive systems of race relations, only two concern us here – those prevailing in southern Appalachia and northern Alabama.[21] In the latter case, Lewis makes clear that the UMWA carefully balanced equal rights for its members within the union with the necessity to outwardly conform to the dictates of white supremacy. Certainly in the first decades of the century, full integration would have spelled political disaster. Inclusive membership and power sharing inside local unions was one thing; "social equality" was quite another, for it handed the miners' foes a powerful weapon.

Lewis builds a persuasive case for this balancing act by examining the UMWA's handling of two signal coal field conflicts, the strikes of 1908 and 1920. In both battles, the miners refused to be split along racial lines, despite efforts to divide them by demagogic pandering to prejudice. In both cases, state authorities justified intervention against the union by referring to its biracialism and the manner in which the militancy displayed by black strikers violated social norms. The specter of armed blacks "conspiring" with whites in a class uprising in a region supposedly organized by caste, Lewis argues, provided a politically

20. Ronald L. Lewis, *Black Coal Miners in America: Race, Class, and Community Conflict, 1780–1980*, Lexington, 1987; Joe William Trotter, Jr., *Coal, Class, and Color: Blacks in Southern West Virginia, 1915–32*, Urbana, 1990.

21. Lewis, *Black Coal Miners*, p. x. The other three systems are southern slavery and convict labor, black exclusion in northern and midwestern mines, and black technological displacement throughout the industry in the post-World War II era.

justifiable reason for crushing the union by force in 1908 and for unabashedly partisan intervention twelve years later. He thus demonstrates that labor conflict in Alabama's mines must be understood in a racial context – but not the one of black exclusion and strikebreaking posited by Hill. The outcome in both struggles was shaped more by southern racism than by racial divisions within the union. Unable to play white and black workers off of one another, operators secured public support for their offensive by appealing to working-class whites' fear of "nigger domination" and middle-class apprehension about the loss of social control.[22]

The public positions taken by the UMWA during these strikes highlight the dilemma the union faced in trying to represent the interests of its black members while deflecting what Lewis terms the "social equality wedge" wielded by the operators. Official pronouncements repeatedly denied accusations that the union favored equality, yet desegregated meetings, offices, and union halls pointed to an element of truth in the charge. After branding the equality allegation a "deliberate lie," one official went on to state that the strike was not

> .... a social fight. We dare not even dream that the time will ever come in the history of Alabama when these coal barons will even consider that the white miners and their families are their social equals.... There is only one race question now in Alabama and that is the race between the United Mine Workers of America on the one hand, standing for a living wage that will enable the miner and his family to live as Americans should, and the Alabama Coal Operators Association, which stands for the lowest wages and most disgraceful living conditions that exist anywhere in America.[23]

More than a clever response to race-baiting, these sorts of statements illustrate the union's tortured attempts to maintain solidarity while avoiding outright violation of racial norms.

Of course in both 1908 and 1920 the UMWA ultimately met with defeat (in Lewis' metaphor, "impaled on the horns" of the dilemma it

22. Lewis, *Black Coal Miners*, pp. 49–66. Important details concerning the way in which state authorities injected the race issue into the 1908 strike are provided in Philip Taft, *Organizing Dixie: Alabama Workers in the Industrial Era*, Westport, 1981, chapter 2. See also Richard A. Straw, "'This Is Not a Strike, It Is Simply a Revolution': Birmingham Miners Struggle for Power, 1894–1908" unpublished PhD dissertation, University of Missouri, 1980.

23. Alabama *Labor Advocate*, 12 Oct 1920, quoted in Taft, *Organizing Dixie*, p. 56.

tried so hard to avoid). These losses had important consequences. The loss suffered in 1908, according to Philip Taft, literally wiped out the union and "seriously hampered understanding between white and black workers," making the rebuilding of the shattered organization considerably more difficult. Following the 1920 setback, the operators initiated a policy of recruiting black laborers from boll weevil stricken plantation districts and housing them in company towns. This conscious attempt to prevent the reemergence of interracial solidarity is testament to the effectiveness of the mine workers' efforts to unite black and white miners.[24]

Throughout the recounting of this history Lewis carefully resists the temptation to romanticize the situation of blacks in the Alabama coalfields. In addition to rigid occupational discrimination (black miners were confined to pick mining and loading) and pay differentials, African Americans contended with political disfranchisement, racial violence, and unequal access to public and private amenities. Moreover, while the union's international and district officials uniformly followed an egalitarian policy, local officers could not claim such consistency. Still, it is hard to dispute Lewis' conclusion that "whatever local discrimination blacks encountered in their dealings with white miners, in the context of southern society the UMWA was the most progressive force in their lives."[25]

Paradoxically, the situation of black miners in southern Appalachia was both bleaker and brighter than in Alabama. On the positive side, they received equal pay for equal work, participated in electoral politics, and encountered a much lower level of racial violence. In the mountain hollows and hills of the region, "blacks came closer to finding economic equality than in any other coalfield, and perhaps anywhere else, in America." Yet, this optimistic assessment must be tempered: blacks were barred from certain job categories, denied use of new high-yield technology, and subject to *de facto* social segregation. Further, mine operators here successfully manipulated racial tensions and kept the workforce weak and divided. They routinely employed spies, gun thugs, and dynamite in their campaign to keep the UMWA out of the region; and they virtually controlled state government for much of the early twentieth century, and repeatedly used its armed might (and occasionally that of the federal government) to crush union organizing

24. Taft, *Organizing Dixie*, p. 29; Lewis, *Black Coal Miners*, Spero and Harris, *The Black Worker*, pp. 359–66.

25. Lewis, *Black Coal Miners*, p. 64. One black UMWA member expressed the same sentiment in this manner: "the miner's union has done more and is doing more for the negro than all the secret orders combined." *Labor Advocate* 4 Sept 1908, quoted in Taft, *Organizing Dixie*, p. 30.

campaigns. Indeed, the largest and bloodiest armed conflicts between labor and capital in American history occurred here. Although lynching was a remote possibility, a black miner stood a fairly good chance of being shot or wounded in strike situations at Cabin Creek, Matewan, or Blair Mountain.[26]

The African American response to this situation is treated fully in Trotter's study of southern West Virginia. Extending themes developed in his earlier work on black proletarianization, he shows how black miners supplemented their union activities with a variety of responses aimed at countering workplace inequality. These included high productivity when faced with white worker competition (short of rate-busting), willingness to work in non-union mines (but not necessarily to scab), and alliance with the small but influential black middle class (especially in the political arena). As in Alabama, blacks joined the union in proportions that equalled, and sometimes exceeded whites. They held office, participated fully in internal union affairs and fought successfully against white rank-and-file prejudice. But because the UMWA did not succeed in cracking the Appalachian fields until the 1940s, the union simply did not carry the same import as it did elsewhere.[27]

As a result, Trotter's focus is more upon the miners themselves than upon the union. Although he examines the UMW's infamous 1921 "armed march" in Logan County, discussing in considerable detail the role of black rank-and-file leadership, the bulk of his study revolves around the workplace and the community. In these non-institutional settings, it is clear that black miners thought and acted in *both* racial and class ways. Instead of depicting workers as choosing one of these identities over another, Trotter shows how the two categories overlapped and interpenetrated. For example, when discussing the miners' political alliance – through the Republican Party – with the state's small but influential black professional elite, Trotter emphasizes the class-determined limits of this sort of racial solidarity. The "commitment to working class solidarity," he maintains, developed "within the framework of black unity." At the same time, it is important to recognize that black

26. See the succinct comparison between the two regions in Joe W. Trotter, Jr., "Class and Racial Inequality: The Southern West Virginia Black Coal Miners' Response, 1915–1932," in Zieger, *Organized Labor in the Twentieth Century South*, p. 78. Quotation from Lewis, *Black Coal Miners*, p. 121; for operators tactics see chapters 7 and 8. For the role of violence, see Daniel P. Jordan, "The Mingo War: Labor Violence in the Southern West Virginia Coal Fields, 1919–1922," in Fink and Reed, *Essays in Southern Labor History*; and Corbin, *Life, Work, and Rebellion*, pp. 195–224.

27. The focus upon southern West Virginia is not as narrow as it first might seem. Close to seventy percent of the 88,000 blacks who lived in the central Appalachian coalfields (covering portions of Virginia, West Virginia, Kentucky, and Tennessee) in 1920 resided there; Lewis, *Black Coal Miners*, p. xi. Trotter's work on proletarianization began with *Black Milwaukee: The Making of an Industrial Proletariat*, Urbana, 1985.

miners' loyalty to the GOP, weakened or at least rendered problematic class solidarity with the Democratically inclined white workforce. Similarly, when black miners responded to white racism by pursuing the strategies outlined above, they did not abandon entirely their class identities, but realized these through the social reality of a work process shaped by racial difference.[28]

In providing detailed regional histories, and in offering ways of comprehending the differential responses to racial inequality, Lewis and Trotter have significantly advanced our understanding of both class formation and the dynamics of race within the working class. The insights contained in these books suggest that a comparative perspective on black labor in the industrial era has much to offer. Indeed, Trotter concludes his study with a concise, programmatic statement calling for comparative studies of black proletarianization across regional boundaries, and an implicit plea for the conceptual situation of this process within the larger context of international capitalism. He approvingly quotes historical sociologist Edna Bonacich, who notes that what is at stake is not the primacy of race versus class "but rather the way in which capitalist development shaped the interests and actions of various class-race segments, and how those interests and actions in turn shaped the directions capitalist development took."[29] While neither author advances an agenda for future research, several topics suggest themselves. Most obvious is the need for work on Kentucky's coalfields, home to over 15,000 blacks by 1914, and an area almost entirely neglected by historians. Relations between African American and immigrant miners similarly await exploration (especially after the cinematic treatment it received in John Sayles recent film "Matewan"). Finally, the mine workers' successful early 1930s organizing drive – carried out under the slogan "The President Wants You to Join a Union" – deserves attention, for it undoubtedly contains clues about the interracial legacy forged during the bloody coal field wars twenty years earlier.

If the mine workers long tradition of interracial organizing naturally attracted historians interested in organized labor's relationship with blacks, another major topic of recent writing is more of a surprise. Southern waterfront workers and their unions form the subject of

---

28. Trotter, *Coal, Class, and Color*, p. 114. Many of these points are raised by David Roediger in his review of Trotter's book, *Labour/Le Travail*, vol. 28, Fall, 1991, p. 363.

29. Edna Bonacich, "Capitalist and Racial Oppression: In Search of Consciousness," in *Research in Urban Sociology*, vol. 1, *Race, Class, and Urban Change*, Jerry Lembcke and Ray Hutchinson, eds., Greenwich, 1989, quoted in Trotter, *Coal, Class, and Color*, pp. 267–68.Trotter more recent edited collection, *The Great Migration in Historical Perspective: New Dimensions of Race, Class, and Gender*, Bloomington, 1991, represents an uneven start in the direction of a comparative regional perspective on African-American life in the first decades of the twentieth century.

several books and articles produced by the new history. New Orleans figures prominently in this literature, for in addition to being the South's most important port, it was there in 1892 that black and white workers cooperated in conducting a successful general strike that represented the climax of Gilded Age interracial solidarity. The general strike has fascinated scholars for quite some time – but traditional accounts hold that the events of '92 marked the beginning of the end for Crescent City workers. According to the conventional wisdom, white racism in the next few years drove blacks out of and away from trade unionism, and the race riots of 1894 and 1895 brought the port in line with the rest of the South. However, fresh research by Eric Arnesen and Daniel Rosenberg suggests that, on the waterfront, interracial cooperation survived the troubled 1890s and persisted intact until the destruction of union power in 1923. Examining the volatile mix of class and race on the New Orleans docks during the tumultuous 1930s, Bruce Nelson's recent work suggests that for black longshoremen viable unionism ultimately meant a conservative defense of hard-won employment gains through the corrupt vehicle of the AFL rather than an alliance with whites behind the social unionism of the CIO.[30]

The conceptual orientation of these studies parallels the model employed by Trotter and Lewis. Indeed, Arnesen explicitly engages with the theoretical dilemma arising out of the race/class dichotomy. Declining to privilege or assign dominance to either category, he instead argues for a wholly different approach. Refusing to regard white racism as a static factor in the working-class experience, he maintains that racial ideologies must instead be seen as fluid, ever-changing historical products rooted in specific sets of social relations. "The historian's task," he writes, "is to reconstitute historically-specific racisms, to trace their continuities and discontinuities, and to account for concrete forms that racism assumes and to evaluate its particular salience in given contexts." Thus, the key question

30. Roger W. Shugg, "The New Orleans General Strike of 1892," *Louisiana Historical Quarterly*, vol. 21, April 1938; C. Vann Woodward, *Origins of the New South, 1877–1913*, Baton Rouge, 1951, pp. 231–32, 267; and David Paul Bennetts, "Black and White Workers: New Orleans, 1880–1900," unpublished PhD. dissertation, University of Illinois-Urbana, 1972, represent this traditional view. For the new scholarship, see Eric Arnesen, *Waterfront Workers of New Orleans: Race, Class and Politics, 1863–1923*, NY, 1991; Arnesen, "To Rule or Ruin: New Orleans Dock Workers' Struggle for Control, 1902–1903," *Labor History*, vol. 28, no. 2, Spring 1987; Arnesen, "Longshore Workers in the Gulf Ports: The Evolution of Biracial Unionism in the Early Twentieth Century," in *Power Relations and Racism in the Labor Market: Historical Perspectives*, Marcel van der Linden, ed., Leiden, 1994; Daniel Rosenberg, *New Orleans Dockworkers: Race, Labor, and Unionism, 1892–1923*, Albany, 1988; and Bruce Nelson, "Class and Race in the Crescent City: The ILWU, from San Francisco to New Orleans," in *The CIO's Left-Led Unions*, Steve Rosswurm, ed., New Brunswick, 1992.

concerns not the relative power of race versus class, but how particular groups of workers defined themselves. How did notions of racial identity inform workers' understanding of their class identity and vice versa?[31]

The advantages of this conceptual shift become clear in Arnesen's fresh coverage of familiar territory – the power sharing arrangement hammered out by white and black waterfront workers in the 1880s and 90s. Instead of celebrating the establishment of the Cotton Men's Executive Council as a triumph of class over race, he shows how organizational cooperation built upon – and, in fact, codified – racial division within the workforce. Two separate locals, one black and the other white, gained a solid hold in those sectors where both races labored. Dividing work equally, receiving the same wages and negotiating with employers as a single unit, these workers fashioned a "biracial" rather than interracial system.

By including a number of worksites, and extending his focus to other ports, Arnesen shows how whites pursued conflicting strategies of inclusion or exclusion. Initially, their rejection of color bars in New Orleans had less to do with ideological than concrete structural factors. Solidarity prevailed because blacks occupied strategic positions in the labor process of cotton loading and screwing; they therefore could not be ignored. Moreover, the highly competitive nature of waterfront capital coupled with great numbers of skilled black workers meant that whites-only unionism was a weak program – accommodation to Jim

---

31. Arnesen, *Waterfront Workers*, pp. ix–xi; quotation from "Longshore Workers in the Gulf Ports." Arnesen takes his lead from the theoretical insights of Barbara Fields, who argues that race is a "complicated and far from obvious concept .... the notion of race, in its popular manifestation, is an ideological construct and thus, above all, a historical product. A number of consequences follow. One of the more far-reaching is that the favorite question of American social scientists – whether race or class `variables' better explain `American reality' – is a false one. Class and race are concepts of different order, they do not occupy the same analytical space, and thus cannot constitute explanatory alternatives to each other. At its core, class refers to a material circumstance: the inequality of human beings from the standpoint of social power ... the reality of class can assert itself independently of people's consciousness, and sometimes in direct opposition to it.... Race, on the other hand, is a purely ideological notion." Fields, "Ideology and Race in American History," in *Region, Race, and Reconstruction: Essays in Honor of C. Vann Wodward*, J. Morgan Kousser and James McPherson, eds., NY, 1982, pp. 150–51. The idea that different racisms can be understood only through reference to the political and economic structures that produce them can be counterposed against Herbert Hill's assertion that "systems of racial oppression acquire their own dynamic ... they develop an independent life of their own which sustains stratification within the working class." Hill, "Race, Ethnicity and Organized Labor," p. 32. Fields responds dismissively, stating that to attribute to the idea of race "a transhistorical, almost metaphysical status ... removes it from all possibility of analysis and understanding," "Ideology and Race in American History," p. 144.

Crow at one pier soon would be undermined by black non-union labor at others.[32]

While this analysis revises our understanding of working class race relations in the 1890s, the treatment of the early twentieth century carries even greater significance. Both Arnesen and Rosenberg allow that biracial unionism suffered a severe setback in the mid–1890s, but they attribute the breakdown of solidarity to economic depression and an employer's offensive rather than capitulation to white supremacy. By the end of the decade, they maintain, workers began to rebuild their shattered movement. Away from the docks, white craft unionists formed a Central Trades and Labor Council, affiliated with the AFL and drew a strict color line. On the waterfront, however, longshore unions responded by resurrecting the biracial arrangement in the form of Dock and Cotton Council.

Again resisting the temptation to explain these different outcomes by referring to the power of class over race, the authors suggest several tangible reasons for the reconstitution of the workers' alliance. Foremost among these was an intensification of the waterfront labor process that began during the mid-decade economic downturn. Desperate to cut operating costs, shipping agents attempted to boost productivity by restructuring the work of the highly skilled screwmen, the "aristocrats of the levee," who manually packed bales of cotton into the holds of steamships. Taking advantage of technological and engineering changes, employers sought to deskill the screwmen and replace them with cheaper longshore workers. This assault on their trade forced black and white screwmen to "amalgamate" again in order to maintain control over work.[33]

Amalgamation assumed an interesting and historically significant form. Reasoning that the key to success lay in preventing employers from playing the races off of one another, workers sought to eliminate all possible divisions between the black and white unions. Without contemplating the erasure of the color line, the Dock and Cotton Council negotiated a "half-and-half" agreement whereby the two unions equally shared all work. The white screwmen would labor on the starboard side of all ships arriving in port; the black union would assign its members to the port side. Longshore gangs would be apportioned in a similar fashion. Waterfront workers endured two lockouts and a major strike as employers attempted to resist this formula and maintain for

32. In addition to his published work cited above see the concise summary of this period in Eric Arnesen, "Learning the Lessons of Solidarity: Race Relations and Work Rules on the New Orleans Waterfront," *Labor's Heritage*, vol. 1, no. 1, January 1989.

33. For the screwmen's struggle over control, see Rosenberg, *New Orleans Dockworkers*, 52–55; and Arnesen, "To Rule or Ruin," pp. 145–49.

themselves the advantages of a segmented labor market. Technological change did occur – but workers insulated themselves from its worst effects by cooperating. Thus, on one level, economic survival strategies impelled both races toward unionism and led them to break with the racial standards of the dominant culture.

The second key factor behind the remarkable "half-and-half" arrangement concerns the way in which workers learned from their own lived experience. In the early twentieth century, dock union leaders, both black and white, recognized that only an alliance across the color line would allow them to wrest control of the labor process from capital and maintain high wages. Rank-and-file waterfront workers, despite their racial feelings, recognized that the riots of 1894/95 ushered in an era of deteriorating conditions and hardship. Drawing on an earlier tradition of labor solidarity, they accepted a significant degree of equality on the job. Blacks did not forget the hostilities of the past decade, but clearly, as Arnesen suggests, they "saw themselves as both *black* workers and black *workers*; white workers similarly saw themselves as working men who were white and as whites who were workers."[34]

Biracial unionism was a complex phenomenon. Nelson perceptively notes that it often reflected the strong preference for autonomy that has always charactarized black self-organization and not, necessarily, the strength of white racism. Arnesen's ongoing work on other Gulf ports shows that it involved no single strategy or set of arrangements. Nevertheless a pattern is clear: where independent black unions wielded sufficient strength, white unions were compelled to carve out equitable deals with them. "We are in the union today because the white man had to take us in for his own protection," one black longshore official bluntly admitted in the 1930s. This was the case in New Orleans. But elsewhere – most notably in Mobile – the biracial structure "served less to promote interracial collaboration than [it] did to isolate black and white locals from one another" and thus sustain rather than challenge racial inequality in the economic sphere.[35]

Other industries need to be examined, especially in the transportation sector, before these sorts of generalization can be refined. Equally as important is the need for additional research into the way in which national unions encouraged – or undermined – local power sharing arrangements. Again, Arnesen has pointed the way in his comments on

34. Arnesen, *Waterfront Workers*, pp. x–xi.
35. Nelson, "Class and Race in the Crescent City," p. 45. See Arnesen's "Longshore Workers in the Gulf Ports" for discussion of Mobile and Galveston. His "Following the Color Line of Labor: Black Workers and the Labor Movement Before 1930," *Radical History Review*, vol. 55, Winter 1993, contains further discussion of the phenomenon of biracial unionism. Quotation from Spero and Harris, *The Black Worker*, 199.

the machinations of the International Longshoremen's Association, but this represents a first step. Largely missing from these fine studies, though, is an attempt to understand the various forms unionism assumed by examining community dynamics. Both Arnesen and Rosenberg downplay the importance of community – indeed, readers never learn where black and white dock workers resided, what sorts of social organizations may have bridged the divide between the worlds of work and community, or how these institutions might have contributed to the labor movement. This is the critical juncture where African American and labor history meet, but unfortunately it remains hidden and opaque. This lacuna must be filled if additional questions about the specific makeup of both black and white working-class identity are to receive sustained treatment. How, for instance, did the Irish ethnicity of many white waterfront workers shape both their relations with blacks and their self-identification as whites? How did Louisiana's French-Creole heritage influence lower-class race relations? That these questions remain unanswered does not detract from the contributions of these writers. Rather, it testifies to the power and depth of their insights and to the way in which they have fashioned the agenda now guiding historical inquiry.[36]

Of course, the experience of workers in the South's ports and coal mines does not tell the entire story; and certainly none of the scholars shaping the new history would maintain that interracialism was the order of the day in the progressive era South. The tradition of biracial unionism that existed in certain sectors of the economy was matched in others – on the railroads and in many of the building trades, for instance – by a gradual but relentless exclusionary drive. Nonetheless, it is now clear that interracial cooperation persisted in a number of locales long after the establishment of legal and institutional segregation. Indeed, it is no longer possible to speak of a "solid" South when it comes to working-class organization.

On the whole, southern labor remained weak and internally divided. Numerous writers have argued that this allowed the region's industrial-

---

36. Two recent prize-winning books on longshore work gloss over the important topic of national union policy and local practice. Bruce Nelson, *Workers on the Waterfront: Seamen, Longshoremen, and Unionism in the 1930s*, Urbana, 1988; and Howard Kimmeldorf, *Reds or Rackets?The making of Radical and Conservative Unions on the Waterfront*, Berkeley, 1988. An important but overlooked contribution to such a project is David Lee Wells, "The ILWU in New Orleans: CIO Radicalism in the Crescent City, 1937–1957," unpublished MA Thesis, University of New Orleans, 1979. David Roediger raises precisely this point about ethnicity in his review of Arnesen in *In These Times*, 27 March–2 April 1991; see also his pioneering *The Wages of Whiteness: Race and the Making of the American Working Class*, London, 1991, for a discussion of the close relationship between racial identity and class consciousness up to 1877.

ists to keep wages down and thus compete effectively with the northern capital for (at least) the first three decades of the twentieth century. The shock of the Depression unleashed social forces that simultaneously boosted the attractiveness of southern industry and undermined the conditions which made it competitive. The collapse of the rural economy forced thousands of black workers into southern cities just as northern manufacturers, eager for cheap labor and wanting to escape the union revival, began shifting their operations to Dixie. By the mid–1930s, the northern working-class upsurge assumed a disciplined, controlled form under the institutional umbrella of the CIO. Intent upon the organization of mass production industry, aware of the need to erase the regional wage differential and necessarily committed to interracialism, the CIO represented the greatest challenge to the southern order since Reconstruction.[37]

Yet, until very recently astonishingly little had been written on the CIO's southern organizing drive. Horace Cayton and George Mitchell's *Black Workers and the New Unions* appeared in 1939 and, despite its many cogent insights, must be considered a primary source; and Ray Marshall's *Labor in the South* was written just before the emergence of the "New Labor History" and is largely unconcerned with social dynamics. As recently as the mid–1980s, the most useful volume remained the idiosyncratic personal account of Lucy Randolph Mason. Moreover, general treatments of the CIO emphasized the organization's departure from the craft unionism of the AFL, stressing the innovations in tactics necessitated by an industrial model of organization and often explaining the labor history of the New Deal era in terms of the rivalry between the two federations. While this approach has a certain validity, it slights the CIO's radical break with the racial practices of the AFL, downplays the importance of black initiative in sparking the new movement and slights the role of black leadership in sustaining it.[38]

A number of important studies have appeared in the last five years

37. This framework is essentially that advanced by Michael Honey in his "Labor and Civil Rights in the South." For the South's low wage competitive advantage, see Gavin Wright, *Old South, New South: Revolutions in the Southern Economy Since the Civil War*, NY, 1986, chapter 1.

38. Horace R. Cayton and George S. Mitchell, *Black Workers and the New Unions*, Chapel Hill, 1939; F. Ray Marshall, *Labor in the South*, Cambridge MA, 1967; Lucy Randolph Mason, *To Win These Rights: A Personal Story of the CIO in the South*, Westport, 1972. The relative paucity of work on the CIO in the South is illustrated in Robert Zieger's excellent review article, "Toward a History of the CIO: A Bibliographical Report," *Labor History*, vol. 26, no. 4, Fall 1985. For general treatments exemplifying this point, see Walter Galenson, *The CIO Challenge to the AFL: A History of the American Labor Movement, 1935–1941*, Cambridge MA, 1960, and Joseph Rayback, *A History of American Labor*, NY, Free Press, 1966. Again, I am indebted to the framework suggested by Michael Honey.

that fill crucial gaps in our knowledge of the CIO's fortunes in the south. Finely textured local studies of Memphis and Winston-Salem, ongoing work on southern steel and packinghouse workers, and renewed interest in Alabama's miners have revised the standard portrait of the CIO.[39] Moreover, while previous accounts depict black workers as participants in coalitions headed by whites, these studies place them at the very center of the new union movement. Not only did blacks provide the CIO with its strongest and most reliable base of support in the south, but black leaders supplied crucial initiative and guidance at every turn. They launched independent organizing efforts, which in many cases preceded the chartering of CIO unions; engineered shop floor strategies and direct action tactics which resulted in the first victories; and forged long-lasting ties with community groups which allowed the CIO to become a general social movement in a number of locales.

These features are most pronounced in meatpacking and tobacco processing. Both industries contained unusually large concentrations of black workers. In the packing houses of Fort Worth, Atlanta and Birmingham, this resulted from employers' conscious and largely successful attempts to undermine the unions formed by white butchers in 1904 and 1921/22. Although black employment had tailed off somewhat during the NRA period, African Americans still accounted for between a third and a half of the workforce. North Carolina's tobacco plants relied upon an even higher proportion of blacks. R.J Reynolds' giant Winston-Salem facility, for instance, employed more than 10,000 workers of which less than a third were white. The key to CIO success in both industries, therefore, lay in the black support.[40]

39. Robert R. Korstad, "Daybreak of Freedom: Tobacco Workers and the CIO, Winston-Salem, North Carolina, 1943–1950," unpublished PhD. dissertation, University of North Carolina at Chapel Hill, 1987; Dolores E. Janiewski, *Sisterhood Denied: Race, Gender, and Class in a New South Community*, Philadelphia, 1985; Honey, "Labor and Civil Rights in the South." Judith Stein, "Southern Workers in National Unions: Birmingham Steelworkers, 1936–1951"; and Rick Halpern, "Interracial Unionism in the Southwest: Fort Worth's Packinghouse Workers, 1937–1954," both in Zieger, *Organized Labor in the Twentieth Century South*. Horace Huntley, "Iron Ore Miners and Mine Mill in Alabama, 1933–1952," unpublished PhD. dissertation, University of Pittsburgh, 1977; Huntley, "The Rise and Fall of Mine Mill in Alabama: The Status Quo Against Interracial Unionism, 1933–1949," *Journal of the Birmingham Historical Society*, vol. 6, no. 1, January 1979; Huntley, "The Red Scare and Black Workers in Alabama: The International Union of Mine, Mill, and Smelter Workers, 1945–1953," in *Labor Divided: Race and Ethnicity in United States Labor Struggles, 1835–1960*, Robert Asher and Charles Stephenson, eds., Albany, 1990; and Robin D.G. Kelley, *Hammer and Hoe: Alabama Communists During the Great Depression*, Chapel Hill, 1990, chapter 7.
40. For the 1904 and 1921/22 unionization drives in the packing houses, see Eric Brian Halpern, "'Black and White Unite and Fight': Race and Labor in Meatpacking, 1904–1948," unpublished PhD. dissertation, University of Pennsylvania, 1989, chapters 2 and 3. Reynolds' employment figures c. 1943 from Korstad, "Daybreak of Freedom," p. 41.

But more than the weight of numbers lies behind black CIO activism in these industries. In both cases, the structural position of black workers in the labor process helps explain their prominence in early organizing efforts. From their initial entry into meatpacking, significant numbers of blacks were promoted into skilled knife positions in an effort to diffuse solidarity among whites. By the mid–1930s, these workers dominated the critical animal killing floors where relentless management pressure and onerous conditions combined to produce a militant outlook. Stoppages in this department proved a particularly powerful weapon owing to the perishable nature of the product. The constantly moving "disassembly" lines allowed small groups of workers to bring production to a halt. After twenty minutes, watchful government inspectors condemned carcasses left hanging on the "dead rail," costing the company thousands of dollars. Prolonged stoppages soon idled adjacent departments by depriving them of meat. Furthermore, management could not readily discharge these workers since many butchering operations required great dexterity, high levels of skill and years of experience. Similarly, the loading dock – another heavily black department – was strategically situated. As one worker explained, "regardless of what happened in the other departments, the product had to be shipped out of the loading dock. If it got blocked there, well, there was no use killing or processing the meat."[41]

A similar dynamic prevailed in the tobacco sheds of the Upper South. There, according to historian Dolores Janiewski, the division of labor "wholly incorporated the racial and gender hierarchy that placed white men on top and black women at the bottom." In the hot and dusty stemmeries, blacks occupied virtually all jobs save supervisory ones. In these vital units, gender played an important role in job assignments: black women stemmed and cleaned the tobacco and fed it through machines, while black men – about a fifth of the workforce – moved the unprocessed product to the work stations and then carted it away to the cigarette machines whose operators were almost exclusively white men. White women tobacco workers operated auxilliary machines or assisted the men. The black female tobacco workers formed the core of CIO pioneers. While not wielding the same kind of power as skilled "knifemen" in the packing houses, they used their control over the labor process to extend union organization and force the first concessions

41. For detailed discussion of the labor process in meatpacking, see Halpern, "Black and White," chapter 1; and Roger Horowitz, "The Path Not Taken: A Social History of Industrial Unionism in Meatpacking," unpublished PhD. dissertation, University of Wisconsin-Madison, 1990, chapter 2. Interview with Frank Wallace by Halpern and Horowitz, 17 March 1986, United Packinghouse Workers Oral History Project, State Historical Society of Wisconsin, Madison WI [hereafter cited as UPWAOHP].

from management. When women tied up the black "tobacco side," production on the white "cigarette side" ground to a halt. Indeed, the ability of these women to control production was so threatening that in the early 1940s, shortly after union recognition, the tobacco companies moved to install new machinery in the stemmeries, thereby undermining shop floor power.[42]

None of this is meant to suggest that no white workers participated in the founding of CIO unions, or that all blacks were pro-union militants. CIO unionism in most southern industries is best understood as an alliance between different segments of the working class. While blacks clearly took the first initiatives, they soon were joined by white activists. In both packing and tobacco, these white unionists tended to come from the more skilled sections of the workforce; and many were trade union veterans of an earlier period of struggle. In Winston-Salem, for instance, a committee of white workers came forward *after* the black women registered their first gains. The group had been meeting independently of the CIO's Tobacco Workers Organizing Committee, and several of its members had previous experience with the AFL's Tobacco Workers International Union. In the packing houses, three types of whites supplemented the core of black union pioneers: older "knifemen" who had participated in the ill-fated 1917 to 1922 drive conducted by the AFL's Meat Cutters; loosely supervised, free roaming members of the mechanical gangs and outdoor stockyard crews; and left-wing activists. Held back by the fear lingering from earlier defeats, by the families they supported and by the stigma of associating with blacks, these white workers formed an important addition to the CIO nucleus.[43]

Many black workers – probably most – initially adopted a "wait-and-see" attitude toward the new unions. Certainly a few, remembering past Jim Crow treatment or unable to overcome their suspicions, remained hostile to the organizing drives. Gender dynamics certainly contributed to many black women's initial ambivalence to a style of unionism which was male-dominated. But at the same time, the contrast between the patriarchal and frankly racist behavior of many AFL affiliates rendered the alternative style pursued by the CIO positively refreshing. Regrettably, few authors have systematically explored the ways in which gender figured into black workers embrace of the CIO. That the deeply-rooted "habits of domination" dividing workers from one another had as much to do with matters of sex as race is indisputable. Labor historians need to recognize the implications of this fact and extend their gender analysis beyond the structural parameters of the

---

42. Janiewski, *Sisterhood Denied*, pp. 100–1, 114; Korstad, "Daybreak of Freedom," pp. 90–95, 321.

43. Korstad, "Daybreak of Freedom," p. 34; Halpern, "Black and White," chapter 5.

labor process into the ideological realm. A few scholars, such as Dolores Janiewski and Jacquelyn Hall, have pointed the way and suggested some approaches to this problem, but for the most part the gendered nature of the workplace and the labor movement have been ignored.[44]

By the time the Second World War ended, though, the vast majority of black workers in unionized industries were firm supporters of the CIO. The strong civil rights orientation of many CIO unions convinced many previously aloof blacks that these were not the same "white man's outfits" that they had encountered in the past. Both the Food, Tobacco, Agricultural, and Allied Workers (FTA), and the United Packinghouse Workers of America (UPWA) were left-wing organizations that did not hesitate to use the union apparatus to bring a measure of equality to their southern locals. The UPWA, for instance, secured contracts which contained strong anti-discrimination language, eliminated in-plant segregation and wage discrimination, and opened up traditionally lily-white departments to black workers. Although these kinds of gains sometimes alienated whites, they secured the unwavering loyalty of blacks. In both cases, this action against discrimination stood in dramatic contrast to the practices of the AFL unions competing for membership and bargaining rights in the two industries.[45]

A second factor contributing to black union activism was the recomposition of the industrial working class during and immediately after the war. Mobilization created an almost insatiable demand for labor and eroded traditional hiring barriers. Thousands of blacks secured factory jobs for the first time. However, in industries like meatpacking and tobacco, where working conditions were highly unpleasant, another dynamic played itself out as well. While more blacks joined the workforce, many whites exited for cleaner, lighter, higher-paying jobs in the

44. In addition to her *Sisterhood Denied*, see Janiewski's "Seeking `a New Day and a New Way': Black Women and Unions in the Southern Tobacco Industry" in *"To Toil the Livelong Day": America's Women at Work, 1780–1980*, Carol Groneman and Mary Beth Norton, eds., Ithaca, 1987. Jacquelyn Hall et al., *Like a Family: The Making of a Southern Cotton Mill World*, Chapel Hill, 1987; see also Allen Tullos, *Habits of Industry: White Culture and the Transformation of the Carolina Piedmont*, Chapel Hill, 1989. Although these last two works deal with white textile workers, they succeed in incorporating the category of gender into their analyses.
45. The Tobacco Workers Organizing Committee (TWOC) became the Food, Tobacco, Agricultural and Allied Workers (FTA) in 1944.Two years earlier, the Packinghouse Workers Organizing Committee (PWOC) received an international charter, becoming the United Packinghouse Workers of America (UPWA). The UPWA's civil rights orientation is detailed in Halpern, "Black and White," but for its anti-discrimination activities in the South, see "Interracial Unionism in the Southwest," pp. 170–76; and Moses Adedeji, "Crossing the Colorline: Three Decades of the United Packinghouse Workers of America's Crusade Against Racism in the Trans-Mississippi West, 1936–1968," unpublished PhD Dissertation, North Texas State University, 1978.

expanding defense sector of the economy. Despite high rates of turnover, older unionists succeeded in transmitting to these newcomers the traditions of shop floor militancy and egalitarianism that characterized the initial organizing era. This younger wartime cohort was instrumental in pressing FTA and packinghouse locals forward on civil rights issues.[46]

This new aggressiveness was further augmented after 1945 by returning black servicemen whose wartime experience had altered their views about the place of blacks in southern society. Eddie Humphrey, a Fort Worth packing house worker, explained, "We died, our blood had been shed for this country, and I felt ... that we should get a better deal out of it. Instead of crumbs we wanted us a slice of the pie." Less willing than the older generation to accept segregation and the incremental gains made by black workers, these militants eagerly took advantage of new mechanisms put at their disposal by their unions. In Humphrey's case, he joined with other local unionists to enlist the assistance of the international union and activists in other packing centers to utilize the nationally negotiated contract and grievance machinery to combat discrimination and open up additional job opportunities. Although these activities clashed with the sensibilities of many white workers, blacks, keenly aware of the backing of the International, stood their ground. "That's about the time that we began to recognize the fact that we had a little bit more muscle, a little bit more people power," one remembered.[47]

The experience of southern black unionists during the 1940s thus offers two important correctives to recent scholarship on the CIO. First, contrary to the view that wartime militancy represented a decomposition of union power, strong evidence suggests that in many industries the CIO was able to preserve and extend the discipline and sense of purpose that characterized the initial organizing era. Second, the "rank-and-filism" that currently dominates writing on shop-floor activism needs to be rethought, for rather than stifling grass roots activity, national union bureaucracies often empowered local activists – especially, as in the case of southern blacks, when they operated in a less than hospitable local climate.[48]

---

46. For detailed treatment of wartime recomposition in meatpacking see Halpern, "Black and White," chapter 7; and Horowitz, "The Path Not Taken," chapter 8.

47. Halpern, "Interracial Unionism," pp. 171–74. Interview with Eddie Humphrey by Halpern and Horowitz, 16 March 1986, UPWAOHP; interview with Frank Wallace by Halpern and Horowitz, 16 March, 1986, UPWAOHP.

48. Both of these dominant tendencies are present in Nelson Lichtenstein's otherwise excellent, *Labor's War at Home: The CIO in World War II*, NY, 1982. See also Joshua Freeman, "Delivering the Goods: Industrial Unionism During World War II," *Labor History*, vol. 19, 1979. On the "rank-and-file" paradigm, see Jonathan Zeitlin's comments on the British historiography, "Rank-and-Filism in Labour History: A Critique," *International Review of Social History*, vol. 34, 1989; and Eric Arnesen's response, "Crusades Against Crisis: A View From the United States on the `Rank-and-File' Critique and Other Catalogs of Labor History's Alleged Ills," *International Review of Social History*, vol. 35, 1990.

Recent studies of two other southern industries – steel and iron ore mining – amplify these points and bring the general contours of CIO unionism into sharp relief. The mining of iron and the production of steel are closely related processes, and in northern Alabama two companies dominated both enterprises – Republic Steel, and the Tennessee Coal, Iron, and Railroad Company (TCI). It is hardly surprising, then, that the CIO's progress in these fields was a parallel process. Although less successful than the campaigns in meatpacking and tobacco, the organizing drives conducted by the Steel Workers Organizing Committee (SWOC) and the International Union of Mine, Mill, and Smelter Workers (Mine Mill) did bring black and white workers together in single unions, resulted in signed contracts and transformed local power relations. Moreover, the relative weakness of industrial unionism in these sectors can be explained in such a way that further highlights the most important features of the CIO's relationship with African American workers.

In the industrial belt surrounding Birmingham, blacks made up nearly half of the workforce in the steel mills and comprised a full eighty percent of the area's 5,000 iron miners. In steel, not only were these workers the lowest paid – earning as little as sixteen cents an hour – they were restricted to the most menial jobs. Black miners, by contrast, received roughly the same wages as whites, but they were restricted to manual jobs, denied access to supervisory and safety positions, and frequently found themselves assigned to inferior ore deposits. In both industries, blacks were the unions' earliest and strongest supporters. Mine Mill, which began organizing in the NRA period, well before the establishment of the CIO, quickly established local unions at Republic and TCI's mines. Both were built around activist cores of blacks; white miners, by and large, opted for membership in the company unions established just after the passage of the National Industrial Recovery Act. With the stage set for racial confrontation, TCI intensified divisiveness by further segregating the workplace, erecting separate pay-shacks for whites and segregating the transportation of miners to their work stations.[49]

Seriously divided, Mine Mill struck prematurely in 1934 for wage parity with coal miners and union recognition. It called its members out again in 1936 over the company's refusal to negotiate over an incentive plan. Although not complete failures – largely because of the intervention of Secretary of Labor Frances Perkins – these conflicts further polarized black and white miners. The red-baiting that accompanied the first strike destroyed what little white support existed for the union. The

49. Kelley, *Hammer and Hoe*, p. 143; Huntley, "Iron Ore Miners," pp. 48–60.

second confrontation, which was more of a clear-cut defeat, strengthened the hand of the white-dominated company union, now chartered as the independent Brotherhood of Captive Miners, and opened the way for the mass discharge of black union leaders. Mine Mill thus entered the CIO era weak and internally divided.[50]

In steel, the situation at mid-decade was slightly different – though equally as bleak. Although the Alabama industry was "entirely dominated by employee representation plans," these unions displayed considerable independence from the companies that sponsored them and drew their representatives from both races. As a result, CIO strategy involved winning over these groups to the SWOC rather than attacking them directly. The racial division that plagued Mine Mill was less of a factor in steel, since significant numbers of whites did join the SWOC. However, here too blacks formed the backbone of the early organization. "The negroes were the first to join and then they were the stickers," recalled one unionist. Yet, because they were kept out of skilled positions in the mills, these union pioneers were unable to utilize the kinds of direct action that allowed black packing house and tobacco workers to entrench their organizations. As a result, SWOC made only limited progress. Indeed, John L. Lewis expectations for southern steel were uncharacteristically modest. He told the SWOC's regional director that he would be satisfied, "if you get results in ten years."[51]

Amongst these black recruits in the mines and mills, though, the union cause "was like the second coming of Christ." Long before the northern black middle class agreed to cautiously back the CIO, Birmingham's black churches and civic organizations gave their wholehearted support to the new unionism. Inside the SWOC, blacks held elected and appointed positions and took every opportunity to assert themselves. In Mine Mill, more blacks were elected to leadership position than any other CIO union, with the possible exception of the UPWA. Their visible and vocal presence, no doubt, alienated many white workers. "I'm not going to join your damn nigger organization," one told an organizer. One clue to the relative strength of white racist sentiment in Alabama's steel and iron industries has to do with the inexperience of the white workforce there. Many, if not most, were first generation industrial workers recruited from the rural portions of the state. Unlike their counterparts in meatpacking or tobacco, few had either worked with blacks in the past or – because of rigid occupational segregation – labored alongside them performing

---

50. Huntley, "Iron Ore Miners," pp. 58–82, 87–94; Taft, *Organizing Dixie*, pp. 111–14.

51. Taft, *Organizing Dixie*, p. 103, Reuben Farr quoted on p. 106; John L. Lewis quoted in Stein, "Southern Workers," p. 183.

similar jobs. The common ground upon which unionism was built was much narrower here than in the other industries.[52]

As with mining, the steel companies manipulated pre existing racial prejudice in an effort to forestall the organization of their mills. They disseminated propaganda portraying the SWOC as a "nigger union," circulated rumors amongst whites about black designs on their jobs and invoked municipal legislation against the union. "The first meeting I ever had with a colored group, the law came to arrest me," recalled Reuben Farr, a white leader of the TCI local. In nearby Fairfield and Gadsden, local authorities obliged the steel companies by strengthening ordinances prohibiting race mixing in order to place SWOC union meetings beyond the legal pale. These measures largely backfired, as SWOC organizers carried on and engaged in civil disobedience, publicly demonstrating the depth of their commitment to equality. Indeed, the arrest of twenty-nine unionists in Gadsden for violating a rarely enforced statute forbidding the meeting of blacks and whites for the purpose of breaking a law, "the advocacy of miscegenation or social equality between the races forbidden by law, or to advocate or propose any measure of movement looking to the destruction of state, county, or city government" brought national attention to the SWOC's efforts and made local heroes of those detained.[53]

SWOC received an enormous boost in the 1937 when it secured a contract with Tennessee Coal and Iron. Significantly, this breakthrough had little to do with the union's strength in TCI's mills and shops, but resulted from a decision by its parent company, United States Steel, to accommodate rather than combat the CIO. Again, affiliation with a national organization pushed forward southern union progress. This victory marked a turning point in the steel union's fortunes as white workers began deserting the company unions and coming over to the SWOC. A successful sit-down strike at the Alabama Casting Company, organized wholly by rank-and-file workers, coupled with TCI's transparent use of the 1937/38 recession to inflict heavy layoffs amongst union activists, further accelerated this process. Also helpful in winning white support were the educational efforts of the local WPA staff who, in close cooperation with the union, offered labor education courses,

52. Rob Hall quoted in Kelley, *Hammer and Hoe*, p. 142; information on community support, ibid. Quotation from Robert J. Norrell, "Caste in Steel: Jim Crow Careers in Birmingham, Alabama," *Journal of American History*, vol. 73, December 1986, p. 673. On the inexperience of southern steelworkers, see Stein, "Southern Workers," pp. 185–86. For discussion of a similar dynamic involving rural whites in shipbuilding see Bruce Nelson, "Organized Labor and the Struggle for Black Equality in Mobile During WWI," *Journal of American History*, vol. 80, December 1993.

53. Farr quoted in Taft, *Organizing Dixie*, p. 105. For city segregation laws, see Taft, pp. 106–7; Kelley, *Hammer and Hoe*, p. 142.

classes on public speaking and lessons in parliamentary procedure and grievance presentation. At the peak of the program, seventy-six instructors were holding classes for Alabama steelworkers.[54]

The CIO's problems in Alabama were far from over, though. Just as the SWOC was gaining a foothold in Alabama, national policy imperatives intervened to stall further progress. The northern steel campaign entered full swing in the summer of 1937, and the small southern staff was trimmed as all available resources came to bear on "Little Steel." Although a union nucleus was in place at Republic Steel, the plant remained largely unorganized and would remain so until the first years of the Second World War. Likewise in iron ore mining, union growth in the late 1930s was incremental and came about largely as a result of external forces. In the dark days after the disastrous 1936 strike when the situation seemed hopeless, the National Labor Relations Board ordered TCI to reinstate discharged unionists with full backpay. This victory bolstered Mine Mill's prestige at a critical juncture and led to the collapse of the Brotherhood. By the fall of 1938, the union signed its first collective bargaining agreement with TCI, allowing it to make further inroads among white miners. In addition to picking up new recruits at TCI, union locals at many of the region's smaller companies reported sizeable increases in membership.[55]

Although Mine Mill was on the move again, the divide between black and white ore miners proved too great to bridge. Ironically, the new white recruits caused considerable tension. Unhappy about the prominent role played by blacks in the union, they attempted to wrest control from the local's officers and reverse the policy of evenly splitting executive positions along racial lines. Although this effort failed, white unease festered and soon turned to bitter rancor. The company nurtured these racial grievances by changing its hiring policy and enforcing segregation practices with greater vigor. From 1938 onwards, TCI hired whites almost exclusively in a concerted effort to "lighten the complexion of the workforce" and thus undermine black control of Mine Mill. At the same time, the company encouraged a new "independent" union, the AFL-affiliated Red Ore Miners, which competed for the loyalty of whites. Mine Mill remained overwhelmingly black through the 1940s and prey to company inspired racial polarization.[56]

54. Stein, "Southern Workers," pp. 189–90; Kelley, *Hammer and Hoe*, pp. 143–44; Taft, *Organizing Dixie*, p. 108.

55. Stein, "Southern Workers," pp. 189–90; Taft, *Organizing Dixie*, p. 110; Huntley, "Iron Ore Miners," pp. 92–96; Kelley, *Hammer and Hoe*, p. 146.

56. Huntley, "Iron Ore Miners," pp. 96–99, 111–13, 122; "Rise and Fall of Mine Mill," pp. 5–6; Kelley, *Hammer and Hoe*, p. 146. Huntley's argument about TCI's manipulation of the workforce is born out by the statistics on the racial composition of Jefferson County's industrial workers in Norrell, "Caste in Steel," p. 676.

The examples of the SWOC and Mine Mill in Alabama direct attention to two important features often overlooked by labor historians. First, an examination of the labor process and the position of key groups of workers within it can help explain the ebb and flow of union organization. This observation takes on particular salience in a racially (or ethnically) charged situation, such as the one prevailing in Birmingham's steel mills where black workers, despite their numbers, could not exercise the kind of shop-floor power so vital to industrial union success. Integrated work departments – such as those in the packing houses – generate shared experience and common grievances amongst workers that can, in certain situations, counter fragmentary forces. In southern steel, occupational segregation made the project of solidarity all the more difficult by giving whites an economic stake in the preservation of inequality.

Second, the experience of iron and steel demonstrates the leading role played by black workers in CIO unionism. In the case of the former, whites proved to be the union's Achilles heel, from both without and within Mine Mill. Capital exploited this situation from the start, and was largely successful in keeping white miners out of the union. In the case of steel, blacks again provided much of the dynamism behind the SWOC. Indeed, black initiative – such as the sitdown at Alabama Casting – forced the union's normally cautious white bureaucrats to reluctantly endorse direct action tactics. Similarly, black grassroots militancy, prompted these leaders to adopt an aggressive civil rights stance, which at times included the defiance of local law authorities. As with the left-leaning UPWA and the FTA, black southerners reaped enormous gains out of all proportion to their local strength due to their membership in national organization, even though that organization was decidedly centrist. Additional case studies are required (especially of the UAW in the South) before anything like a complete picture emerges, but even at this early stage it is clear that black workers played a far more important – and complex – role in the establishment of industrial unions than previously believed.

Blacks who joined CIO unions in the 1930s were motivated by more than simple economic considerations. To be sure, better pay, improved working conditions and greater dignity were appealing goals, but the CIO also offered a vehicle with which to attack racial discrimination, both on and off the job. For white workers, especially those in the South, the imperatives of interracial unionism forced a certain recognition of black rights and often led to a modification in conduct. Opinions and attitudes might not have been reversed – racists did not become promoters of social equality – but the material benefits of unionism necessitated tolerance of, and even limited support for, the redress of black grievances. One CIO activist in meatpacking succinctly expressed this point: "Overcoming prejudice didn't mean anyone got invited to somebody's house for Christmas dinner. But so far as on the job and in the union.... See, we were making a *religion* of racial unity."[57]

The convergence of black and white interests around material benefits allowed industrial unions to emerge. "Making a religion of racial unity" was vital to their success, at least in industries where both races were represented in large numbers. And the minimum measure of success for CIO unions was the securing and enforcing of collective bargaining agreements. These contracts inevitably involved an erosion of the color line and allowed black workers to register significant advances. Shop-floor rights embodied in the union contract had radical implications within the context of traditional southern race relations. Carefully enforced seniority eliminated the practice of discriminatory layoffs and enabled blacks to rise into skilled jobs previously reserved for whites. Similarly, by directing the company to "pay the job not the man," many of these agreements abolished at a single stroke the often considerable wage differential between white and black workers. And the grievance system provided minorities with a collective means of addressing discriminatory practices. The industrial "citizenship" and implied egalitarianism of the union contract generated a rights consciousness that encouraged black workers to utilize these new institutional mechanisms. "When the union came, it was just like being reconstructed," recalled Ruby D. Jones, a Winston-Salem tobacco worker and FTA member.[58]

In meatpacking, where employer intransigence forced local unions to rely upon their power at the point of production to enforce the contract, job actions tended to promote interracial solidarity, not just through the active involvement of the rank-and-file but because white workers throughout the plant depended upon the predominantly black killing floors for crucial support. "They really had the push," one white worker recalled, "we had a strong union because of the black people." Even in an industry like steel a similar dynamic frequently made itself felt.

57. Les Orear quoted in Lizabeth Cohen, *Making a New Deal: Industrial Workers in Chicago, 1919–39*, NY, 1990, p. 337. Another rank-and-file worker remarked of his conservative white fellow unionists: "They didn't come in and hug 'em and kiss 'em ... but they knew they had to be together, period. Even though some of them were anti-negro, they still knew you had to be together to form a union and to win some of their demands." Joe Zabritski quoted in Rick Halpern, "The Iron Fist and the Velvet Glove: Welfare Capitalism in Chicago's Packinghouses, 1922–1933," *Journal of American Studies*, vol. 26, no. 2, August 1992, p. 183.

58. Robert Korstad and Nelson Lichtenstein, "Opportunities Found and Lost: Labor, Radicals, and the Early Civil Rights Movement," *Journal of American History*, vol. 75, no. 3, December 1988, pp. 787, 790. Ruby Jones quoted in Janiewski, "Seeking a New Day," p. 175.

When TCI fired the white head roller in the guide mill, his entirely black crew stopped work and successfully forced his reinstatement – a victory that swelled support for the union amongst whites.[59]

White workers tended to back attacks on discrimination as long as they were articulated through the union in terms of seniority and job rights. Thus, in the summer of 1945 when Armour unfairly discharged seven black butchers at its Fort Worth facility, the entire plant walked out. "What management does to Negroes today it will do to white workers tomorrow," the union paper announced. Yet there existed clear limits to this kind of interracialism. In the same Texas plant, blacks moved into skilled jobs in already integrated departments, but others areas of the plant remained white preserves. When two black women transferred into the sliced-bacon department, for example, angry whites engaged in a sit-down strike, demanding their removal. Management complied and union leadership, fearing a white backlash, acquiesced. Similarly at Reynolds Tobacco in Winston-Salem, the FTA local declined to push forward demands for plant-wide seniority and settled for a department-based system so as not to provoke white resistance.[60]

Similarly, there were boundaries to the social integration practiced by CIO unions in the South. Local committees generally contained representatives from all groups; and meetings were conducted on a non-segregated basis. Occasionally mixed dances and picnics took place, in brazen violation of local custom. Yet at the same time, even advanced unions like the UPWA declined to challenge the standard practice of maintaining separate dressing rooms for black and white workers, Jim Crow water fountains, and partitioned plant cafeterias until the 1950s. In Memphis, the CIO itself did not end the segregation of its own headquarters until pressured to do so in 1950 by General Counsel Arthur Goldberg.[61]

As long as union goals and civil rights aims ran parallel, a delicate equilibrium prevailed. White workers did not oppose black challenges to economic discrimination as long as they were articulated in traditional trade union terms. But attempts to push beyond the fairly narrow language of the contract met with resistance. Because black workers did not push too hard during the initial organizing era, the racial accommodation did not collapse. In many industries, though, wartime recomposition of the workforce disrupted this balance. In Fort Worth, for example,

59. Interview with Mary Salinas by Halpern and Horowitz, 18 March 1986, UPWAOHP; TCI example from Stein, "Southern Workers," p. 191.

60. Halpern, "Interracial Unionism in the Southwest," p. 168; Korstad, "Daybreak of Freedom," p. 170.

61. Halpern, "Interracial Unionism," pp. 168, 172–74; Adedeji, "Crossing the Colorline," pp. 40–43. For Memphis, see Honey, "Labor and Civil Rights," p. 490.

the aggressive civil rights activities of Eddie Humphrey and other veterans caused a white disaffiliation movement that spread to other packing house locals across the South. Mine Mill suffered through a similar episode when disgruntled whites cloaked their racist motives in an anticommunist mantle and succeeded in gaining CIO support for a secessionist revolt. In packing, the International union succeeded in neutralizing the racist opposition, but the internecine strife permanently crippled Mine Mill.[62]

If black activism within the workplace was limited by the racial conservatism of southern whites, out in the community it faced fewer restrictions. In a number of locales, black workers used their unions to mobilize community support for direct assaults on Jim Crow. In Winston-Salem, FTA members revitalized a nearly defunct NAACP branch, transforming an ineffective middle-class club of 100 members into a mass organization of nearly 2,000. They then used this vehicle to challenge black disfranchisement by allying with the CIO Political Action Committee's voter registration drive. Unionists challenged the power of local clerks to assess the eligibility of black applicants and conducted citizenship classes to prepare would-be voters for qualification. Before FTA's campaign, only a handful of black names adorned the voting rolls. In 1944 blacks accounted for more than thirty percent of the electorate. Two years later, FTA support proved crucial in the victory of a liberal Democrat over strong conservative opposition; and the following year the local succeeded in electing the first black to city council since the end of Reconstruction.[63]

In the mid–1940s many labor activists believed that they were well on the way to extending union organization to all sectors of the economy and, in so doing, transforming the American political economy. Many black unionists confidently believed that the "Double V" – victory against fascism abroad and Jim Crow at home – was within their grasp. This buoyant optimism is illustrated in the 1944 report of a correspondent for the *Pittsburgh Courier* who wrote after a visit to Winston Salem, "I was aware of a growing solidarity and intelligent mass action that will mean the dawn of a New Day in the South. One cannot ... mingle with the thousands of workers without sensing a revolution in thought and action. If there is a `New' Negro, he is to be found in the ranks of the labor movement."[64]

---

62. Halpern, "Interracial Unionism," pp. 173–75; Huntley, "Iron Ore Miners," pp. 123–72.

63. Korstad, "Daybreak of Freedom," pp. 221–28, 248–50; Korstad and Lichtenstein, "Opportunities Found and Lost," pp. 792–93.

64. *Pittsburgh Courier*, 3 June 1944, quoted in Korstad and Lichtenstein, "Opportunities Found and Lost," p. 793.

Needless to say, the CIO did not succeed in organizing the bulk of southern industry, nor did black unionists succeed in bringing a new day to African Americans. The first task remains unaccomplished and, indeed, seems further from realization than ever before. The second task required the emergence of a new civil rights movement in the later 1950s, one that drew its strength and moral power from the black church rather than the labor movement. A number of factors combined in the late 1940s to send the CIO into decline. The most important one was a conservative offensive against labor that used the issue of Communism to split away liberal support from the CIO and isolate left-wing unions. This had devastating consequences for black labor activism in the South, especially as union civil rights activity became identified with proof positive of Communist domination. The degeneration of the CIO's much-heralded "Operation Dixie" into an assault upon left-led unions sealed the fate of both the labor movement and the emerging, worker-led freedom struggle. By abandoning the effort to organize the unorganized, the CIO ceased being a labor *movement*; and this, in turn, deprived civil rights activists of political and social space in which to operate.[65]

The study of black workers and unionism in the South is currently in the midst of exciting change and ferment. The old framework of southern distinctiveness is being modified to account for an energetic history of labor organizing that often transcended the supposedly primal divide of race. Little questioned opposing formulas – class vs. race, solidarity vs. fragmentation, white unions vs. black workers – are coming under close critical scrutiny and found wanting. As the New Labor History begins to "bring the unions back in," fresh questions about social context and workers' consciousness are reinvigorating a field which seemed only a short time ago to have reached a dead end. And as African American history starts to explore the way in which the workplace formed a primary arena of racial contact and conflict, "black workers" are shedding their one-dimensionality and are acquiring a new complexity and sense of historical agency.

While it is too early to discern any sort of synthesis, new generalizations are displacing old ones. The major contours of an emerging revision are distinguishable: the racial policies of organized labor in the early twentieth century were far from monolithic; black workers were an integral part of the industrial union upsurge of the 1930s; their relationships with their white co-workers were less antagonistic and far

65. For elaboration see Korstad and Lichtenstein, "Opportunities Found and Lost," pp. 800–1, 811; and Michael Honey, "The Labor Movement and Racism in the South: A Historical Overview," in *Racism and the Denial of Human Rights*, Martin Berkowitz, ed., Minneapolis, 1983.

more complex than previously assumed; and it was through labor struggles that blacks made their most important progress towards equality in the years before the emergence of the "modern" civil rights movement. A great deal more work remains to be done on both the local and regional levels before these positions are more than provocative hypotheses supported by scattered evidence. Several theoretical debates need resolution; and many interpretative features require sharpening. As this new history assumes a refined and nuanced shape in the years to come, it undoubtedly will influence other fields – business and politics come instantly to mind – and prompt further revisionist initiatives.

Part II
The Rural South

–3–

The Legal Basis of Agrarian Capitalism: The South since 1933

Pete Daniel

The Civil War destroyed the grids that bound together the antebellum South, forcing all southerners, black and white, men and women, to reconstruct a new society based on free labor. Former masters and slaves, as well as their white neighbors, understood the importance of controlling the sale and proceeds of their crops. When conservative whites regained political supremacy and ended the First Reconstruction in the 1870s, they immediately seized control of crops by subordinating the sharecropper's lien for wages to the landlord's claim on rent and advances. The struggle over control of the crop persisted, and the resulting crop lien system endured until, in the guise of the New Deal, federal policies undermined its legal foundation. The positive, albeit exaggerated, federal role in the Second Reconstruction – the civil rights movement – masked a dramatic shift from state lien laws to federal agricultural policies, an abrupt legal transformation that lubricated the gears of agribusiness.

If state law adjudicated in courts was the legal foundation of the crop lien system, agribusiness ripened in the collusive atmosphere of government subsidies, land-grant university patronage, and corporate drumming. By the middle of the twentieth century, capital-intensive agriculture had largely reconfigured the southern countryside. Science, technology, and government agricultural policies administered by a corpulent and obfuscating bureaucracy destroyed the labor-intensive rural order born of Reconstruction.

Through a powerful but almost invisible network that stretched from the U.S. Department of Agriculture (USDA) in Washington to the thousands of county and local agricultural committees throughout the country, the bureaucracy preserved the ideology and power of the white elite. Even as civil rights laws erased public discrimination, this subterranean stream of racism flowed through the USDA bureaucracy. "The rules may be color blind," attorney Patricia J. Williams cautioned, "but people are not."[1]

1. Patricia J. Williams, *The Alchemy of Race and Rights*, Cambridge, 1991, p. 120.

This essay explores some of the implications in the displacement of state lien and labor laws by federal rules. Under federal regulations, county committees composed of the local white elite diluted the role of state courts as mediators in the relations between landlords and tenants. *Ad hoc* bureaucratic rulings at the committee or county appeal level rapidly supplanted state statutes and case law, and (since these decisions were not published) committees easily politicized their verdicts. These procedures not only strengthened the white elite but also replaced overt discrimination with institutional racism in southern agriculture. Finally, and appropriately, some emergency agricultural programs themselves became commodified. Taken together, these federal policies became the legal basis for agribusiness, part of a new grid that along with science and technology, replaced the crop lien system.

The implications of this transition from state law to federal regulations must be viewed within the larger context of changes brought on by more familiar factors. In this scenario, the tractor and the mechanical cotton harvester are the icons, long-dreamed-of engines of change that by the 1950s allowed planters to substitute capital for labor. The final alchemy, herbicides, destroyed weeds and, ultimately, eliminated the jobs of those who had chopped them. Science and technology, supported by federal subsidies, marched through the cotton, tobacco, rice, and sugar fields, powerful agents of capitalism ordered to drive out inefficiency. The mainstay of the old system, sharecropping, dwindled to the point that after 1954 the Census Bureau did not even report the category.[2]

Locating the ideology that informed this program explains to some extent its content. The USDA urged that farms should be organized as businesses. There was in the USDA an eagerness to please larger farmers and those who sold to them and, it follows, an ill-disguised contempt for small-scale farmers. For such arrogant bureaucrats the disappearance of sharecroppers, embarrassing unwashed victims of the plantation system, was an unmixed blessing, an answer to their prayers. Such sentiment should not be surprising, given how harmoniously the racial and class biases of the southern white elite resonated with USDA bureaucrats. By the end of World War II, this powerful segment of the USDA bureaucracy and its allies in Congress had dismembered both the Farm Security Administration (FSA) and the Bureau of Agricultural Economics (BAE), the only internal threats to its pro-business agenda.

---

2. Jack Temple Kirby, *Rural Worlds Lost: The American South, 1920–1960*, Baton Rouge, 1987, p.70.

The road was cleared for the destruction of sharecropping and the creation of a new system.[3]

Yet sharecropping was a way of life, a culture that emerged from poverty. That culture produced, among many others, Robert Johnson and Jimmie Rodgers, personifications of blues and country music. Bureaucrats, and the constituency they served, saw in such people not culture or even resources but obstacles to the new order. Recognition of the richness of southern rural culture is a recent phenomenon that arrived after that way of life was doomed. The USDA preferred to portray sharecroppers as depraved victims of a primitive culture that would mercifully be destroyed by "progress."

During the spring of 1933, millions of southern farmers started out under the old system – sharecroppers bickering with landlords and every family planting all that it could tend in hopes of offsetting low prices.[4] The Agricultural Adjustment Act, passed in May, caught farmers in the fields tending growing crops. For the remainder of the year they witnessed the birth of a confusing and discomforting federal system that promised immediate reimbursement for plowing up portions of the cotton crop and higher prices that fall. The next year the Agricultural Adjustment Administration (AAA) froze commodity production areas by awarding acreage allotments to landowners. Using a complicated formula based on supply and demand, the AAA each year licensed these landowners to plant a prescribed number of acres and denied other farmers allotments. County AAA committees composed of prosperous white landowners largely replaced state courts as they settled disagreements over allotments and over the division of money from other federal programs.[5]

---

3. On the Farm Security Administration, see Sidney Baldwin, *Poverty and Politics: The Rise and Decline of the Farm Security Administration*, Chapel Hill, 1968; on the Bureau of Agricultural Economics, see Richard S. Kirkendall, *Social Scientists and Farm Politics in the Age of Roosevelt*, Ames, 1982. Also, see Pete Daniel, "Going Among Strangers: Southern Reactions to World War II," *Journal of American History*, vol. 77, 1990, p. 888.

4. On the class structure of that era, see Arthur F. Raper, *Preface to Peasantry: A Tale of Two Black Belt Counties*, New York, 1968 ed.; "Cultural Reconnaissance, Greene County, Georgia," 18 September 1944; and Frank D. Alexander, "Cultural Reconnaissance Survey of Coahoma County, Mississippi," n.d. Farm Population and Rural Welfare Sample Counties, Reconnaissance Surveys, Box 250, Records of the Bureau of Agricultural Economics, RG 83 (National Archives).

5. On the domestic allotment program, see Harold F. Breimyer, "Agricultural Philosophies and Policies in the New Deal," *Minnesota Law Review*, vol. 68, 1983/84, pp. 338–39, 343–44. Breimyer observed (p. 338) that W.T. Spillman of the USDA, John D. Black of the University of Minnesota and of Harvard, and M.L. Wilson of Montana State College "began to think in terms of applying a truly industrial instrument to the rural-agrarian sector, namely collective management of farm output through both super-cooperatives and a national farm program. Toward this end they devised a `domestic allotment' plan."

Prior to the committee system, state laws and courts had played an important, albeit often contradictory, role in mediating class tension. The rural social and economic structure that emerged after the Civil War was solidly grounded in law that gave planters control over land, crops, and labor.[6] Indeed, it is one of the bedrocks of Reconstruction history that when conservative whites regained power, they enacted legislation that subordinated the laborers' lien for wages to that of the landlord for rent and advances.[7] Landowners used crop lien laws along with exorbitant interest rates and innovative methods of labor control, while sharecroppers fought back with liens for their labor and a barrage of what James C. Scott labeled "everyday forms of peasant resistance" – "foot-dragging, dissimulation, false compliance, pilfering, feigned ignorance, slander, arson, sabotage, and so on."[8]

While this "offstage" story is yet to be written about the South, a glance at state laws circumscribing tenants and sharecroppers suggests, in Scott's term, that they employed "weapons of the weak." It was a misdemeanor to sell or conceal any part of the crop, to buy or sell cotton between sunset and sunrise, to entice away a laborer before the annual contract expired, and in North Carolina to buy or sell cotton in less than bale quantities. Such laws suggest ways that poorer farmers fought back against lien laws and high interest rates that eroded their income. As late as 1939 a report came from Floyd County, Virginia, that a tenant "sold without the landlord's knowledge enough fence post timber from the farm to buy it."[9]

---

6. Labor laws, like lien laws, varied from state to state and evolved over time. The works of Harold D. Woodman and William Cohen, as well as some of my work, have explored labor and lien laws, but there is no work that treats the South from the Civil War to the civil rights movement. The best analysis of the development of lien law is Harold D. Woodman, "Post-Civil War Southern Agriculture and the Law," *Agricultural History*, vol. 52, 1979, pp. 319–37. I am indebted to Woodman for reading and commenting on an earlier version of this paper. On labor laws, see William Cohen, *At Freedom's Edge: Black Mobility and the Southern White Quest for Racial Control, 1861–1915*, Baton Rouge, 1991; Pete Daniel, *The Shadow of Slavery: Peonage in the South, 1901–1969*, Urbana, 1972.

7. A.B. Book, "A Note on the Legal Status of Share-Tenants and Share-Croppers in the South," *Law and Contemporary Problems*, vol. 4, 1937, p. 541. See also, C. Vann Woodward, *Origins of the New South, 1877–1913*, Baton Rouge, 1951, pp. 180–85; Eric Foner, *Reconstruction: America's Unfinished Revolution, 1863–1877*, New York, 1988, pp. 406, 408–9, 594–95; Steven Hahn, *The Roots of Southern Populism: Yeoman Farmers and the Transformation of the Georgia Upcountry, 1859–1890*, New York, 1983, pp. 173–76. As Hahn points out (p. 175), "The law embodies and legitimizes relations of power; it does not neatly determine day-to-day social reality."

8. James C. Scott, *Weapons of the Weak: Everyday Forms of Peasant Resistance*, New Haven, 1985, xvi.

9. Book, "A Note on the Legal Status," p. 542; Scott, *Weapons of the Weak*; interview with Kyle Weeks, Floyd County, Virginia, Virginia Legal Study, 1939, Land Tenure Section, Records of the Bureau of Agricultural Economics, RG 83 (National Archives).

State laws and resulting court cases demonstrate that control of crops was contested terrain for the two-thirds of a century from the end of Reconstruction to the Second World War. Although the judges and juries were all-white, the state court system nevertheless heard disagreements involving both whites and African Americans, at least those who could afford to bring cases.[10] Given the poverty and powerlessness of sharecroppers and the landlord's superior lien and prerogative of keeping accounts, one should not claim too much glory for courts, but over the years before the New Deal the interplay between legislative and judicial bodies remained spirited.[11]

Tenants sometimes won concessions not reflected in the law. Some landlords, for example, customarily enforced only the lien on cotton lint and not seeds. Allowing tenants or sharecroppers to keep seed money saved planters or creditors the bother of furnishing additional cash to finish out the crop year. "A man's cottonseed is customarily exempt from liens," Alabama planter and gin owner T.R. Kelly explained. "Frequently that is the only cash a man gets out of his crop." A Mississippi ginner and planter explained that tenants always kept seed money even when they owed money on their accounts. Many farmers, according to a Georgia ginner and planter, looked to cottonseeds "as paying his ginning, and paying for his picking, and usually leaving him a little reserve." A 1941 article insisted that because "the bulk of the lint is mortgaged by the small farmers before maturing, the only actual cash that passes into their hands at the end of the year is that derived from the sale of the seed. This is due to the general practice of exempting cottonseed from crop mortgages."[12]

No doubt many landlords or creditors did enforce the lien on cottonseed. Still, the custom of tenants keeping seed money entered into the folklore and vocabulary of Southerners. Southern Tenant Farmers Union leader H.L. Mitchell remembered that sharecroppers kept half the seed money and on the way to the gin would say, "Git that white man's cotton off my seed." Oscar Johnston, the manager of the Delta and Pine Land Company in Mississippi, summed up the practice: "The cotton-

---

10. For an overview of such laws, see 52A *Corpus Juris Secundum*, St. Paul, 1968, Sec. 793–95, Sec. 820–21. For an overview of such scholarship on African-American history, see Harold D. Woodman, "The Economic and Social History of Blacks in the Post-Emancipation South," *Trends in History*, Fall 1982, pp. 37–55.

11. Mississippi *Code* (1972), sec. 85–7–1; Arkansas *Code* (1987), ch. 41, sec. 18–41–101 through 18–41–108; Alabama *Code* (1975), Sec. 35–9–30, 35–11–91, 35–11–92; 13 *Alabama Digest*, 23–33.

12. T.R. Kelly testimony, Mississippi, 2520; J.C. Hallman testimony, Mississippi, 7096; W.E. McDougald testimony, Georgia, 1255, *Investigation of the Cottonseed Industry*, Senate Docs., 71 Cong., 2 Sess. See also M.J. Cliett testimony, Alabama, 2584; W.W. Jackson testimony, Alabama, 2637; W.C. Coker testimony, Alabama, 2676–77; Sam Epstein testimony, Arkansas, 13564, 13566, ibid.

seed crop is the cotton producers' only unmortgaged asset. It supports the producer during the harvest season and the money from it is more widely distributed than is the money paid for lint."[13] Whether exempting seed money was a case of convenience proving more useful than enforcing the law or sharecroppers' hard-won concession awaits further research.

State law and even state and local customs were not static but represented constant conflict. Even in the 1920s southern state courts were still undecided over whether sharecroppers were simply wage laborers or tenants. According to a 1938 analysis by A.B. Book, three states – Arkansas, South Carolina, and Georgia – regarded the cropper as an employee who had no claim on the crop until the landowner settled for the year. Dominated by the landlord's first claim on the crop, a sharecropper in these states only maintained "as a laborer, a statutory lien on the crops which his labor produces." Three other states – Texas, Tennessee, and sometimes Mississippi – held sharecroppers "tenants in common." As such they had legal standing that allowed them to participate in dividing crops and either to mortgage or to sell their share of the crop. In Mississippi, the legal standing of sharecroppers remained "offstage," for all cases before 1934 involved landlords or tenants. Alabama and North Carolina law made no distinction between share-tenants and sharecroppers.[14] Granted, lien laws were class legislation that usually favored landlords, but these laws were interpreted by judges, a step removed from the political process, and their precedents were recorded in state reports.

13. On evidence of lien holders who did not waive the lien on seeds, see, E.S. Morris testimony, Oklahoma, 11365; T.R. Hupp testimony, Oklahoma, 11357, *Investigation of the Cottonseed Industry*. H.L. Mitchell, *Mean Things Happening in this Land: The Life and Times of H. L. Mitchell, Cofounder of the Southern Tenant Farmers Union*, Montclair, N.J., 1979; *Cotton and Cotton Oil Press*, 5 August 1939, vol. 40, p. 12. I am indebted to Lynette Wren for these citations on cottonseed.

14. Book, "A Note on the Legal Status," pp. 542–45. Under the 1923 Alabama state code revision, "all share-cropper agreements create the relation of landlord and tenant between the parties," except for the one exception when, if both contributed labor, the relations would be "tenants in common of the crop." Quoted in A.B. Book to Paul W. Bruton, 27 March 1934, Cotton, Landlord-Tenant, Records of the Secretary of Agriculture, RG 16 (National Archives). In Mississippi the law was less specific, but only because the issue had never been settled. "Of the five cases considering this question," one of Book's memorandums revealed, "the first two hold that the parties are tenants in common of the crop, the succeeding two cases hold that the relationship of landlord and tenant was created, and the last case (1926) while refusing to decide the conflict in the authorities, treats the situation there under consideration as making the parties tenants in common." A.B. Book to Paul W. Bruton, 24 March 1934, ibid. See also John Charles Crow, "Cropper and Tenant Distinguished in Missouri," *Missouri Law Review*, vol. 24, June 1959, pp. 330–36; Jack A. Bornemann, "Crop Lien and Privileges in Louisiana," *Tulane Law Review*, vol. 14, 1939–40, pp. 444–51.

Even as the New Deal began, a three-tiered case in Humphreys County, Mississippi, between landlord, tenant, and sharecroppers attested to the mediating power of state courts and showed as well the complexity of such disputes. In 1933, tenant W.R. Jenkins, as he had for twenty years, rented Mrs. M.E. Jackson's farm. Jenkins agreed to pay a thousand dollars standing rent and received advances to finance his operation. He hired four African American sharecroppers and, as the opinion explained, "made the usual share-crop contract, which was that the landlord [presumably Jenkins] would furnish the land, teams, plow tools, and 'furnish' to make the crops; the tenants to furnish the labor therefor; the proceeds to be shared, half and half, the tenants first paying the 'furnish' out of their half of the proceeds."

Jenkins also owed Mrs. Jackson over $2,300 in back debts. He sold the cotton and turned over all of the proceeds to Mrs. Jackson. The judge observed that this covered the thousand dollar rental, her "'furnish' to Jenkins, to enable him to farm the place; and, in addition, Jenkins' 'furnish' to these sharecroppers to enable them to make and gather their crops," and $1,127 owed to the sharecroppers. Mrs. Jackson applied the sharecroppers' portion to Jenkins' back debt. The Mississippi Supreme Court ruled in favor of the sharecroppers, declaring that they "had a lien on the crops produced by them for the payment of their shares thereof, paramount to all liens and incumbrances or rights of any kind created by, or against Jenkins, except the lien of Mrs. Jackson for her rent and supplies furnished Jenkins." The court awarded the four sharecroppers their respective shares plus six percent interest.[15]

This legal niche, a claim on the crop, took on new significance when coupled with AAA rules relating to government payments. Federal rules, like lien laws, indisputably favored landowners, although cash renters and tenants also received direct government payments. Sharecroppers, on the other hand, were in a legal twilight zone, for, as we have seen, state laws varied dramatically in assigning legal control of the crop. Jerome Frank and other liberals in the USDA Office of General Counsel hoped to strengthen sharecroppers' claims on government payments. In the spring of 1934, as farmers went about preparing their land for the new cotton crop, Frank's office conducted a study of state landlord-tenant laws and discovered the vague but substantial legal standing of sharecroppers. In Arkansas, where abuses and unresolved complaints ignited the Southern Tenant Farmers Union, Frank's team discovered that over the years Arkansas state courts, at least in legal theory, had eroded the absolute power of landlords and allowed for the

15. The proceeds were distributed as follows: Doss Jefferson, $260.03; Horse Gowdy, $389.03; Ellie Jefferson, $178.68; Sam Willis, $299.78, "with six percent interest on each of the amounts from January 1, 1934." *Jackson v. Jefferson et al.*, 158 So. 486, 487.

disagreements and complicating factors that inevitably arose in land-lord-sharecropper relations. Some arrangements were treated as "tenants in common," where sharecroppers had "a title interest in the crop" or in others as "an employee with a mortgageable inchoate inter-est." The cropper thus not only had a lien for his wages (settlement), but also a lien on the property (the crop). The report on Arkansas, as well as those covering other southern states, concluded that "the cropper should be given a share of the option money."[16] The Office of General Counsel thus uncovered a potential legal solution to one of the AAA's most vexing problems involving landlord-sharecropper relations.[17] Paradoxically, state statutes and court opinions offered sharecroppers a lever to secure federal benefits. If AAA rules would incorporate such state laws, rural power relations could be turned upside down.

By the fall of 1934, however, this initiative was too late. To gain control of AAA benefits, landlords appropriated government payments, evicted unneeded sharecroppers, changed the status of others to wage laborers, and dominated local AAA committees. After the purge of Jerome Frank and other liberals from the Office of General Counsel in February 1935, federal rules – not state laws – became the legal battle-ground for landlords and tenants.[18] This purge of liberals from the USDA left power in the hands of, for want of a better term, the agricul-tural establishment – land grant universities, the federal extension service, farm editors, large farmers, farm organizations, county commit-tees, and their servant, the USDA. Secretary of Agriculture Henry A. Wallace viewed agriculture through his experience as an Iowa farmer,

16. On the evolution of crop lien laws, see memorandum to Paul W. Bruton, n.d., Cotton, Landlord-Tenant, Records of the Secretary of Agriculture, RG 16 (National Archives). Attorney Margaret S. Bennett discovered that "some of the cases seem to indi-cate that once the crop is made, the cropper at once has an interest as an owner of so much of the crop as exceeds in value the landlord's claim for advances." Since the cropper "is the one actually producing the crop," she concluded, "the cropper should be given a share of the option money." She reviewed the AAA rules, and the option payment went to one who had legal ownership of the crop. "If, therefore, a sharecropper is a part owner of the crop, he could have become a party to the contract in a capacity other than as a lien claimant. On that basis he would be clearly entitled to a share of the option money." Margaret S. Bennett, memo to Bruton, 7 March 1934, ibid. For a recent discussion of lien laws, see David W. Dewey, "Federal Law to Preempt Crop Lien Provisions of the Uniform Commercial Code," *Alabama Law Review*, vol. 38, 1987, pp. 503–8.

17. Baldwin, *Poverty and Politics*, p. 78. See enclosure, "General Conditions in the Mississippi Delta with Special Reference to Plowing up Cotton Crops," in John P. Davis to Secretary, 23 April 1934; and Secretary to Davis, 13 June 1934, Cotton, Landlord-Tenant, Records of the Secretary of Agriculture, RG 16 (National Archives). For an exam-ination of how landlords cheated tenants in the early years of federal programs, see Harold Hoffsommer, "The AAA and the Cropper," *Social Forces*, vol. 13–14, 1935, pp. 494–502, esp. 495, 497, 499.

18. Anthony J. Badger, *Prosperity Road: The New Deal, Tobacco, and North Carolina*, Chapel Hill, 1980, pp. 89–94, 125–26, 220–29; Kirkendall, *Social Scientists*, pp. 100–2.

farm editor, and advocate of science and technology.[19] The AAA, if successful, would replicate Iowa across the land. When this midwestern formula confronted the South with its sharecropping and racism, it empowered white landlords who most closely resembled businessmen. Because they controlled local AAA committees, landlords used USDA bureaucracy to institutionalize their ideas of race and class into federal regulations.

The AAA bypassed state courts and established an administrative network that stretched from Washington through states to county and local committees. Although touted as the embodiment of grass roots democracy (Secretary Wallace proudly labeled the plan "economic democracy"), local AAA committees in every county were collusive creatures of the agricultural establishment. At best it was only a democracy of landowners; at worst it had the odor of oligarchy. The Secretary of Agriculture appointed state committees, and in the South the Extension Service dominated every level of AAA operations, often controlling the nomination and election of state, county, and local committees. County committees assigned acreage allotments, adjusted disputes over AAA benefits, and heard landlord-tenant disputes. Through AAA committees, the rural elite perpetuated its ideology, which included race and class assumptions.[20]

A 1947 study of Wilson County, North Carolina, and of Darlington County, South Carolina, revealed how extension agents and AAA committeemen came to dominate local policy. Both white and black farmers attended AAA meetings and voted in referendums. Several tenants served on community committees but no sharecroppers or African Americans were elected at any level. The landless came to view committee elections "as a function primarily of landowners." Because committee work involved record keeping, younger and better educated farmers quickly dominated committees, and, as interest in elections waned, the same people were elected year after year. Although some

19. See Breimyer, "Agricultural Philosophies and Policies in the New Deal," pp. 347–48; and on Henry A. Wallace, see Deborah Fitzgerald, *The Business of Breeding: Hybrid Corn in Illinois, 1890–1940*, Ithaca, 1990.

20. On the creation of local committees, see Gladys L. Baker, Wayne D. Rasmussen, Vivian Wiser, and Jane M. Porter, *Century of Service: The First 100 Years of the United States Department of Agriculture*, Washington, 1963, pp. 159–61. On the workings of the committees, see Hoffsommer, "The AAA and the Cropper," pp. 496–97. "The farmers selected are usually operators of relatively large farms and are practically all landowners," Hoffsommer revealed. "In general, the County Agents were instructed to select men of character and ability in the community and in sympathy with the program.... Few, if any, croppers ever became members of these committees." See also Badger, *Prosperity Road*, pp. 125–26, 220–23; James C. Cobb, "'Somebody Done Nailed us on the Cross': Federal Farm and Welfare Policy and the Civil Rights Movement in the Mississippi Delta," *Journal of American History*, vol. 77, 1990, pp. 914–15.

AAA administrators suggested hiring blacks for responsible positions, one remembered that "every time we raised the question of hiring Negroes, the Extension Service would turn us down with the explanation that they were charged exclusively with the educational functions under the law." With the support of the Extension Service, the elites in these two counties and others throughout the South dominated the AAA committees and directed federal policy.[21]

A disgruntled farmer no longer sought relief in a state court but, if dissatisfied with the county committee's decision, appeared before a county review committee, composed of three other powerful local white farmers, sometimes the very people named in his complaint.[22] An aggrieved party could appeal to Washington, or, as a last resort seek judicial review in a federal court. Whatever the efficacy of such a program in Iowa, in the class-ridden and racist South it empowered landowners best prepared to make the transition to agribusiness. As early as the fall of 1934, the newborn bureaucratic network stymied sharecroppers from successfully appealing cases of extortion and eviction. William R. Amberson, a professor at the University of Tennessee Medical School in Memphis, watched the Arkansas cotton country turn into a battlefield as AAA policies pitted sharecroppers against landlords. "Bad as the conditions used to be, before the federal government entered the picture, the present situation is worse," Amberson revealed. To incite racial feelings and encourage mischief in the integrated Southern Tenant Farmers Union, landlords, who had years of practice at using race to confound issues, substituted black sharecroppers for whites. Meanwhile, Amberson discovered, planters forced contracts on sharecroppers "in which they are asked to agree to pay rent for acres already rented to the government."[23]

Although the USDA ignored Amberson's charges of fraud, a state case concerning the 1935 crop suggested that money from federal programs offered irresistible temptations. In Mississippi County, Arkansas, F.M. Dulaney rented a 567-acre farm from Mrs. B.W. Thweat, agreeing to pay eight dollars per acre and share with her any

21. Robert Earl Martin, "Negro-White Participation in the A.A.A. Cotton and Tobacco Referenda in North and South Carolina: A Study in Differential Voting and Attitudes in Selected Areas," unpublished Ph.D. diss., University of Chicago, 1947, pp. 242–43, 259, 263, 259–60, 267. I am indebted to Anthony Badger for bringing this study to my attention. See also Arthur F. Raper, *Preface to Peasantry: A Tale of Two Black Belt Counties,* New York, 1968, p. 249.

22. Kirkendall, *Social Scientists and Farm Politics,* p. 92; Pete Daniel, *Breaking the Land: The Transformation of Cotton, Tobacco, and Rice Cultures since 1880,* Urbana, 1985, pp. 101–2.

23. William R. Amberson to Paul Appleby, 21 November, 29 November 1934, Cotton, Landlord-Tenant, Records of the Secretary of Agriculture, RG 16 (National Archives).

income from land he rented to the federal government. Dulaney then contracted with a dozen sharecroppers and, as the judge recounted, "furnished the teams, tools and supplies to enable the sharecroppers to make the crop and received one half of the crop therefor." He also rented 155 acres to the federal government but did not, as his contract stipulated, share it with Mrs. Thweat. She then seized seven hundred dollars worth of cotton raised by the sharecroppers to satisfy Dulaney's government account. The sharecroppers sued. The Arkansas Supreme Court decided "that the statute is a rule of natural and exact justice in a case like the instant one wherein the landlord will not be permitted to take more than the contract fixed." Once the eight dollars per acre rental fee had been paid the sharecroppers had no further obligation. Since they only owed $122.11, the dozen sharecroppers divided $577.89 for their year's work. As other sharecroppers were being evicted and cheated throughout the state in violation of federal guidelines, the Arkansas Supreme Court upheld the sharecroppers' lien for their labor.[24]

Tenants who managed land, such as F.M. Dulaney in the Arkansas case, often benefited from USDA programs, and not all such tenants were white. "We have cases where the negro rents land from the land owner to be paid in cotton at the end of the harvesting season," the Chairman of the East Baton Rouge Cotton Production Control Association and President of the Farm Bureau complained to Henry A. Wallace in March 1935: "That negro is sub-renting that same land to the United States Government, collecting the rent in cash and spending it as he pleases." The USDA replied that while this was "an important question," any tenant, regardless of race, could dispose of government rental income as he pleased.[25] Such tenants, a step above sharecroppers, had greater opportunity to profit from USDA programs.

Sharecroppers had but one weapon to challenge landlords who appropriated federal money, changed their status to wage hands, or evicted them. They complained to Washington. In the mid–1930s some 400 letters per week arrived in Washington, but they were redirected to local AAA committees for redress. Thus, most complaints were disposed of by the very people complained of. As one Washington official admitted in December 1934, the AAA had "dismissed each complaint by simply writing a reply instructing the complaining tenant

24. *Dulaney et al. v. Balls et al.*, 102 S.W. 88, 89–90.

25. Wilmer Mills to Henry A. Wallace, 28 March 1935; C.H. Alvord to Mills, 4 April 1935, AAA, Rice, Records of the Agricultural Stabilization and Conservation Service, RG 145 (National Archives).

that he should see his county agent and county committee."[26] At times, it seems possible to hear the echo of bureaucratic chuckling even today, for the self-investigation policy endures. Since 1987, the USDA Office of Advocacy and Enterprise conducted sixteen on-site-investigations of the three thousand complaints it received. The others it referred to the civil rights offices of the agencies involved and incorporated the findings and recommendations in the decision letter to the complainant.[27]

Landowners and the USDA, ignoring the precedents of state law, cut the legal ground from underneath sharecroppers and tenants. Bureaucracy rushed into the breach. Federal agricultural policy rapidly displaced a body of law that had evolved over three-quarters of a century. State cases relating to landlord-tenant conflicts dropped abruptly after 1933.[28] The AAA embodied class legislation with an insatiable appetite that fed on itself, first swallowing sharecroppers and tenants, then devouring African Americans, and finally consuming landowners. Such small farmers had been given a death sentence, and every federal policy combined to insure that the execution was carried out.[29]

Instead of involving the division of crops between landlord and tenant, disagreements increasingly involved government benefits and acreage allotments. The allotment and appeal process over time became a legal arena, for there was a finite amount of farmland. By 1953, allotments were not based entirely on the farm's historical production but included the farm's total land in cultivation.[30] Acreage reserves, up to ten percent of the county allotment, gave local committees a tool to pacify those who complained and to reward those who demonstrated trends such as irrigation and mechanization.[31] Judge John R. Brown,

26. D.P. Trent, memorandum for C. C. Davis, 28 December 1934, AAA, Production Control Program, Landlord-Tenant, 1933–38, Records of the Agricultural Stabilization and Conservation Service, RG 145 (National Archives). Of the 2,098 complaints received by this time, only 347 were adjusted by county committees, 215 settled by field investigators; 1,512 were dismissed, and only 24 contracts were cancelled. See Daniel, *Breaking the Land*, p. 102; Donald H. Grubbs, *Cry from the Cotton: The Southern Tenant Farmers' Union and the New Deal*, Chapel Hill, 1971, pp. 3–61.

27. Mike McGraw and Jeff Taylor, "Pledges, Not Changes, Made," Kansas City *Star*, 11 December 1991.

28. The Alabama *Digest* for 1960 records only eight cases after 1933, although one, *Metropolitan Life Ins. Co.v. Reconstruction Finance Corporarion*, 162 So. 379, suggests the prominence of agribusiness.

29. State courts could hear cases arising from disputes over federal rules, but federal law superseded state. *Lee v. De Berry et al.*, 65 S.E. 2d 775 (1951).

30. Stephen Pace to D.W. Brooks, 2 December 1953; D.W. Brooks to Ezra Taft Benson, 3 December 1953, Cotton, Acreage Allotments, Market Quotas, Records of the Secretary of Agriculture, RG 16 (National Archives).

31. C. Michael Malski, "Agricultural Law: Appealing Agricultural Allotments," *Mississippi Law Journal*, vol. 41, 1970, pp. 422–24.

who presided over a major Texas allotment case, admitted that allotment policy was contained "in a legislative structure so abstruse that ... it sets forth a formula which, to the tutored, reflects the product hammered out in the legislative process, but to the uninitiated, appears to be an unintelligible stream of words."[32]

While federal courts heard some cases, most disputes were settled administratively at the local, state, or federal level. The lack of codified administrative decisions presents one of the most significant problems in the shift from state law to federal rules. As recently as 1989, allotment decisions at the top level (Deputy Administrator for State and County Operation – DASCO) were inaccessible except through a Freedom of Information Act search. A search turned up 1,200 decisions, often contradictory. Instead of being reported to the public and based on *stare decisis*, the DASCO rulings were *ad hoc* political decisions masked by their inaccessibility. This set of concealed decisions raises questions that begin with favoritism and end with the effectiveness of particularly adept lobbying.[33] As farming evolved into agribusiness, the power to allot acreage became the power to dictate farm survival. The county Agriculture Stabilization and Conservation Service took on increasing importance as a source of capital. Over time, both government agricultural programs and allotments became commodities that possessed inherent financial value. An allotment became far more than a license to grow crops. Since their introduction in 1933 as an emergency device to reduce surplus commodities, allotments have evolved, in the words of one legal scholar, "into a new variety of transferable wealth." In all commodity programs, except for rice, the allotment was particularized to a farm and landlord. As allotments evolved from a temporary recovery device into a commodity, they attained value. In the 1960s, for example, a tobacco farm took on seven thousand dollars in additional value for each acre of tobacco allotment. Cotton and rice values ran from five hundred to a thousand dollars.[34]

The rice exception deserves a brief comment. Rice allotments originally went to producers (farmers), in many cases tenants who owned

32. *Fulford v. Forman*, 245 F. 2nd 149. For an overview of price support policy, see Wayne D. Rasmussen and Gladys L. Baker, *Price-Support and Adjustment Programs from 1933 through 1978: A Short History*, Washington, 1979, USDA, ESCS, Agriculture Information Bulletin no. 429.

33. Karen Sorlie Russo, "Farm Clients Beware of ASCS Mysteries," *The Compleat Lawyer*, vol. 8, 1991, pp. 57–60. For the appeal route, see John H. Davidson, ed., *Agricultural Law*, vol. 1, sec. 1.25, "Appeal Regulations."

34. David Westfall, "Agricultural Allotments as Property," *Harvard Law Review*, vol. 79, 1966, pp. 1188–89; 11 Harl, *Agricultural Law*, Sec. 91.02[3], "Transfers of Allotment." For a recent analysis of the ASCS, see Neil D. Hamilton, "Legal Issues Arising in Federal Court Appeals of ASCS Decisions Administering Federal Farm Programs," *Hamline Law Review*, vol. 12, 1989, pp. 633–48.

machinery and moved annually to take advantage of crop rotation opportunities. In 1949, the state Production and Marketing Administration (PMA), which replaced the AAA in 1945, took the allotments from tenants and in Arkansas and parts of Louisiana assigned them to farm owners. Reassigning the allotments, which by this time had monetary value, required only the recommendation of the state PMA committee and approval of the Secretary of Agriculture. It was a purely bureaucratic decision, a reassignment of capital that went practically unnoticed because rice allotments were not being used at the time.[35]

For years allotments were assigned to a particular farm and could not be alienated from that land. As farm structure changed and farmers consolidated operations, allotments became more liquid. In 1962, Congress authorized leasing tobacco allotments within counties. In 1965, it sanctioned selling cotton allotments from the land and approved liberal leases and, in 1982, permitted selling tobacco allotments. The original award in 1933 thus generated wealth to a certain class of farm owners and their descendants, "economic grandfather clauses" in the words of attorney David Westfall. He concluded a legal article by observing that the largest landowners "received the lion's share of benefits."[36] Allotments could also be used as collateral to secure advances for production credit, with the creditor obtaining a lien on the allotment. "The Food and Agriculture Act of 1965," Brainerd S. Parrish revealed, "permits a farmer to assign all payments that he may receive under the allotment as security for cash or advances to finance crop production. Thus a creditor can get a lien on the allotment, as well as obtain an assignment of the federal price-support and acreage-diversion payments."[37] Federal agricultural policies transcended rules and metamorphosed into commodities that, in turn, underwrote the production costs of farm commodities. Over time other USDA programs became commodified. Complex laws combined with farmers' lever-

35. Murray R. Benedict and Oscar C. Stine, *The Agricultural Commodity Programs: Two Decades of Experience*, New York, 1956, pp. 141–44; Daniel, *Breaking the Land*, pp. 276–77, 280–81. On the reorganization of USDA programs, see Baker *et al.*, *Century of Service*, pp. 482–83, 487.

36. Westfall makes the point that licensed businesses are similar, such as the right to engage in certain enterprises: taxicabs, liquor stores, TV stations. "For rice," he observed (p. 1181), "the rules are still more liberal: no legal obstacle bars a would-be rice baron from buying up all rights to produce the crop in an entire state, even though he acquires no land." David Westfall, "Agricultural Allotments as Property," pp. 1180–1206. For a discussion of the changes in the cotton plan in 1965, see Brainerd S. Parrish, "Comment. Cotton Allotments: Another 'New Property,'" *Texas Law Review*, vol. 45, 1967, pp. 734–53. Parrish examined the implications of the rule on bankruptcy and income tax. See also Daniel, *Breaking the Land*, pp. 269–70.

37. Parrish, "Comment. Cotton Allotments: Another 'New Property,'" pp. 734–53.

aged position led large operators to offer "crops to be grown, growing crops, and/or harvested crops" as collateral.[38] There is still a crop lien system, but since the demise of sharecroppers it is the owners who are now the vulnerable parties.

Throughout the 1940s and 1950s, the AAA and its acronymic successors, the Production and Marketing Administration, Commodity Stabilization Service, and Agricultural Stabilization and Conservation Service, drastically cut acreage in order to raise prices and reduce the surplus. Even as it forced farmers to cut acreage, the USDA poured millions of dollars into research to increase yield per acre, in its self-serving words, "to feed a starving world." Having their cropland frozen, farmers over time intensified their inputs: fertilizer, irrigation, and chemicals. By 1975, cotton farmers produced 453 pounds per acre, three times as much as in 1930.[39] While this might seem an irreconcilable contradiction, it meant that farmers could maximize their production per acre with better seeds, herbicides, insecticides, and machinery. They idled their least productive land and intensified production on their best acres. USDA policies, by encouraging well-capitalized farmers to take advantage of science and technology, supported programs that increased production as well as programs that reduced it.

The benefits of these contradictory policies were not equally distributed. Acreage cuts hurt small farmers proportionally more than larger farmers. A North Carolina cotton farmer complained in 1954 that a fifteen percent reduction in his small allotment cut his productive acreage by fifty percent.[40] Small farmers had less capital, smaller allotments, and less input in policy, but they continued to contest allotments. In the estimation of federal judge John R. Brown, in the mid–1950s allotment disputes in Texas took on "much of the character of earlier cattle-sheep disputes of the Western range."[41] When the Eisenhower Administration mandated drastic production cuts to erase surplus commodities, small farmers tightened their belts to the last

38. "Mortgages on Future Crops as Security for Government Loans," *Yale Law Journal*, vol. 47, 1937, pp. 98–111; Keith G. Meyer, "Potential Problems Connected with the Use of 'Crops' as Collateral for an Article 9 Security Interest," *The Agricultural Law Journal*, vol. 3, 1981–82, p. 115.

39. *Agricultural Statistics, 1967*, Table 85, "Cotton: Acreage, yield, production, value, and foreign trade, United States, 1866–1966," p. 74; *Agricultural Statistics, 1977*, Table 78, "Cotton: Area, yield, production, and value, United States, 1959–76," p. 59.

40. T.E. Swann to Hugh Alexander, 3 December 1954, Cotton, Acreage Allotments, Marketing Quotas, Records of the Secretary of Agriculture, RG 16 (National Archives).

41. *Fulford v. Forman*, 245 F.2d. 145, 147.

notch. The knife that had earlier carved millions of sharecroppers from the southern countryside cut into small farm owners.[42]

In the 1950s, the transition to agribusiness more and more affected formerly secure family farm owners. As civil rights marched toward center stage and African American farmers fled the South, it was entirely fitting that Ezra Taft Benson presided over the final unraveling of the sharecropping system and escalating attack on small landholders. Isolated from the impact of USDA policy, Benson had no comprehension of the stress and pain inflaming the southern countryside in the 1950s, and, in his 1962 autobiography *Cross-Fire*, did not even acknowledge the existence of African Americans. It did not faze Benson, or President Dwight D. Eisenhower either, that the decade of the 1950s came in with 10.7 million southern farmers and departed with seven million, including a decline of over fifty percent in African American farmers. While paying lip service to family farmers, the first Republican Administration in twenty years tailored agricultural policies even more to help larger commercial farmers.[43]

It was a measure of how class alignments had shifted in the twenty years since the New Deal began that even though many of these complaining farmers owned land and worked tenants, there was a shrill

42. A Louisiana cotton farmer complained that the cut from thirty-one to eighteen acres meant that he could not pay his machinery notes or give work to the seventeen people on his farm. In Arkansas a cotton farmer got only a five-acre allotment for three sharecropper families and predicted, "they will be ready for the soup line soon." He had complained to his local committee, but when he got no relief suspected discrimination. An exasperated African American Louisiana cotton farmer asked his Congressman how he could support four tenants with an eight-acre allotment. "That will be exactly 1.6 acres for each of us." Harry Himel to Russell Long, 2 March 1954; R.G. Lamb to John L. McClellan, 11 December 1953; Alex Noflin to James H. Morrison, 14 December 1953 (?), Cotton, Acreage Allotments, Marketing Quotas, Records of the Secretary of Agriculture, RG 16 (National Archives). See also Ted C. Jackson to James H. Morrison, 14 December 1953, ibid.

43. Ezra Taft Benson, *Cross Fire: The Eight Years with Eisenhower*, Garden City, 1962; *Farm Population Estimates, 1910–70*, Table 5, "Total and farm population of the United States by regions, divisions, and states, for decade years, April 1920–70," pp. 28–31, USDA, Rural Development Service, Statistical Bulletin no. 523, Washington, 1973. In October 1953 Secretary Benson slashed the national cotton allotment by thirty percent to 17.9 million acres. Immediately, cotton state Congressmen attacked Benson, none more vehemently than Mississippi's Jamie L. Whitten. Whitten successfully increased allotments to 21.4 million acres for the 1954 crop year and insisted that large western growers from Texas to California should not permanently benefit from their increased production when controls were off from 1951 to 1953. See Jamie L. Whitten to Ezra Taft Benson, 12 October, 5 December, 21 December 1953, 5 January 1954; Benson to Whitten, 21 December 1953, 12 January 1954, Cotton, Acreage Allotments, Marketing Quotas, Records of the Secretary of Agriculture, RG 16 (National Archives); "The Decline of Black Farming in America," Report of the U.S. Commission on Civil Rights, February 1982, Table 1.1, "Farms Operated by Blacks and Whites," p. 3. See also Benedict and Stine, *Agricultural Commodity Programs*, pp. 35–41.

note of resentment and distrust. One outraged South Carolina tobacco farmer proposed to study allotments in his county "comparing the acreage of the committee members, their relatives, politicians, and those who work in the office with the rest of us, who have no political pull or other unfair means of getting extra acreage." J. True Hayes's request to examine records of the county committee drove nervous USDA scriveners to draft a series of responses that both stonewalled and promised limited access to records. The response epitomized the Janus-faced USDA claim of democracy and openness on the one hand and elite secrecy on the other. Unfortunately, the fruits of Hayes's investigation are not in the file.[44]

Defenders of the committee system made much of its grassroots operation. Judge John R. Brown explained: "Congress meant to establish an initial and a reviewing agency of *local* people having *local* responsibility for decisions concerning *local* factors having a definitive *local* impact." Translated into everyday operation, this meant that local politics guided agricultural policy, and in many areas of the South local disputes dominated farm life. With reserve acreage to distribute, county committees and review committees could reward and chastise. The unpopularity of committee decisions is reflected in the approximately six thousand review proceedings in 1954 and fourteen thousand a year later.[45] The local nature of policy implementation meant that local ideology informed decisions, yet such decisions could be cloaked in bureaucratic language. Local leaders took credit for successes and blamed the federal government for failures.

Wealthy investors in agriculture could even commodify losing money, declaring a farm loss to offset profits in other areas. As full-time farmers faced acreage cutbacks, they castigated wealthy investors who farmed for income tax purposes. Mrs. Leigh Kelly of Fort Smith, Arkansas, wrote a long and pointed letter to Benson arguing that "cattle & chicken farms can not compete with the doctors, lawyers, oil men etc. who are running model farms to take a loss on their income taxes." A Texas farmer complained that "an ever increasing number of individuals" who were "millionaires or near-millionaires" entered rice farming to avoid income taxes. The result, he speculated, "will surely be bankruptcy for hundreds of farms."[46]

44. J. True Hayes to Benson, 15 July 1954; J.J. Todd to Hayes, 24 July 1954; Hayes to Benson, 6 August 1954; Benson to Hayes, 25 August 1954, General Correspondence, 1906–70, Tobacco, Acreage Allotments, Marketing Quotas, Records of the Secretary of Agriculture, RG 16 (National Archives).

45. *Fulford v. Forman*, 245 F. 2d. 145, 151, 152n20.

46. Mrs. Leigh Kelly to Benson, April 1953, Farm Program, Records of the Secretary of Agriculture, RG 16 (National Archives); Gene Andrew to Benson, 26 January 1956, Rice, AAA, Records of the Agricultural Stabilization and Conservation Service, RG 145 (National Archives). On this subject, see Sally Hanlon, "Joint Economic Committee Investigates 'Tax-Loss Farming,'" Tax Notes, vol. 31, 5 May 1986, p. 443.

The more USDA officials spoke of preserving the family farm the less such farms survived. Hoping to relieve some of this frustration, Secretary Benson asked farmers to write about their concerns. He got more than he bargained for. Mrs. J.O. Lawson of Covington, Georgia, asked Benson, "Why do big men like you sit around and study up something to hurt a poor mule farmer?" She had raised eight children but admitted that "we have nothing after twenty eight years of married life." A forty-six-year-old farmer wrote from Alabama, "all the Record that i know of ... is to make the rich richer and the poor poorer." It was unfair, he charged, for "bankers merchants lawyer senators congressmen and doctors farmin for thay are Rich people."[47] Twenty years after Iowan Henry A. Wallace launched the AAA, Wilbert McReynolds of DeRidder, Louisiana, looked around at all the farmers who had failed. "These failures," he indignantly suggested to Benson in 1953, "may be the result of trying to make an Iowa plan fit Louisiana."[48]

The Soil Bank created in May 1956 opened another cash window for those who controlled cropland, and it demonstrated that land not farmed could be as valuable as that in production. Landowners could take acreage out of production, put it in the Soil Bank, and receive a conservation payment. A South Carolina farmer complained that local landowners, much like those twenty years earlier, were forcing tenants off the land so they could place all of their cotton allotment in the Soil Bank. "To my mind," he wrote, "there is nothing more reprehensible." Assistant USDA Secretary Marvin L. McLain (an Iowa native) replied, as had USDA officials twenty years earlier, that tenant rights were safeguarded. His bureaucratically correct letter assured the South Carolinian that it was "the responsibility of the county committees to determine whether or not the participation in the Program by a producer has or will result in a reduction of the number of tenants or sharecroppers on the farm."[49] The comfortable collusion between Washington and county committees stamped the federal imprimatur on local discrimination and outright illegalities.

For most farmers it only required paperwork – not illegalities – to bank soil. Linda Flowers, who grew up in eastern North Carolina, recalled the story of a farmer who rented "every available acre a big landowner had for twenty-five hundred dollars, and the `very next damn day,' as my father tells the story, put it in the Soil Bank for six thousand

47. Mrs. J.O. Lawson to Benson, 16 April 1953, Farming 2; M.N. Andrews to Benson, 24 January 1956, Economics 2, Cost Squeeze, Records of the Secretary of Agriculture, RG 16 (National Archives).

48. McReynolds to Benson, 26 January 1953, Farm Program, 1953, ibid.

49. Otis A. O'Dell to Olin D. Johnston, 18 October 1956; Marvin L. McLain to Johnston, 7 November 1956, Farm Programs 2, ibid.

dollars, thus clearing a bundle without so much as cranking his tractor – and there was nothing illegal about it." "If the decimation of tenantry was not the purpose of the Soil Bank," she concluded, "it was certainly its effect."[50] The USDA rewarded larger farmers who had more land and capital. With enough marginal land to bank and enough productive land to farm intensely, larger farmers could cut labor costs and use machines and chemicals to intensify operations. In the right hands, of course, ledgerbooks could show a profitable tax loss.[51]

Given their importance, the composition of county and review committees bears closer scrutiny. The systematic exclusion of African American farmers (and probably poor whites as well) from committee positions originated in the Washington bureaucracy. By 1964, the Secretary of Agriculture had never appointed an African American to a State Committee in the South (there are no statistics for sharecroppers). State bureaucracies followed the headquarters' lead. In the eleven southern states no African American had been elected as a county committeeman, and in 1964 only seventy-five of 37,000 community committeemen in the South were African American. In 1964, an effort by the Congress of Racial Equality (CORE) to aid black Mississippi farmers to run for ASCS county committees led to intimidation and violence. But there has been progress of a sort: in 1989 there were nineteen black county ASCS committee members – out of a total of 8,713.[52]

Whites also dominate the county office workforce. As late as 1987, only thirty-three out of 2,520 county ASCS directors in the nation were black. One of these county directors revealed that he had been

50. Linda Flowers, *Throwed Away: Failures of Progress in Eastern North Carolina*, Knoxville, 1990, pp. 59, 60.

51. For a statement of present USDA programs, see 11 Harl, *Agricultural Law*, Sec. 91.02, "Acreage Allotments, Marketing Quotas and Parity-Based Price Supports"; Sec. 91.03, "Production Control and Price Support Programs"; Sec. 91.04, "Production Control and Price Support Programs for Specified Agricultural Commodities."

52. A law review article explained the committee system. Three farmers composed the committee with two alternates and they served three year terms, appointed by community committeemen, who were elected "by all eligible farmers of the respective communities. At these elections, nearly all-white community committees are elected; these in turn elect nearly all-white county committees, which play the central role in the program." While there are institutional barriers to blacks – incumbents supervise elections, inadequate notice given of elections, and ballots sometimes defective – there was also the class position of landlord against tenant or sharecropper. "In the few cases where Negroes have been organized to vote in ASCS elections, local whites have responded with coercion and with subterfuge." "The Federal Agricultural Stabilization Program and the Negro," *Columbia Law Review*, vol. 67, 1967, pp. 1121–36. U.S. Commission on Civil Rights, *Equal Opportunity in Farm Programs: An Appraisal of Services Rendered by Agencies of the United States Department of Agriculture*, Washington, 1965, p. 90; August Meier and Elliott Rudwick, *CORE: A Study in the Civil Rights Movement, 1942–1968*, New York, 1973, p. 342; "Current Membership of ASCS County Committeemen by Ethnic Groups," 1989, USDA, Office of Advocacy and Enterprise.

previously rejected for director some thirteen times. "Most of the offices are staffed by white women," he explained, "and the white-dominated committees just don't want to put a black man in charge." By 1986, ASCS nationally employed 765 African Americans out of a work force of almost 23,000. Institutional racism affected USDA employment overall, for as recently as September 1991 African Americans were only 8.9 percent of a USDA permanent workforce of nearly 100,000, compared to the federal government average of 17.2 percent.[53]

By 1967, with pressure from civil rights laws, seventy-three African Americans won seats on southern ASCS review committees. Even in the mid–1960s, many poor blacks and whites did not know their right to appeal, nor would they eagerly confront elite committeemen. Reflecting the institutional bias against blacks, in 1965 only half as many African Americans as whites appealed ASCS rulings. To escape bureaucratic gravity, an aggrieved farmer could insist on judicial review and take the case to federal court, but that entailed the risk of retaliation from ASCS county and review committees as well as bearing court expenses. Congressional legislation or USDA practices that denied black participation in the ASCS system would violate the Constitution, yet the USDA achieved the same end through institutional racism.[54]

The presence within the USDA of a civil rights office created a convenient bureaucratic mask to disguise old practices. During the first six years of the Reagan administration, for example, the USDA Civil Rights office had eight directors and a new reorganization plan each year. Such bureaucratic inertia preserved old patches of discrimination and provided fertile soil for new growth. As recently as September 1990, the USDA ranked at the bottom of federal departments in minority employment (seventeen percent), and near the cellar but improving in women employees (thirty-nine percent).[55] The institutional bias so evident in the ASCS permeated the entire agricultural establishment. For example, from their beginning in 1890, black land grant colleges were underfunded, and the implementing legislation that created both

53. Ward Sinclair, "Old-Boy Network Still Haunts Agriculture's Problem Child," *Washington Post*, 21 September 1987, A13; "FY 90–91 Changes in Work Force EEO Profile by PATCO"; "Comparison of Government-Wide, USDA, and ASCS Employment Representation as of June 1986," USDA Office of Advocacy and Enterprise.

54. "The Federal Agricultural Stabilization Program and the Negro," pp. 1126–31.

55. Ward Sinclair, "Lyng Laid Down the Law, but is the USDA Enforcing It?" *Washington Post*, 21 September 1987, A13; Mike McGraw and Jeff Taylor, "Through Much of USDA it's a White Male Bastion," *Kansas City Star*, 11 December 1991.

experiment stations and the Federal Extension Service marginalized African Americans.[56]

As Welchel Long put it in 1987, "they didn't put any money in these black colleges, like they don't now. About like a rabbit and a mule. They say 50-50, one rabbit, one mule." Long, an African American agricultural teacher and farmer from Elberton, Georgia, had a long and bitter struggle with the Farmers Home Administration (the legatee of the New Deal's underfunded Farm Security Administration). A World War II veteran educated at Tuskegee Institute and at the University of Georgia, Long in 1952 began teaching agriculture at Bowman High School. Two years later, he started farming part-time. In 1960, he approached T.K. Wilson, head of the county Farmers Home Administration for a loan. Wilson told him that he did not qualify. Over the next twenty years Long attempted to fight bureaucratic inertia and racism.

At first Wilson discouraged Long from applying, then he refused to give him an application form, and finally he misled him into thinking he would get a $13,000 operating loan. At a hearing before state Farmers Home officials, Long endured racist epithets and was warned that if he referred his case to the Civil Rights Division of Farmers Home that his "job might be in jeopardy." He pressed on. An investigator heard his story, but the report languished. "It seems to me," Long accurately reflected, "that there is a systematic unwritten policy or conspiracy on the part of the National Administration to let this trend continue. To drag out complaints and charges with the hope that they will just disappear." In 1985 another investigation fizzled. "They finally found that there wasn't nothing wrong with what they did," Long concluded.

The Long case epitomizes how county agricultural personnel continued to discriminate against African Americans using the federal bureaucracy to absorb complaints. Long encountered the same obfuscation and

---

56. In 1964 the Soil Conservation Service (SCS) employed 6,100 people; twenty of the forty African Americans it employed in the South were listed as professionals on active duty. *Equal Opportunity in Farm Programs*, pp. 84–86. By 1990, the number of African Americans in the SCS permanent work force had grown to 926 out of 12,821, 670 of whom (forty-three women) were in professional jobs. Douglas Helms, "Eroding the Color Line: The Soil Conservation Service and the Civil Rights Act of 1964," *Agricultural History*, vol. 65, 1991, pp. 48, 51, 52. In 1968, predominately black land-grant colleges received seventy million dollars in federal and state aid annually, while the white land-grant institutions in the same states got $650 million. Formula funds (Morris-Nelson, Hatch, Smith-Lever, Bankhead-Jones, etc.) to white institutions in 1967 were $59.3 million; to black schools, $1.4 million. Frederick S. Humphries, "1890 Land-Grant Institutions: Their Struggle for Survival and Equality," *Agricultural History*, vol. 65, 1991, pp. 3–11. See also Grant Seals, "The Formation of Agricultural and Rural Development Policy with Emphasis on African Americans: II. The Hatch-George and Smith-Lever Acts," *Agricultural History*, vol. 65, 1991, pp. 12–34.

discrimination at every level of the USDA. Farmers Home investigators predictably found nothing amiss with Farmers Home policy. When Long arrived in Elbert County in 1952, there were nearly four hundred black family farm units, mostly sharecroppers, and in 1987 there were two, counting Long, who himself no longer farmed.[57]

Farmers Home policies suggest why this decline continues. In January 1992, only 417 blacks served on Farmers Home county committees nationwide out of a total of 6,611 (6.3 percent). Such numbers become more relevant when analyzing the continual decline of farm ownership loans awarded to African Americans: in 1990, there were nine.[58] The system that Long battled had perfected institutional racism, and only Long's intelligence and stubbornness kept him hammering away at it.

Such cases of racial discrimination abound, but Welchel Long, with his education, teaching position, and tenacity, in many ways was atypical. Henry Woodard, an African American who owns land in the Mississippi Delta, personifies a farmer caught in an encompassing network of racism. When oral historian Lu Ann Jones and photographer Laurie Minor arrived at his farm near Tunica, Mississippi, in October 1987, Woodard was anxiously waiting for help to harvest his rice. Laurie Minor photographed him half buried in a golden rice field as he told his story. Woodard had farmed since 1948 when he sharecropped with his father on his forty acres of Delta land. During the Korean War, he recalled, farming "boomed into big multi-farming." Machines, chemicals, and government programs, he suggested, gradually ended sharecropping. The peak years, he remembered, were during the civil rights movement: "that's when they went tearing the houses down and moving us off the farm." At the time of the interview in 1987, only fifteen black farmers were left in the county. In earlier years, FmHA "was doing the furnishing," but "to my knowledge, hasn't furnished any black farmer in Tunica County this year."

57. Interview with Welchel Long, Madison County, Georgia, 16 April 1987, by Lu Ann Jones, Oral History of Southern Agriculture, National Museum of American History; statement of Welchel Long, Elbert County, Georgia, n.d., in Oral History of Southern Agriculture files.

58. Statement of Welchel Long; William C. Payne, "Institutional Discrimination in Agriculture Programs," *The Rural Sociologist*, vol. 11, 1991, pp. 16–17; "County Committee Data by Race/National Origin and Sex as of January 9, 1992"; Farmers Home Administration, "Committees in Selected States, 1981–1987"; Farmers Home Administration, "Distribution of Loans Made by Six Specified Types by Race or Ethnic Group, 1990," USDA, Office of Advocacy and Enterprise. For a recent analysis of the Farmers Home Administration, see Martha A. Miller, "The Role of the Farmers Home Administration in the Present Agricultural Crisis," *Alabama Law Review*, vol. 38, 1987, pp. 587–623.

Ten years earlier, in 1977, Woodard started growing rice, then a booming crop in the Delta. For "ten year ago," he recalled,

> I had a, it wasn't a dream. I don't know just really what it was. It may've been a dream but I was woke. Something shaked me and woke me up. It felt like a man caught me by my arm and shook me and woke me up. Then the voice said, he said, "If you want success, plant rice."

Woodard went to the county agent to get advice. "And they told me: `Can't no nigger grow no rice, Henry.'" Woodard persisted, so the county agent suggested he talk to the owner of the grain elevator. "And I went and talked with him. He told me, `Naw, I ain't got no room for your rice.'" Again Woodard persisted. Finally the grain elevator owner told him, "Go on and plant it but when I get through docking you, you'll hate you ever saw rice." The next year he planted rice and contracted to have a crop duster apply chemicals. A friend who worked at the flying service told him "you ain't getting your chemicals. They're flying over you, but it's not in there." In 1982, his rice well burned, but the interview ended before he could explain the circumstances.

At the time of the interview Woodard owed FmHA $228,000. Yet he had learned the year before when he attended a Farm Aid rally in St. Louis that his was not an isolated case, nor were black farmers the only rural folks in financial trouble. He had assumed that white farmers "knew what was happening." Black farmers, he stated, "don't have no input on setting no priorities ... what to make the crop on and what the government is doing, 'cause we don't have but a very few black elected officials. And none of 'em is in no policy-making position."[59] Woodard is one of some 22,000 African American farmers and 15,000 farm owners left in the U.S., and only 4,400 of these make more than the $10,000 in gross sales that place them in the commercial category. By comparison, in 1910 there were over 200,000 black farm owners in the South.[60] Given the significance of plantation slavery and the central position of African Americans in agriculture until the 1930s, their disappearance from the countryside is remarkable. If African American farmers had left agriculture at the same rate as white farmers since 1920, there would still be 300,000 black farmers.[61]

59. Interview with Henry Woodard, Tunica, Mississippi, 5 October 1987, by Lu Ann Jones, Oral History of Southern Agriculture, NMAH.

60. U.S. Bureau of the Census, *Census of Agriculture, 1987*, vol. 1, *Geographic Area Series*, pt. 51, *United States Summary and State Data*, tables 32, 33, 34; Loren Schweninger, *Black Property Owners in the South, 1790–1915*, Urbana, 1991, p. 174.

61. William C. Payne, Jr., to author, 12 February 1992.

It would not have surprised Henry Woodard to learn that at the height of the civil rights movement in 1967, as his neighbors were fleeing the land, that in nearby Sunflower County six thousand families lived in poverty. They received $446,000 for food relief and $8,676 for manpower development. Planters in the county divided $10.2 million, two-thirds of it for not cultivating land. Senator James O. Eastland pocketed $168,524.52. "Today," an Arkansas farmer admitted in 1987, "we get more money from the government than we do out of our crop."[62]

Despite their reliance on federal largesse, many larger farmers boasted of their independence and self-reliance. At every opportunity, they directed a constant stream of calumny at big government (the hand that feeds them), and they were especially irate at the government for disbursing food and welfare (much less elaborately) to the descendants of sharecroppers who were dispossessed by the very USDA policies that enriched them. Today's farmers profit from the commodity programs that established a new context for social, economic, and political relations in the southern countryside.

The layers of USDA policies over the years have created a bureaucratic tangle of contradictions. Yet the transformation in southern agriculture was anything but accidental or haphazard. The USDA rewarded landowners and encouraged mechanization, and it also restructured agricultural law. Instead of checking the abrupt transformation to agribusiness and ameliorating the human costs, federal policies encouraged the landowning elite to gain absolute control over local agricultural policy and direct its benefits. No body of published decisions clarified precedents or provided predictability. Politics, not precedent, informed decisions. The substantial spoils of government programs – now commodified – are divided among wealthy landowners by wealthy landowners. As he stood in his rice field in 1987, Henry Woodard recalled scenes from the Farm Aid rally in St. Louis: "And I saw white crying and blacks crying. We all is at the mercy of the government."[63]

62. Cobb, "Somebody Done Nailed us on the Cross," p. 919; interview with L.D. Brantley, Coy, Arkansas, 30 September 1987, by Lu Ann Jones, Oral History of Southern Agriculture, NMAH.

63. Interview with Henry Woodard.

–4–

The Legal System and Sharecropping: An Opposing View

Martin Crawford

The main problem confronting any commentator presented with a paper on twentieth century southern agriculture by Pete Daniel is that Daniel probably knows as much about the subject as anyone alive. His essay on "the Legal Basis of Agrarian Capitalism" complements and extends the investigations into southern agriculture that he began as a doctoral student in the 1960s, and which received outstanding expression in *The Shadow of Slavery* (1972) and, more recently, in the award-winning *Breaking the Land: The Transformation of Cotton, Tobacco, and Rice Cultures since 1880* (1985). I say "complements" deliberately, because what is particularly impressive about this essay is its author's determination to move beyond existing synthesis – much of which he has created – to offer a new perspective on southern rural development in the middle and late decades of the twentieth century.

The broad landscape of Daniel's argument is a familiar one: during the depression decade of the 1930s, the traditional patterns of southern agricultural life were undermined and a process of rural "modernization" initiated. The main catalyst of change was the federal government, which through innovative policies such as acreage restriction, direct benefit payments, and soil conservation all but destroyed the farm tenure system that had evolved in the wake of the Civil War and whose most distinctive feature, sharecropping, had proved remarkably impervious to the momentous changes that were transforming rural society elsewhere in the United States. Those southern farmers able to take advantage of price supports and other New Deal programs belatedly discovered that the way to increased efficiency was through greater mechanization. As the cost of credit continued to decline, large landowners gradually abandoned the old labor-intensive methods and with them the sharecroppers and tenants upon whom they had traditionally relied. While the transition to capital-intensive farming was slow and uneven, it was inexorable: by 1950, nearly a quarter (23.4 percent) of southern farmers operated tractors, a four-fold increase on the 6.3

percent of 1940, but a figure that still left the South lagging well behind the rest of the country.[1] At the same time, these changes induced a predictable concentration in southern landholding: by 1970, only a little over 900,000 farms were operating in the former Confederate states, a far cry from the two and a half million plus that had existed at the onset of the New Deal.

As has already been recognized, therefore, capital-intensive agriculture had, in Daniel's own words, "largely reconfigured the southern countryside" by the middle of the twentieth century. What has been less apparent is the extent to which this transformation had an unequal impact upon southern African Americans in a period when they had begun to mount a successful challenge – via the agency of the civil rights movement – to the twin oppressions of segregation and disfranchisement. An examination of agricultural statistics for the period 1930 to 1970 confirms that the decadal rate of contraction among African Americans invariably exceeded that for southern farmers as a whole. During the 1930s, for example, the number of black farmers declined by 22.4 percent as compared to an overall figure of 8.1 percent. These statistics provide no encouragement for anyone who might think that, with the increasing empowerment of African Americans, the decline could be stilled or even reversed. In the 1960s, the number of African American farmers fell dramatically from just over a quarter of a million (259,000) to approximately 82,000, a decline of 68.3 percent that was more than double that for southern farm operators as a whole.[2] The extraordinary collapse in black farming clearly persisted throughout the 1970s and 1980s, confirming, if confirmation were required, the personal testimony of such men as Henry Woodard and Welchel Long whose courageous struggles against "bureaucratic inertia and racism" Daniel has so well described.

Pete Daniel's essay is most persuasive, therefore, in documenting the racial impact of rural transformation in the post-New Deal South. As public discrimination was progressively outlawed, federal intervention encouraged the consolidation of white landowning power through local agricultural committees in collusion with a "corpulent and obfuscating" federal bureaucracy. The composition and ideological assumptions of these local committees invariably ran counter to the interests of poor, mainly African American farmers, and the result, as has been seen, was the marginalization and virtual elimination of African American agriculture in the southern states. Progress in diluting the white exclusivity of local power structures has been pitifully slow, with, as Daniel notes,

1. Gilbert S. Fite, *Cotton Fields No More, Southern Agriculture, 1865–1980*, Lexington, Kentucky, 1984, p. 184.
    2. Calculated from tables in Fite, *Cotton Fields No More*, p. 238.

only nineteen African American ASCS [Agricultural Stabilization and Conservation Service] members by 1989 out of a total of 8,713.

It is important to recognize, nonetheless, that Daniel's narrative of rural transformation also embraces an argument about the changing role of southern law and, in particular, what he terms "the displacement of state lien and labor laws by Federal rules." Following New Deal intervention, he maintains, county agricultural committees, acting under federal license, largely replaced state courts as the arbiters of landlord-tenant conflict, and, in Daniel's opinion, this change served to weaken the ability of sharecroppers and other tenants to establish proper claims. Of course, as he notes, such disagreements were now less about crop liens than about government benefits and acreage allotments, the rules for the allocation of which had been established by the federal agencies themselves: "Landowners and the USDA, ignoring the precedents of state law, cut the legal ground from underneath sharecroppers and tenants. Bureaucracy rushed into the breach. Federal agricultural policy rapidly displaced a body of law that had evolved over three-quarters of a century."

In his desire to indict federal policy for its role in destroying the sharecropping culture (a culture he cryptically describes as having "emerged from poverty"), Daniel has, I believe, considerably overestimated the extent to which state law, and the court system that construed and enforced it, acted to protect the rights of the region's farm tenant population in the pre-New Deal era. Some of the language he employs, indeed, seems to indicate uneasiness at upholding such a view, including his suggestion that state laws and courts "played an important, albeit often contradictory, role in mediating class tension." Too good a historian to ignore the weight of his own evidence, Daniel appears uncertain as to the impression he wishes finally to convey of a system that has traditionally evoked little liberal or radical admiration. "Given the poverty and powerlessness of sharecroppers and the landlord's superior lien and prerogative of keeping accounts," he argues, "one should not claim too much glory for the courts, but over the years before the New Deal the interplay between legislative and judicial bodies remained spirited."

Despite these ambivalences, Daniel is nonetheless still keen to argue that, prior to the intervention of President Roosevelt's "corpulent and obfuscating bureaucrats," the southern legal system offered some protection for the region's African American sharecroppers in their perennial battle against their white landlord masters. That being the case, it is necessary to examine the evidence he presents to back up this belief in the "mediating power of state courts." That sharecroppers did fight back is self-evident, as the rash of post-Redeemer counter-legislation against such potentially subversive activites as selling cotton after dark demonstrates. That they were aided in their resistance to any measurable extent by the courts is a much more doubtful proposition.

While Daniel admits that the model of rural relations "defined by law" was subverted by the exertion of power by the local elite, he continues to insist that tenants could profit both from the complexity of legal deliberations and, more intriguingly, from the fact that "laws were interpreted by judges, a step removed from the political process, and their precedents were recorded in state report" (p. 84). In any event, the two legal judgements that he invokes in support of his argument – the W.R. Jenkins case of 1933 and the F.M. Dulaney case of two years later – both occurred after the New Deal had begun and, more importantly, neither could be said to stand as representative of the difficulties that sharecroppers and laborers historically faced in validating their lien against that of the landlord. In the first case, the landlord, Mrs. Jackson, had unwarrantably applied the sharecroppers' portion of the proceeds from the sale of the cotton crop to the back debts of her tenant, Jenkins, a claim the Mississsippi Supreme Court surely had little hesitation in denying, as the award of six percent interest over and above the rightful share of the crop perhaps confirms. In the Dulaney case, which was also "three-tiered," the landlord, Mrs. Thweat, again acted unjustifiably in depriving the sharecroppers of their due share of the proceeds in order to satisfy her claim against her tenant.

Although both judgments do clearly uphold the laborer's lien, in the first case in particular the landlord's claim was for debts unrelated to the sharecroppers' contract and thereby likely to be discounted even under the prejudicial rules that applied in Mississippi. Only in the 1935 case, perhaps, do we find some progress in that, as is traditional in such three-tiered affairs, the sharecropper's lien would not take effect until the tenant who hired them had paid his rent. The fact that the disputed claim derived from land rented to the federal government suggests that the decision of the Arkansas Supreme Court could well have been influenced by the changing political climate induced by Roosevelt's rise to power. Here perhaps it is possible to find some endorsement for the legal protections glimpsed by Jerome Frank and other USDA liberals, as they tried to strengthen sharecropper claims on government payments. On the other hand, Frank's idea that state precedents could play an effective role in transforming power relations seems thoroughly naive.

As historians have long acknowledged, southern sharecroppers and laborers traditionally had little legal security against the landlords and merchants who resourced and provisioned them. To invoke a body of state precedent in this area, in fact, is to invoke a burden of argument weighing heavily in favor of a landlord-merchant class whose local authority remained largely undiminished in the decades preceding the New Deal. Although state laws did originally establish that liens for advances were valid only against the crop for which they were made, this constraint was soon circumvented as landlords demanded and received from the courts increased protection for their rights as lenders. This meant, for example, that crop proceeds would soon be applied to previous years' debts, which in turn forced tenants into negotiating progressively more unfavorable loan terms and also, most damagingly, into accepting advances for basic personal items such as food and clothing. While legislative and judicial practice undoubtedly varied from state to state throughout the South, as Harold Woodman in particular has shown, a sharecropper's ability to accumulate an annual surplus and thus liberate himself from the debt cycle was seriously eroded by court action. In a 1911 case cited by Woodman, advances for such items as snuff and tobacco were deemed to be covered by the landlord's lien. In Arkansas, a similar judgement included a family sewing machine. Nor did the advent of so-called personal exemption laws provide much assistance, since most provided that exemption did not apply to debts from rents or advances made by a landlord.[3]

Of course, sharecroppers and laborers did find means to resist this oppressive system, but their primitive rebellions served only to reinforce the determination of the landlord class to retain control over the agricultural process and even to fortify the instruments employed for that purpose. In this, landlords were again aided by state courts.[4] It is not my purpose to criticize Pete Daniel concerning the enforcement of state anti-enticement and contract labor laws, since his own research has done so much to uncover and contextualize this dark aspect of southern history. However, it is necessary to remind him of the crucial role played by southern courts in strengthening state legislative action to restrain tenant and laborer rights. In the early twentieth century, southern courts routinely upheld state laws against the breaking of contractual obligations, laws that generally imposed criminal penalties for what were after all civil offenses. Although most of these laws were patently unconstitutional, they survived well into the mid-twentieth century principally because of endorsement by state supreme courts. In fact, the major challenge to this systematic oppression came not from the state courts but from the federal judiciary. In January 1911, the U.S. Supreme Court struck down an Alabama contract labor statute in the famous *Alonzo Bailey* judgment. The constitutionality of the law in

3. Harold D. Woodman, "Post-Civil War Agriculture and the Law," *Agricultural History*, vol. 53, 1979, pp. 319–37.

4. See Woodman, "Post-Civil War Agriculture and the Law," for detailed documentation of activity by state courts.

question had earlier been upheld on three separate occasions by the Alabama court.[5]

As Neil McMillen has recently argued in his study of African American Mississippi life during the Jim Crow era, it was only through the "agility" of the state's judiciary that such blatantly discriminatory contract labor laws were shielded from constitutional sabotage. Even on the rare occasions when the state supreme court invalidated such laws – as in the *Armstead* case of 1912 – it did so on the narrowest possible grounds, leaving intact the more savage "false-pretense" law whose real purpose, in McMillen's words, was not so much to punish fraud, "but to restrain tenant mobility by imposing criminal penalties for civil contract violations and [thus] sanctioning, if only indirectly, imprisonment for debt." In the post-*Bailey* and *Armstead* era, in fact, the use of the false-pretense law and its close cousin, the anti-enticement statute of 1890, were both regularly upheld by Mississippi's highest court as legitimate exercises of state police power. Finally, in the *Thompson* case of 1927, only five years before FDR's election, the court managed both to invalidate restrictive labor practices while at the same time upholding the restrictive anti-enticement law that sanctioned them. As McMillen concludes: "No doubt an occasional curtsey to the Thirteenth Amendment was good exercise for any Mississippi judge. It might even appease a higher court. But for black tenants, there were few practical benefits to be derived from coy declamations against `slavery in any form.'"[6]

State courts may in some cases have mitigated the worst impact of legislative repression, therefore, but in general their role was materially to sustain the traditional authority of the South's rural white elites. For most poor sharecroppers and laborers, moreover, legal redress through the court system was hardly to be considered, as the eloquent testimony of Ned Cobb ("Nate Shaw") confirms. Cobb, an intelligent and resourceful man, was frequently at odds with his landlord and supply merchant, but he rarely appears to have considered employing the legal process in order to protect his tenancy rights. As he himself observed, remembering the time when his father's stock and farm tools were seized by a furnishing agent, "it was out of the knowledge of the colored man to understand that if you gave a man a note on everything you had, exactly how you was subject to the laws. Because the colored man wasn't educated to the laws for his use; they was a great, dark secret to him." Ned Cobb, in fact, did become "partly" educated to Alabama's

---

5. See Pete Daniel, *The Shadow of Slavery, Peonage in the South, 1910–1969*, Urbana, 1972, pp. 65–81.

6. Neil R. McMillen, *Dark Journey, Black Mississipians in the Age of Jim Crow*, Urbana, 1989, pp. 140–47.

laws, but the knowledge that he acquired was of little use in sustaining him against the landlords and merchants who conspired to keep him in debt servitude. Not suprisingly, Cobb initially welcomed the federal intervention of the 1930s, as "I knowed I stood a better chance with the government than I did with any of these folks here, absolutely. I wouldn't turn around to look at any of them if the government was beckonin me to come in with them. *They* knowed it too, and they didn't like for the government to come into this country and meddle with their hands."[7]

It has not been my intention in this response to split legal or constitutional hairs with Pete Daniel. I also acknowledge that, in some areas – including, for example, that relating to the laborer's lien – he openly disagrees with historians such as Harold Woodman upon whom I have generally relied. Rather, I have wished to point out what seems to be a tendency in Daniel's essay to over-characterize the pre-New Deal era – practically to the point of idealization – as a means of discrediting, through contrast, the Federal interventions of the 1930s and after. Perhaps much of what Daniel regards as sharecroppers' culture was worth preserving. A good deal of it undoubtedly was not, and, like all great economic and social transformations, that which modernized southern agriculture involved enormous human dislocation. Yet changes in southern agrarian society were bound to come, irrespective of whether Franklin D. Roosevelt was elected in 1932 or not. As Gavin Wright has reminded us, the displacement of farm tenants and their absorption into an urban labor market would have occurred sooner or later if only because by 1950 there was "little promise in the future of cotton agriculture" in the southeast.[8] What historians must ultimately decide, therefore, is whether southern agriculture could have been modernized in a way that advanced rather than, as Pete Daniel's essay implies, retarded the economic and social progress of the region's farm population and, in particular, the extent to which such a process could have contributed to ending the perpetuation of racial disadvantage in the South. Preserving a traditional peasant culture, we should remember, was not the aim of federal farm policy after 1933, however equitably or inequitably such a policy was ultimately administered.

In conclusion, therefore, I would suggest that there was far more continuity between the pre- and post-New Deal eras than Daniel's fine essay allows. The source and nature of the power wielded by local agricultural committees after 1933 surely replicated in essential respects

7. Theodore Rosengarten, *All God's Dangers: The Life of Nate Shaw*, New York, paperback ed., 1974, pp. 33, 303, 305–6.
8. Gavin Wright, *Old South, New South, Revolutions in the Southern Economy since the Civil War*, New York, 1986, pp. 247–49.

that of earlier landlords. Their local hegemony, after all, derived not merely from the everyday functioning of the farm tenancy system and the control of credit, but also, crucially, from the support and protection they received from a conservative, and undeniably racist, judicial and political system. The administration of the rules may have changed after 1933, therefore, but the consequences, for large numbers of poor, predominantly African American southerners, remained depressingly familiar.

–5–

The Disappearance of Sharecropping: A South African Comparison

William Beinart

An historian of Southern Africa necessarily has many anxieties in responding to Pete Daniel's essay, rooted as it is in a deeper and more varied historiographical tradition. For a long time, Southern African historians have been accustomed to be influenced by the approach to a variety of issues taken by their American counterparts. More recently, a number of scholars, mostly American, have attempted comparative exercises: George Frederickson on colonization; John Cell on segregation; and Stan Greenberg on *Race and State in Capitalist Development*.[1] This latter work has most relevance to Pete Daniel's thesis and will be discussed at a later stage.

Daniel's paper does raise important issues for historians of South Africa, and it also has some bearing on contemporary problems in that country. Until very recently, blacks have been barred from purchasing or hiring land in most of South Africa. Now that South Africa may be on the brink of democratization and the extension of civil rights to blacks, it is very instructive to read what has happened in the last few decades in the southern states of the U.S.A. where civil rights were won but the agrarian world has hardly changed.

A number of recent advances in the historiography of South Africa may also raise questions about the experience of agrarian change in the U.S. The first has to do with the longevity of sharecropping; the second with the dissolution of this and related forms of tenancy. Daniel suggests the centrality of the judiciary and the state for both processes. He places great emphasis on the relatively sympathetic approach to tenants in the courts prior to the 1930s depression. Subsequently, New

1. George M. Frederickson, *White Supremacy: A comparative study in American and South African History*, New York, 1981; John W. Cell, *The Highest Stage of White Supremacy: The Origins of Segregation in South Africa and the American South*, Cambridge, 1982; Stanley B. Greenberg, *Race and State in Capitalist Development*, New Haven, 1980.

Deal legislation and the bureaucracy acted to the detriment of both black tenants and landowners, and in favor of white groups intent on accumulation, who also controlled the local state.

His emphasis on the local state – local farmers' committees, officials, and those who police the countryside – is very useful. Although historians of South Africa have explored the local dynamics of settler power in the early phases of colonization, they have perhaps placed too much emphasis on the center, the "apartheid state," when discussing more recent years. But one point that has emerged forcefully from recent writing on the South African countryside is that legislation does not easily change social relationships. Twentieth-century South African general history often reads like a list of legislation, yet there is a book to be written about laws that were only very partially implemented. It would also be rewarding to ask questions about the importance of related forces that Daniel touches on but does not develop – notably the priorities and preferences of sharecroppers themselves in the context of changing forms of production. Both in relationship to the nature of sharecropping arrangements and their dissolution, it is necessary to look much more closely at the "weapons of the weak" and how their armory affected social processes. Finally, some of the most exciting material in Daniel's paper has to do with the intersection between technical intervention – ideas of efficiency and conservationism – and changes in property and tenancy relationships. These are issues of great importance in the history of southern Africa.

If South African sharecroppers are viewed through the lens of the American experience, it is possible to see the same kind of phenomenon. The biography of Nedd Cobb ("Nate Shaw"), probably the most famous American sharecropper of all, has provided the model for one of the most interesting exercises being undertaken in South African history at the moment – an extended biography of a sharecropper named Kas Maine.[2] Much of the material seems similar: the desire for self-improvement, the drive for independence, and the fact that both of these men were not just laborers or tenants but saw themselves as using their labor to accumulate. Both aimed at "getting a footing where I wouldn't have to ask nobody for nothing."[3]

It is important, however, to emphasize the difference between types of sharecropping which is, after all, a very widespread and varied

2. Theodore Rosengarten, *All God's Dangers: the Life of Nate Shaw*, New York, 1974; M. Nkadimeng and G. Relly, "Kas Maine: the story of a black South African agriculturalist" in B. Bozzoli, ed., *Town and Countryside in the Transvaal*, Johannesburg, 1983; C. van Onselen, "Race and Class in the South African Countryside: Cultural Osmosis and Social Relations in the Sharecropping Economy of the South Western Transvaal, 1900–1950," *American Historical Review*, vol. 95, 1990.

3. See Rosengarten, *All God's Dangers*.

phenomenon.[4] South African sharecropping was probably in its heyday between the 1880s and the 1910s. It did not arise from a post-slavery society. There were imported slaves in South Africa, but in a fairly restricted area of the Cape where, in general, they became wage laborers rather than tenants after abolition. Sharecropping in South Africa, in contrast to the American South, developed mainly out of the relationship between recently conquered African communities and whites who assumed ownership of the land. This form of tenancy attracted some of the most innovative African peasants who transformed their patterns of production by adopting ploughs, ox-draught, woolled sheep, new crops, wagons and horses.[5]

These sharecroppers were welcomed on undercapitalized and under-utilized white-owned farms as they had their own implements and seeds, and became involved in transforming the countryside from below – almost, indeed, counter-colonizing areas from which conquest had threatened to exclude Africans. They looked to accumulate cattle and, in turn-of-the-century South Africa, this gave them a degree of independence. The great maize-farming revolution in South Africa thus initially depended partly on sharecroppers. It was only after a few decades that white farmers, financed partly by the rent from black sharecroppers, were able to reshape relationships decisively in their own favor.

The African origin of South African sharecroppers was evident in their control and discipline over extended families – essential in order to achieve twice subsistence production, and often very much more. African patterns of patriarchy, together with African marriage and property relations, helped make this possible. Moreover, indigenous knowledge of soil and land, and the drive to invest gains in cattle, meant that sharecropping can be seen as an intensified form of the peasant systems that were developing on African reserve lands. This distinguished it from sharecropping in the American South, where there was far less interest in investing in livestock.

Pride of place in the dissolution of South African sharecropping has traditionally been assigned to the Natives' Land Act of 1913, which restricted African rights to buy land outside small areas reserved for them. Most of the reserves were under communal or non-alienable forms of tenure, so individuals were unable to buy land there either. The

---

4. A.F. Robertson, *The Dynamics of Productive Relationships: African Share Contracts in Comparative Perspective*, Cambridge, 1987.

5. Timothy J. Keegan, *Rural Transformations in Industrialising South Africa: The Southern Highveld to 1914*, London, 1987; S. Trapido, "Putting a Plough to the Ground: A History of Tenant Production on the Vereeniging Estates, 1896–1920," in W. Beinart, P. Delius and S. Trapido, eds., *Putting a Plough to the Ground: Accumulation and Dispossession in Rural South Africa 1850–1930*, Johannesburg, 1986.

Act also specified that Africans could not be tenants on white-owned farms unless at least ninety days labor per year was given to the landowner. Solomon Plaatje charted the effects of this Act in *Native Life in South Africa* (1916), which became highly influential in subsequent historical interpretation.[6] He emphasised the rapid displacement of sharecroppers from farms and the social dislocation that resulted.

It has become clear from recent academic research, however, that the Natives' Land Act was rarely enforced in the years immediately after its passing. It really only had an effect where landowners in any case were trying to transform relationships and dissolve sharecropping to replace it with labor tenancy or wage-labor. Moreover, sharecroppers' ownership of implements and cattle, and their control over family labor, allowed them a good deal of mobility. Some were able to move beyond the areas close to rail lines or markets, where landlords were demanding far more labor, and to establish themselves elsewhere. Sharecroppers retained their independence in the peripheral regions of the Orange Free State, the Transvaal, and Natal despite the Act. Very often they survived on the farms of poorer Afrikaners. As one white English speaker said of Afrikaners: "so long as these landowners are willing and do not consider it infra-dig to enter into partnership with the niggers [*sic*], any amount of legislation will not stop the practice."[7] Most historians now agree that sharecroppers survived because of some landlords' incapacity to transform the relationship and their dependence on sharecroppers for income.

The South African judiciary has had some tradition of independence. The Supreme Court invalidated the Natives' Land Act in the Cape in 1917, for a number of complicated reasons having to do with the way it restricted Africans from achieving the property qualification that would allow them a vote. There is little evidence, however, of the kind Daniel cites in the United States, that South African courts extended protection through their interpretation of contracts. Van Onselen's work dealing with Kas Maine and the peripheral regions of the Transvaal suggests that the relationship survived precisely because both parties avoided the courts. There was collusion between landlords and their sharecropping tenants not to take issues to court that might find both in contravention of stated law.

Sharecropping survived for decades in peripheral districts with very limited legal sanction until agrarian change, including tractors, displaced it (though never completely) even there. As in the United States "tractors and sharecroppers do not go together."[8] It is difficult to imagine that the Swanepoels and the Labuschagnes of Wolmaranstad

6. Sol T. Plaatje, *Native Life in South Africa*, London, 1916.
7. Van Onselen, "Race and Class in the South African Countryside," p. 107.
8. Greenberg, *Race and State in Capitalist Development*, p. 114.

and Schweizer-Reneke had had the kind of sympathy for their share-croppers that Nate Shaw found from Hattie Lou Reeve. The names sound unpromising on the Afrikaner side. But it seems, in fact, that they did, and that the "cultural osmosis" between poorer Afrikaners and their tenants rivaled that which one might find between some landlords and sharecroppers in the American South. Solomon Plaatje recognized this especially in his chapter on "our indebtedness to white women" – although the argument of this chapter was not in harmony with his broader analysis, which tended to blame racist Boers rather than accumulators whether they were Englishmen or Afrikaners.[9]

A series of questions emerge from these comparisons about the role of the judiciary in the American South. Could sharecropping have been maintained without access to the courts? How mutual was the self-interest of croppers and landlords? Why were tenants so litigious, and successfully so, in the post-Reconstruction racial order? Did the composition of the courts change after the 1930s depression, as they did in the Apartheid era after 1948 in South Africa?

Clearly, the skills and preferences of tenant families themselves deeply influenced the survival of the relationship. South African historians, in trying to deal with both sharecropping and labor tenancy, have emphasized that these were a social compromise. Some landowners wanted sharecroppers, but even those who wanted more labor were not easily able to command it. There were "hidden struggles" on many farms.[10] If landowners tightened the noose too sharply, tenants could move not only to less controlled farmlands but also onto African reserves, thus threatening the landowners' supply of rent and labor.

Although the reserves were not very large – eight to ten percent of South African land in the early years of the century – they included some of the richest and (a point not often acknowledged) most well-watered land. Sharecroppers and labor tenants came from recently conquered chiefdoms. Some still held in their minds phantom pre-conquest districts or the remnants of the old chieftaincies as alternative social orders. These existed in some form within the reserves. The state did not, in fact, discourage such trends and, in the segregationist era, held out the promise that more land would be bought for blacks and added to the reserves. Some African political movements explored the potential of ethnic claims to land in the reserves. As long as such options remained in a very unevenly developed agricultural sector, rigid controls over tenancy were difficult. By looking at such patterns of mobility, historians can help to insert the notion of "struggle" more directly into an understanding of tenancy relationships.

9. Plaatje, *Native Life*, Chapter 6.
10. H. Bradford, *A Taste of Freedom*, New Haven, 1987.

Similar processes need to be taken into account in analyzing the demise of South African sharecropping. Fascinating material is being gathered on conflict and tension within black rural families in the colonial area.[11] Homestead heads required great control and discipline at just the time when other social forces were undermining their power. Smallholder or peasant production often throws the burden of labor control onto the family, rather than other social institutions, and can entail exploitation of family and child labor. But sons and, to a lesser extent, daughters began to escape from the control of their fathers. Often, they moved to town: urban labor markets significantly influenced agrarian change.

Legislation in 1932 allowed the tenant head of household to bind by contract children up to the age of 18, by which time farm children had been working for some years. Both tenants and farmers had an interest in controlling child labor. But as demands for crops, rents, or labor increased, an internal dynamic towards the dissolution of tenant families, and even the tenancy relationship, was set in motion. Relatively high demand for young men in mining and industrial employment at wages considerably higher than the agricultural pittance – which was in any case usually controlled by their fathers – hastened these processes.

A direct parallel with the American South emerges here. Greenberg notes the emphasis of some African Americans, most prominently Booker T. Washington, on the benefits of industrial employment.[12] Rates of migration by southern blacks suggest that many might have seen this as an alternative to a demeaning relationship in which they were extremely weak and where social improvement was deeply constrained by racial barriers. I would not want to minimize the agency of modernizing landowners and farmers in squeezing and removing their tenants. Yet there are a series of questions about the priorities, options, and struggles of sharecroppers themselves that might profitably be inserted into an analysis of the timing and character of the dissolution of tenancies.

The discussion of technical issues in Daniel's essay certainly has parallels with South African material. In 1940, the historian De Kiewiet – who had already migrated to the USA – wrote wryly that "South Africa came increasingly to be farmed from the two capitals, Cape Town and Pretoria."[13] He exaggerated, of course, but the Department of Agriculture had tremendous influence as state revenues rocketed by virtue of the gold bonanza after South Africa left the gold standard.

11. Especially Keegan, *Rural Transformations*.

12. Greenberg, *Race and State in Capitalist Development*, p. 210.

13. C.W. de Kiewiet, *A History of South Africa: Social and Economic*, London, 1941, p. 253.

South African literature, however, suggests that it was the depression in the 1930s – and not post-depression intervention, as Daniel maintains in the case of the American South – which eliminated many poorer farmers. Thereafter, a co-operative system, locked into national marketing boards that administered price-supports, was developed. The co-operatives that emerged, dominated by whites and usually Afrikaner farmers, became important and powerful financial institutions. They excluded blacks and provided a strong momentum towards agricultural modernization.

In South Africa, even before the era of extensive price supports, there was a history of technical intervention that was unfriendly to tenants of all kinds. The control of animal disease (scab, Texas redwater, East Coast fever) drew the state into the countryside so that almost every farm animal, both sheep and cattle, in rural South African was dipped frequently by 1920. Farmers feared infection of their herds and flocks by tenants' cattle and deployed the same metaphors of contagion that justified the segregation of blacks in town. Control of fire, ridge terracing of fields, fencing, dams, encouragement of paddocking and discouragement of transhumance – all assisted by government legislation and propagandised by officials before the 1930s – worked against the security of smallholding tenants.

Was there more such intervention in the American South before the depression in the 1930s and New Deal than Daniel suggests? Ideas of soil conservation were an important justification for state intervention in South Africa and these were drawn partly from the USA.[14] Conservationists developed a powerful critique of all African farming because it did not easily fit into the new vision of a planned and ordered countryside.

A final question: was opinion about agrarian strategies within the agricultural bureaucracy and government circles as uniform as it appears in Daniel's essay? Did liberal impulses die with the exclusion of Jerome Frank? Were there not other influences, albeit weak ones? One example might be the romantic anti-industrial agrarianists such as Louis Bromfield and Edward Faulkner, who seemed to be pushing a more Jeffersonian ideal as well as a more organic form of farming.[15] More recently, have not free marketeers argued against the kind of collusive controls illustrated in the paper, which might be construed to inhibit efficiency? In South Africa, there have been challenges from both left

14. W. Beinart, "Soil Erosion, Conservationism and Ideas about Development: a Southern African exploration 1900–1960," *Journal of Southern African Studies*, vol. 11, 1984.

15. Louis Bromfield, *Pleasant Valley*, 1945, and *Malabar Farm*, London, 1949; Edward Faulkner, *Ploughman's Folly*, London. 1945.

and right in the last fifteen years that have led to extensive rethinking – although as yet little action – on state subsidies and the agrarian structure as a whole.

In the debates about the history of segregation and Apartheid in South Africa, it has long been argued that racial legislation and coerced labor systems were an intrinsic part of capitalist development, perhaps essential to its success in an economy dominated by primary production. The demise of sharecropping, assisted by legislation, was an important aspect of the new racial order. The liberal counter-argument suggested that if South Africa had not succumbed to Afrikaner rule and a tight racial order, growth would have been quicker and more equitable, with greater political incorporation and social permeability.

The experience of the American South raises very serious questions about that counter-argument. It is true that there was racial legislation in the South, but it was not as harsh and as hard. The congruence between race and class was not as great as in South Africa. Yet the capacity of the local state, with the technical backing of the central state, to ensure that blacks were excluded from the agrarian world both as tenants and landowners suggests that a relatively free land market, and relatively color-blind legislation, is no guarantee of wider distribution of farming resources.

This point leads us back to the problem of reconstruction in South Africa. The Natives' Land Act and similar legislation was abolished in 1991 but the government is trying to push through a series of changes that might pre-empt more radical agrarian reform. The state is moving towards privatization and away from very heavy agricultural subsidies. Agricultural economists criticize the powerful para-statals and cooperatives, whose hold is already weakening. Economic forces, particularly high interest rates and low commodity prices, have tended to weaken the hold of white farmers on the land in the 1980s. Daniel's paper suggests that the freeing up of markets might not go very far in itself in giving blacks a chance of getting a stake in the seventy-seven percent or so of land that whites came to own as their exclusive preserve. As yet, it is unclear how large a demand for land there may be in the current economic climate. But, if the American South is any yardstick, blacks are going to need powerful local representation in democratic institutions to satisfy even a small demand. They are going to need representation and a measure of control within the bureaucracy and they might very well need much more than that.

Part III
Race, Class and Culture

6

"We were no class at all": Southern Women as Social Reformers

Valeria Gennaro Lerda

Anne Firor Scott maintains that in order to understand Southern women, it is necessary to differentiate myth from reality through analysis of their "invisible" lives.[1] A number of autobiographies, notably those by Katharine Du Pre Lumpkin and Belle Kearney, help us penetrate the hidden world of doubts and feelings of young middle-class Southern women who grew up during the Civil War and experienced the post-bellum social and economic transformation of their region.[2] The "new women of the New South" had to learn to mediate between the "paradise lost" of the plantation world, as recalled by many of their parents and grandparents, and the hardships endured by their section at the end of the Civil War: ruined railroads, burned depots, and mutilated buildings, together with – for many – the loss of land, property, and slaves. They were also obliged to cope with the rules and prejudices established by white male society to protect Southern womanhood. According to these, the "proper sphere" of Southern women was to take their place "on the pedestal" and "to sit silent when men were speaking."[3] In return for their acceptance of a subordinate position, white Southern women acquired patriarchal protection. Such protection began to appear especially essential after emancipation. The racist dogmas that emphasized the primitivism of African American males and the threat they posed as rapists began to affect the outlook of white women. Myths of this kind helped blind such women to the impact of the ideology of white supremacy on the South's biracial society.

It took a long time for middle-class Southern women to come to terms with problems such as white poverty and African American

1. See Anne Firor Scott, "Historians Construct the Southern Woman," in *Sex, Race and the Role of Women in the South*, ed. Joanne V. Hawks and Sheila L. Skemp, Jackson, 1981, p. 96.
2. See Katharine Du Pre Lumpkin, *The Making of a Southerner*, New York, 1946; and Belle Kearney, *A Slaveholder's Daughter*, London and New York, 1900.
3. Darlene Clark Hine, "Foreword," *The Making of a Southerner*, viii.

oppression. Modernization of the South's rural postwar society slowly awakened them, compelling them to confront and overcome some of the barriers within which white patriarchy had confined them. After becoming involved in what they saw as issues arising out of domesticity and their maternal duties, many women found they had to campaign for both social reform and their own emancipation.[4]

This essay examines the reform activities of a group of Southern women, including Rebecca Latimer Felton (Georgia), Madeline McDowell Breckinridge (Kentucky), and Belle Kearney (Mississippi), who devoted their energies to campaigning for reforms to promote social justice, temperance, and women's suffrage in the Progressive Era. It deals especially with the issue of race in the reform movement to which they belonged and the manner in which this influenced their attitudes and ideas. Women who became reformers were, on the whole, more successful at overcoming barriers of gender and class than those of race. Their attitudes toward African Americans were very much influenced by the patriarchal outlook that, in other respects, they had rejected. Many, indeed, condoned lynching as a way of protecting their own position. As Lumpkin observed in her autobiography (with considerable irony), while no women actually "approved of mob lynching" many concluded that "the occurrence of lynchings was entirely understandable": an expression of "the noble motive of outraged white males attempting to protect white Southern womanhood."[5]

The title of the essay is drawn from a comment by Jessie Daniel Ames who, after her own marriage, discovered the weak legal position of married women. In 1905, she was compelled to deal with the objections of a Texan bank cashier who was unable to appreciate her need to open a savings account without her husband's permission. This episode, recounted in Jacqueline Dowd Hall's biography of Ames, is a revealing one because it shows the reaction of a Southern middle-class woman who was no longer prepared to accept a submissive role. "I hit the ceiling!," Ames recalled, "I said, "No it's my money."" Ames summarized the married woman's plight: "The husbands owned everything – the clothes on her back! She owned absolutely nothing ... women were considered not second-class citizens – ye gods, we were third class, we were no class at all after we were married."[6]

---

4. The importance of family ties, of kinship and community is, for example, central to the diary of Magnolia Wynn Le Guin. See Charles A. Le Guin, ed., *A Home-Concealed Woman,The Diaries of Magnolia Wynn Le Guin, 1901–1913*, Athens, Geo., 1990.

5. Du Pre Lumpkin, *The Making of a Southerner*, p. 179.

6. Quoted in Jacquelyn Dowd Hall, *Revolt Against Chivalry: Jessie Daniel Ames and the Women's Campaign Against Lynching*, New York, 1979, p. 27.

The extremely weak legal position of married women in Kentucky has been well-described by Helen Deiss Irvin:

> When all other States permitted a married woman to make a will, Kentucky still denied her this right. If a woman owned property, on her marriage, all of it became her husband's, to dispose as he wished.... If a husband died the wife inherited a third of his personalty and a life interest in a third of his real estate. But if the wife died, the husband inherited all of her personalty and if there were children, a life interest in all of her real estate.

Moreover, she could not make contracts, sue, or be sued. If she took a job, her husband had the right to collect and spend her wages. Irvin also listed the other rights of her husband, such as guardianship over the children (including a child not yet born) if his wife left him. Moreover, at his death this guardianship could be willed to another male.[7] Ironically, in view of this, Kentucky had been the first state to permit any kind of women's suffrage, however limited, through its law that allowed widows with school-age children to vote in county school districts for school trustees. In 1888, this law was extended to allow tax-paying widows and spinsters to vote for school taxes. In 1902, however, Kentucky again broke new ground, this time by abolishing women's suffrage – the only instance in American history of the right to vote being taken away from women after once being adopted by a state legislature.

7. See Helen Deiss Irvin, *Women in Kentucky*, Lexington, 1979, pp. 96–97. On this issue we must remember that during the eighteenth and early nineteenth centuries, two distinct sets of legal principles governed the status of women in the British-American colonies: the common law and equity law. Under the common law, no married woman could own property, either real or personal, and the husband could spend her money, sell her slaves, and appropriate her clothes and jewelry. He also controlled the rents and profits of all real estate. The only right left to a *femme covert* was that no husband could sell real property without the consent of the wife. During widowhood, this law allowed women only a life interest in one-third of the family real property, no matter what proportion of that property had been hers before the marriage. Therefore, women were powerless under the common law regarding property. But another set of rules was also adopted in British North America, equity law, which allowed "marriage settlements," under which women could control their property through full or partial managerial rights. The "marriage settlements" were intended to preserve large family estates, but they became a usable tool to elevate the legal status of women from subservience to relative independence. On this subject, see Marylynn Salmon. "Women and Property in South Carolina: The Evidence from Marriage Settlements, 1730 to 1830," *William and Mary Quarterly*, vol. 39, 1983, pp. 655–85. And, by the same author, "The Property Rights of Women in Early America: A Comparative Study," Ph.D. Dissertation, Bryn Mawr College, 1980. Each colony and state differed deeply in handling the principles of equity law. See also Suzanne O. Lebsock, "Radical Reconstruction and the Property Rights of Southern Women," *Journal of Southern History*, vol. 43, 1977, pp. 195–216.

In Southern society, still primarily rural and hierarchical, men assigned women a role of silence and devotion, of hard work and obedience – the "home-concealed" womanhood, so well-described in Magnolia Wynn Le Guin's diary.[8] According to the standard set by Southern white male society, a woman was destined to a life within a well-protected household, in the anonymity of private life. She was considered to belong to "no class," or else to a special class that was – in Belle Kearney's words – "inadequate for citizenship."[9]

Southern women were not expected to speak at public meetings and this "voiceless condition"[10] was sanctioned both by civil society and the churches.[11] It is, therefore, surprising to see how many middle-class women felt the impulse to challenge the rules and make their voices heard in the public arena. Their difficulties and achievements were documented in the records of women's clubs, literary societies, voluntary associations, philanthropic groups, foreign and home missions and, eventually, state legislatures. The experience was one that was totally new, emotionally demanding and, on the whole, successful. The transition from silence to the spoken word was well-illustrated in Belle Kearney's acceptance speech on being nominated superintendent and organizer of the Loyal Temperance Legion and the Women's Christian Temperance Union in Mississippi. Kearney clearly felt inadequate to the exposure of appearing before a group of women. "My voice was choked, my eyes were clouded with the mist of unshed tears", she recalled, fully aware of the fact that she had not open, her mouth in public since reading her commencement essay at college eleven years earlier.[12] In subsequent years, Kearney became one of the most successful lecturers for the WCTU and temperance campaigns because, as she remembered of her audiences, "the novelty of a woman speaker was overcome by the holy enthusiasm for the cause of social justice." Her speaking, Kearney observed in another part of her autobiog-

8. See *A Home-Concealed Woman*, passim.
9. See Kearney, *A Slaveholder's Daughter* p. 111.
10. See Anne Firor Scott, *The Southern Lady, From Pedastal to Politics, 1830–1913,* Chicago, 1970, p. 158. Quotation from Mrs J.C. Croly, *The History of the Woman's Club Movement in America,* New York, 1898, p. 227.
11. In 1893, the Southern Presbyterian Church issued a decree that "the session must absolutely enforce the injunction of Scripture forbidding women to speak in churches, or in any way failing to observe that relative subordination to men that is taught in I Corinthians 11–13, and other places." Quoted in Josephine Bone Floyd, "Rebecca Latimer Felton, Champion of Women's Rights," *Georgia Historical Quarterly,* vol. 30, 1946, pp. 81–104. For a detailed analysis of the position of women in Southern churches, see Jean Friedman, *The Enclosed Garden: Women and Community in the Evangelical South, 1830–1900,* Chapel Hill, 1985, and, by the same author, "Southern Women and Reform," *Città e Campagna nell'Età Dorata: Gli Stati Uniti tra Utopia e Riforma,* ed. Valeria Gennaro Lerda, Roma, 1986, pp. 93–103.
12. Kearney, *A Slaveholder's Daughter,* p. 142.

raphy, had been "for deepening and broadening the outlook for young womanhood and the ultimate redemption of mankind from the curse of drinking and the blight of social impurity."[13]

The redemption of mankind was to prove an acceptable female goal. It encouraged women to move outside their domestic surroundings into the world of sin, poverty, and injustice. Setting off outside the safe confines of the home became possible, at the start, under the auspices of church auxiliary, missionary groups, and the WCTU. When, as a result of their own experience, they came to realize that only with the ballot could they guarantee that the measures of social welfare they deemed necessary as reformers would be included in party programs, suffrage became a central issue for Southern women. It also proved a most divisive one because they found themselves divided over the respective claims of progress and conservatism, simultaneously committed both to social justice and the preservation of segregation.

Rebecca Latimer Felton (1835–1930) of Georgia provides a good illustration of activity for the betterment of their society by the first generation of post-bellum Southern women. The process of generational change, as Anne Firor Scott has noted, is an important key to understanding the attitudes of Southern white women toward the race issue. Leaders like Felton or Kate M. Gordon of Louisiana willingly exploited racial prejudice, while a reformer of the next generation, Jessie Daniel Ames, attacked the "false chivalry" of intimidating blacks through violence and threw her energies into an anti-lyching campaign.[14]

In the "stormy years" of her youth, Felton lived through the Civil War, the premature death of four of her five children, and the confusions and disorders of Reconstruction politics in Georgia. Almost by accident, after teaching school and knowing first-hand the decline of her family plantation and the hardship of farm life, she became her husband's secretary, speech writer, and campaign organizer for the Independent Democratic Party. Utilizing her pen in newspaper articles to support Dr. Felton's political approach, she also found herself adopting the spoken word "as a weapon" with increasing self-confidence and authority. "I found myself," she later recalled, "suddenly in the thick of a campaign. I did not stop to think what a radical change this was for a young woman reared on an old-fashioned Southern plantation, where a woman was viewed only as an ornament and as a household mistress."[15]

13. Ibid., p. 153.

14. See Anne Firor Scott and Jacquelyn Dowd Hall, "Women in the South," *Interpreting Southern History: Historiographical Essays in Honor of Sanford W. Higginbothan*, eds. John B. Boles and Evelyn Thomas Nolen, Baton Rouge, 1987, p. 498.

15. See Josephine Bone Floyd, "Rebecca Latimer Felton, Political Independent," *Georgia Historical Quarterly*, vol. 30, 1946, pp. 14–34.

In her public life, Felton campaigned for reforms in the penal system. When the Georgia Legislature abolished the convict-lease system in 1908, after years of effort by male and female reformers, she was proud of the role she had played. "I should be given consideration," she later wrote, "for the incessant fusillade I kept up on this subject ... I was never too busy or too tired to ventilate the atrocity when I could find a place to publish my criticism."[16] She was also active in campaigns for temperance and prohibition, together with women's rights including suffrage. Her activity, however, was fundamentally conservative in character. She did not criticize women's domestic status but tried to enhance the right of women to have the sanctity of the home protected. This was particularly true of her perception of the consequences "when King Alcohol reigns."[17]

When Felton decided to join the Woman's Christian Temperance Union (WCTU), she made her commitment primarily in the hope of capturing new forces from the membership of that organization in her battle to end the convict-lease system. Yet she also saw the consumption of alcohol as another plague at work undermining American society. Felton was raised in a Methodist family; both her family and church were biased against "Demon Liquor." Alcohol appeared an even greater menace in the South because of the myths that had grown up to justify white supremacy. The fear of African American male barbarism, encouraged by drunkenness, seemed to Felton and many others to show the need of additional measures to protect white women. This could best be done through legislation. Banning the sale and production of alcoholic beverages, Felton believed, would be an important means of advancing women's security.

"I believe a woman has a multitude of rights," Felton wrote; "I want her to have and enjoy as well as the right to choose her own rulers, such rights as a sober home and a decent and upright husband."[18] A child also had rights, she argued, the most important being "to be born in a sober home without diseased blood in his little veins."[19] In another text, she compared the casualties due to alcohol to the destruction of war: "Twenty five years have shown the presence of an enemy in this country, that endangers the happiness and welfare of the whole people, even greater than the Civil War." Moreover, "the Drink Evil demands nine hundred millions of dollars of tribute per annum."[20] In a public speech at

16. Georgia Convict-Lease System," manuscript, n.d. Rebecca Latimer Felton Papers, Special Collections, The University of Georgia Library (hereafter cited as Felton Papers).

17. Speech Delivered before the Woman's Christian Temperance Union," n.d., Felton Papers.

18. Manuscript, n.d., Felton Papers.

19. Ibid.

20. A Speech Delivered before the Woman's Christian Temperance Union," Felton Papers.

a WCTU meeting, she directly accused men who allowed conditions to deteriorate in contemporary society: "Men," she asked, "and this you call progress? Call me a crank, if you will, but I'll stand up against such injustice and inhumanity while God gives me breath!"[21]

In making such accusations, Rebecca Felton knew she was leaving the "proper sphere" yet wanted to demonstrate the manner in which men prevented women from defending their rights. She mentioned that she knew men "at the club" used to tell their friends that "they would rope their wives" if they dared to open their mouths in public. She consequently asked the men in the audience to help define her sphere.[22] Felton, despite her courage in challenging the social conventions of Georgia and the South, had still not escaped the dilemma of the Southern middle-class white woman, torn between old codes of female behavior and the apparent need to find new ways of protection without seclusion. Ann Lee Whites argues that Southern women, Felton included, did not fight to change the structures of Southern society but to clean society from political corruption brought about by men. Felton herself, using domestic imagery that limited women's role at the same time as it argued for its extension, perceived "the house of politics" made by men as having become dirty but criticized men for not being willing to permit women to sweep after them.[23]

In the Woman's Christian Temperance Movement, women's efforts were directed towards the political and social world, while they remained deeply influenced by the evangelical religiosity that gave Southern ladies the strength to engage in the battle for a moral society. In the campaign for prohibition, women first decided to use the strategy of "education and persuasion," but later moved towards asking for legal prohibition and supported state and federal legislation. Women in the WCTU started their anti-liquor war supporting the "local option," a measure that passed on to state governments the decision whether to forbid the sale of alcohol within their borders. This measure, however, did not succeed in preventing the importation of intoxicating beverages from other states into the dry counties. As a consequence, women achieved greater understanding of the weakness of any measure adopted as long as they did not have the vote and were

---

21. Ibid.
22. Ibid. For a good historigraphical survey of the "two spheres" issue see Linda Kerber, "Separate Spheres, Female Worlds, Woman's Place: the Rhetoric of Women's History," *Journal of American History*, vol. 75, 1988, pp. 9–40.
23. See Ann Lee Whites, "Rebecca Latimer Felton and the Problem of `Protection' in the New South," typescript kindly given by the author, forthcoming in the volume edited by Nancy Hewitt and Suzanne Lebsock, *Visible Women* (Chicago). Quotation from Felton Manuscript, n.d., scrapbook n. 117, Felton Papers. Also see Floyd, "Rebecca Latimer Felton, Champion."

unable to influence politics directly. The new field of reform in which the WCTU asked women to participate, therefore, was suffrage, first at the local level, making it possible for them to vote for the "local option," and afterwards in state and federal elections. The two reforms, for prohibition and women's suffrage, complemented each other admirably.[24]

Felton, who was mainly responsible for the direction taken by the WCTU in Georgia, recalled that "woman suffrage had its inception in the fight against saloons. The WCTU was pledged to woman suffrage."[25] For many, the right to the ballot was synonymous with the right to vote against the liquor traffic and, consequently, against any force that could endanger the family and community at large. But even when justified in these fundamentally Christian terms, the demand for female suffrage encountered strong hostility from men who believed women lacked preparation for the franchise. To arguments such as these, Felton responded that "the women of this country are preparing to be intelligent voters, and this suffrage movement is simply getting ready to vote when that duty is laid upon the intelligence, the mother-hood and the wifehood of the land."[26] "I claim," she wrote elsewhere, "that [women] were born into all rights that are the property of their brothers, born in the same home and educated in the same way ... [yet] the right to vote is denied to one half of the citizens of the United States." The limitation of her outlook when it came to issues of race showed itself in her desire to have the suffrage granted through state legislation since, in common with many Southern suffragists, she saw a federal amendment to the constitution as an infringement of states' rights and consequently a threat to white supremacy.[27] She had no desire whatever to see African Americans given the vote and remained a convinced white supremacist. "After thirty years of experiment," she declared, "no fact is more clearly understood than the mistake of giving the ballot to the negro before he was ready for it ... the great

---

24. The temperance movement had its inception before the Civil War, and it was orga-nized by Protestant men belonging to "respectable" social classes. Officially, women were not admitted. Only after 1840 were women accepted, and thereafter they became active in the temperance crusade. Frances Willard was the President of the WCTU from 1879 to her death in 1898. See Barbara Epstein, *The Politics of Domesticity: Women Evangelism and Temperance in Nineteenth Century America*, Middletown, 1981; and Ruth Bordin, *Women and Temperance: The quest for Power and Liberty, 1873–1900*, Philadelphia, 1981. For a contemporary view of the movement, see Mrs A.A. Ansley, *History of the Georgia WCTU, 1883–1907*, Columbus, Georgia, 1914.

25. Manuscript, n.d., Felton Papers.

26. Getting Ready to Vote," manuscript, n.d., Felton Papers.

27. Ibid.

bulk of negro voters are as incapable as those who were newly emancipated in 1865."[28]

Southern white women, like Felton, usually allied themselves with men over the issue of excluding African Americans from the polls. "Women with the vote," writes Jacqueline Dowd Hall, "offered no challenge to the [idea] ... of ... racial exclusion."[29] Many conservative Southern ladies did not accept the idea of a federal amendment. For them, the progressive demand for women's suffrage was based on the need to defend domesticity and counterbalance African American votes at the polls.[30] Conversely, Rebecca Felton argued, "the only men who seek to deny suffrage to women are the ones who wish to give it to the negro men."[31] As a result of their racial attitudes, middle-class Southern women did not enter the suffrage campaign until after the passage of the first state constitutional amendments to disfranchise African American voters in the early 1890s, at least a decade behind their northern sisters.

In many ways, Rebecca Felton's life and career mirrored the inner contradictions of post-bellum Southern society. She was able to understand the needs of a changing economy and to foresee the trends toward industrialization, in accordance with the views of leaders of the New South. She also took a stand for women mill workers, demanding equal pay for equal work and the liberty to enjoy their own property.[32] At the same time, she remained a staunch defender of what she perceived as woman's purity and of the basic values of family and community life. It was in the name of these values that Felton, despite her compassion for fellow-women and poorer whites, justified lynching that she saw as "a sheltering arm about innocence and virtue." What was the best way of defending Southern civilization? "I say lynch," Felton declared with passionate intensity in 1897, "lynch a thousand times a week if necessary!"[33]

28. Rebecca Felton shared the Southern position in which suffragists decided to belong to the NAWSA only when state autonomy was accepted by the national organization; in other words, they entered the NAWSA only when the question of white women suffrage was separated from black women suffrage.

29. Hall, *Revolt Against Chivalry*, p. 55.

30. See Kenneth R. Johnson, "Kate Gordon and the Woman-Suffrage Movement in the South," *Journal of Southern History*, vol. 38, 1972, pp. 365–92.

31. Mrs. Ethel to Mrs. Felton, April 1915, Felton Papers.

32. On the question of women workers' rights and morality, Rebecca Felton took a stand against an article which denounced the lack of morality and bad health conditions of women and children working in the textile mills of Georgia and of the South. The article was written by Mrs. De Graffenried, sent as an inspector by the U.S. Bureau of Labor in 1891. On this controversy see Ann Lee Whites, "The De Graffenried Controversy: Class, Race, and Gender in the New South," *Journal of Southern History*, vol. 54, 1988, pp. 449–78.

33. *Atlanta Journal*, 12 August 1897.

Madeline McDowell Breckinridge (1872–1920) played a major role in the campaigns for education, public health, and philanthropy in Kentucky in the early twentieth century.[34] Breckinridge was physically frail, affected by tuberculosis of the bone and lungs, and during her childhood had suffered the loss of a leg. Overcoming these disabilities, she threw herself into social reform. Through the Lexington Civic League, the Associated Charities, and the Federation of Women's Clubs she became involved in regulating child labor, in establishing community centers, playgrounds, kindergartens, and a juvenile court system. She also, for obvious reasons, joined the Kentucky Association for the Prevention and Relief of Tuberculosis and helped found the Bluegrass Sanatorium in Lexington.

After years of opposition to her projects from male politicians, Breckinridge became convinced that only the vote would give women the means to enact the reforms needed to modernize her state and the South.[35] Most of her early efforts in this direction were devoted to the school suffrage question. In an address made before the National Suffrage Convention in Louisville on 2 October 1911, Breckinridge complained about what she perceived as the "retrogression" of Kentucky politics. In 1902, the law granting the school suffrage to a limited class of women was repealed, forcing the women suffragists of Kentucky to fight to regain a right conferred sixty-four years earlier.[36] Breckinridge, as Chairman of the Kentucky Federation of Women's Clubs, organized – according to her biographer – "a campaign for school suffrage during the Summer and Fall of 1911, which undoubtedly surpassed in intensity the campaigns of any of those running for state offices, including the Governor."[37] When the bill passed the legislature in January 1912, by a vote of 62 to 25, she

34. See Melba Porter Hay, "Madeline McDowell Breckenridge: Kentucky Suffragist and Progressive Reformer," Ph.D. Dissertation, University of Kentucky, 1980; Sophonisba Preston Breckinridge, *Madeline McDowell Breckinridge, A Leader of the New South*, Chicago, 1921.

35. Breckinridge, having taken up the cause of woman suffrage, succeeded (1912–1915) Laura Clay as President of the Kentucky Equal Rights Association (KERA), which was founded in 1888; she served as Vice-President of the National American Women Suffrage Association (1913/1914). She was campaigning for suffrage in 1915 when the worsening of her health limited her traveling. In 1919, she was again elected President of the KERA. In 1920, she led the drive for ratification of the Federal Amendment by the Kentucky General Assembly. See Hay, *Madeline McDowell Breckinridge*, passim.

36. Clipping from the *Lexington Herald*, Sunday, January 1914, Box 701; "Address of Mrs Desha Breckinridge at the National Suffrage Convention in Louisville," 29 October 1911 [Breckinridge's husband, Desha B., was editor of the *Lexington Herald*]; both in Madeline McDowell Breckenridge Papers, Papers of the Breckenridge Family, Library of Congress (hereafter cited as Breckinridge Papers).

37. Hay, *Madeline McDowell*, p. 130.

could be justifiably proud of her efforts at lobbying and organization.[38]

The key issue facing advocates of women's suffrage in the South was
the argument over the right means of achieving their objective. The
choice lay between a federal amendment or one adopted by the various
states. In Kentucky, the two opposing positions were clearly marked
out: Breckinridge accepted the idea of a federal amendment, while
Laura Clay, President of the Kentucky Equal Rights Association
(KERA) from 1888 to 1912, regarded such a policy as a violation of
states' rights and a menace to white supremacy. Clay was convinced
that, as Helen Deiss Irvin has written, "state action, rather than federal
amendment, would permit Southern states to deal as they saw fit with
the black woman voter."[39] Clay advocated an educational requirement
for women voters, a measure that would at that time have barred from
the polls a higher number of African American than white women.
Although Clay maintained that states' rights and not race was the basis
of her opposition to any federal interference in the matter of suffrage,
Sophonisba Breckinridge – herself an active member of the suffrage
movement – would write in 1921 that "the question of states' rights in
the decade 1910–1920, as in 1861, was really a question of the negro."[40]
Clay, for whatever reason she fought, did not abandon her position. She
took no part in the campaign for the nineteenth amendment and resigned
from the Kentucky ERA in 1919.

The repeal of the school suffrage law itself had been supported by a
number of women who were afraid of seeing the school boards
controlled by African Americans, and who supported the repeal of the
school suffrage for white women on condition it was also taken away
from black women[41]. Breckinridge, on the contrary, accepted the idea of
a national measure and was active both in the campaign for ratification
and in the subsequent movement for educating women to exercise that
right. She fought strenuously to secure ratification by the Kentucky
legislature of the federal amendment and of a proposal to confer the
presidential suffrage on Kentucky women, while at the same time seeking to prepare the women of her state for their new duties as voters.
Governor Black and his administration were in favor of the federal
amendment, and, in general, the politicians to whom Madeline
Breckinridge wrote declared their support for a national constitutional

38. Breckenridge to her "Fellow Citizens," 16 February 1920, Breckinridge Papers.
39. Irvin, *Women in Kentucky*, p. 103. On Laura Clay see the biography by Paul E.
Fuller, *Laura Clay and the Women's Rights Movement*, Lexington, 1975.
40. Quoted in Irvin, *Women in Kentucky*, p. 104.
41. Cunningham, quoted in Claudia Knott, *Woman Suffrage: The Movement in
Kentucky, 1879–1920*, Ph.D dissertation, University of Kentucky, chapter v, pp. 192–254.

amendment that would eliminate "the anomaly whereby women vote on national questions in some states and not in others."[42]

The divisions within the suffrage movement in the South illuminate some of the contradictions of Southern progressivism. As women struggled in the first place to break their silence and later for social betterment, profound differences appeared within their programs and organizations. Their work for social welfare was continually limited and delayed by strategies to maintain the basic values of Southern society, namely states' rights and white supremacy, as a supposed bulwark against the disruption of family and community.

The delay in women's suffrage – women in the South did not start to show interest until 1880 and not until 1913 did every state have its own suffrage organization – can be explained in several ways. First, advocates of women's suffrage not only had to contend with animosity from the male population, the liquor interests, and organized vice, but also with what they saw as mental laziness on the part of their white sisters and female opponents of suffrage. The empowerment gained by speaking in public could be applied to conservative rather than progressive aims. Breckinridge, in one of her speeches, referred ironically to the efforts of women who were ready "to travel thousands of miles and speak on many platforms to prove that woman's place is in the home."[43] There was also a long history of misunderstandings between the Southern States Woman Suffrage Conference (SSWSC) and the National American Woman Suffrage Conference (NAWSA), with Southern leaders such as Kate Gordon, President of the SSWSC, claiming that they "wished to see the power of the State retained" and the vote gained through state action – a states' rights position criticized by more radical members of the SSWSC.[44]

The success of the national movement in having the demand for women's suffrage, with the support of Woodrow Wilson, included in the Democratic Platform for the 1912 presidential campaign, in many ways marked the final defeat of the Southern branch. Many Southerners declined to accept the vanquishing of "state sovereignty." Gordon, for example, refused to acknowledge the inevitability of the Susan B.

42. Robert Simmons [an attorney in Covington] to Mrs. Desha Breckinridge, 24 July 1919, Breckinridge Papers.

43. Address of Mrs. Desha Breckinridge, President of the Equal Rights Associations of Kentucky, 23 March, 1915, manuscript volume, Reamer, Ida Salley Papers, South Carolina Library, Columbia, South Carolina (hereafter cited as Reamer Papers).

44. During the forty-sixth annual Convention of the NAWSA, held in Nashville, a strong states' rights sentiment prevailed, and the Susan B. Anthony Amendment was replaced with the Shafroth-Palmer Amendment, which asked for a referendum on Woman suffrage everywhere eight percent of the voters had asked for it. See Johnson, "Kate Gordon," p. 369.

Anthony amendment and promised to fight against it "to the last ditch." Gordon herself believed women could achieve successful results in their battle for the betterment of society even without the right to vote. "During the last 15 years," she declared in 1915, "every bit of civic advancement in New Orleans has been brought about by women, though hampered by being without the ballot."[45] The record of Kentucky seemed to prove the same point. In 1894 the state passed a property law allowing married women to make wills. In 1896 it established a separate house of reform for girls with women allowed to serve on its board of directors. In 1900, Kentucky granted married women the right to keep their own earnings; and, in 1910, the age of consent of girls was raised from 12 to 16 years. The same year saw the passage of a co-guardianship law that finally recognized a mother's claim to her own child.[46]

Southern middle-class women moved off the pedestal in the second half of the nineteenth century, but they did not aim to give up their beliefs and Southern social rules while becoming strenuous fighters to remove the defects of their society. Among the values they tried to defend was the image of femininity and grace, and they constantly stressed in their public speeches and writings that the freedom women were asking for "was nothing unwomanly" but rather the freedom "to carry out God's plan when He made women helpmates of men."[47] Belle Kearney's looked to the appearance of a new woman, able to forge a new identity in the community, state, and nation, willing if necessary to face ostracism and "ready for every development, capable of every achievement, strong, earnest, brainy, progressive, comprehensive."[48]

To understand Belle Kearney's belief in the potentialities of Southern women, it is necessary to recall some of her own achievements. During her youth spent in Mississippi, she tried hard to understand the boundaries between the private and the public "spheres" in which society was divided. She felt deeply the contradiction of being a person torn between the old slaveholders' system, for which she was born "too late,"[49] and the new troubled post-bellum society. The war had destroyed her family's wealth. She and her mother moved from the splendor of plantation life to sewing dresses for former slaves in order to make "ends meet." Her eagerness for higher education and her sense of unfairness at being denied the right to attend good, expensive schools – even her reac-

---

45. Ibid., p. 388; speech delivered by Kate Gordon at the meeting of the SSWSC, 9 February 1915, Reamer Papers. Gordon had left the NAWSA and founded the SSWSC in 1909.

46. Irvin, *Women in Kentucky*, pp. 99–100.

47. Proceedings, 26 January 1915, Reamer Papers. Mrs. Valentine was the speaker.

48. Kearney, *A Slaveholder's Daughter*, p. 169.

49. Ibid., p. 57. Kearney stressed the irony of "being born two months and six days too late to be a slaveowner."

tion to the term "female" applied to academies or colleges[50] – emphasized her will to change women's lot.

Among other difficulties that she faced in order to defend her vision
of women's life and rights, she had to overcome the entrenched cultural
tradition that a Southern middle-class white woman never worked
"outside the home." Her father refused to let her attain financial independence on the grounds that the proper place for his daughter was at
home. Kearney's father, who had great respect for his daughter's intelligence, reflected the fear of change, as it was foreseen by conservative
Southern men, who could use the "separate spheres" concept as an organizing device in a patriarchal society. But domesticity offered advantages as well as disadvantages to women, smoothing the way to popular
acceptance of extra-familial activities.[51] Kearney began her career
teaching pupils at home and only in later years was she able to teach in
public schools. When she met Julia Ward in 1884, and Frances Willard
in 1889, she was struck by the experience of women speaking in public.
Their influence on the young school teacher was such that Kearney,
following their example, began to build a career as a public lecturer,
spending much of the rest of her life in advocacy of temperance and
woman suffrage.

Like Rebecca Felton, Kearney moved from temperance work to
crusading for suffrage. The WCTU, for which she was an official
lecturer until 1898, was a great school for women, teaching them the
significance of the ballot. To quote Kearney's words, "The WCTU was
the golden key that unlocked the prison doors of pent-up possibilities," a
key that gave her the courage to address a joint session of the
Mississippi legislature, which in turn opened the way for future
addresses to the legislature by women.[52] As for suffrage, like Rebecca
Felton, Kearney favored the enfranchisement of women who could meet
educational and property qualifications as a means to perpetuate white
supremacy.[53]

When the nineteenth amendment to the federal constitution was
submitted to the states, a new stage in the women's suffrage campaign

50. Kearney wrote, "The word 'woman' is strong and dignified, and suggests courte-
ous consideration. 'Female' is weak and almost insulting." Ibid. pp. 40–41.
51. See Carl N. Degler, *At Odds: Women and the Family from the Revolution to the
Present* (New York, 1980), passim.
52. Kearney, *A Slaveholder's Daughter*, p. 118. Kearney spoke for thirty minutes and
her talk was interrupted by frequent applause. Despite her eloquent plea, the legislation
she had suggested for a two year trial period was defeated, although she had opened the
way for future addresses to the legislature by women. On this subject see Nancy Carol
Tipton, "'It's my Duty': The Public Career of Belle Kearney," M.A. Thesis, University of
Mississippi, 1975, p. 46.
53. See Kearney's address, "The South and Woman Suffrage," delivered on 25 March

in Mississippi developed. In spite of the work of many women, it resulted in failure since the amendment went into effect in August 1920 without the consenting vote of the Mississippi legislature. However, the passage of the federal amendment gave American women not only the right to vote but also the ability to stand for election to offices previously open only to men. Kearney, already a nationally known lecturer and reformer, announced her candidacy for the United States Senate seat, vacated through the retirement of Mississippi planter-politician John Sharp Williams. Kearney now committeed her oratorical abilities to a new "special mission": cleaning up corruption in state politics. In a difficult campaign, with James Kimble Vardaman as an opponent, she ran on a platform emphasizing social reform: education, restricted immigration, child welfare, protective legislation for women in industry, public health, federal aid for farmers, labor legislation, and commitment to the League of Nations.[54] In the primary election of 15 August 1922, although able to claim she had demonstrated that "women in politics are as true as steel," Kearney was beaten by Vardaman. As William F. Holmes writes, "Belle Kearney was the first woman in Mississippi history to run for the Senate, and her sex eliminated her from all serious consideration as a candidate."[55] Fewer than three months after the primary election, Kearney became a candidate once more, this time for a senate seat in the Mississippi legislature. Her platform focused on philanthropic, educational, and governmental reforms, stressing the need for a strict enforcement of prohibition. This election she won, becoming in the process the first woman in the South to be elected to a state senate.[56]

It is instructive to compare Kearney's career with that of Rebecca Felton, who became the first female member of the United States Senate, following the death of Tom Watson in 1922. The symbolic honor offered her by the Governor of Georgia made her remark about the irony of going to Washington to receive a senate seat after a long life of political campaigning without the right to vote. The brevity of her senate career, which was achieved through appointment rather than the ballot, demonstrates, as William Chase notes, "the disparity between the shadow and the substance of female power."[57] But both Kearney and Felton, long before their official involvement in the practice of politics, had been instrumental in promoting both social legislation and the gender rights of women. Belle Kearney's two terms in the Mississippi

54. Tipton, p. 95.

55. See William F. Holmes, *The White Chief, James Kimble Vardaman*, Baton Rouge, 1970, p. 375.

56. Tipton, p. 118.

57. William Chafe, *The American Woman, Her Changing Social, Economic, and Political Roles, 1920–1970*, London, 1972, p. 39.

Senate allowed her to fight for further social legislation in response to the needs of her constituents in the eighteenth District. When her term expired in 1926, Kearney continued to lecture and be active in the field of women's rights until her death on 27 February 1939. The *Madison County Herald* of 3 March 1939 assessed her life in these terms: "She was the daughter of a slave holder, but came to be the champion of freedom. Born in the days of war, she became an advocate of peace. Brought up in an era of heavy drinking and intemperance of all kinds, she became a champion of temperance."[58]

The study of the movement for social justice in the South is, in many ways, an analysis of Southern womanhood. For here was an issue, in John C. Ruoff's words, "central to the process of self-definition of Southern society." Moreover, "Southern womanhood was a product of the forces which shaped the South into a self-conscious region," encompassing "a set of values and symbols by which Southerners defined the region's character."[59] Since Barbara Welter's path-breaking essay on the "cult of true womanhood," this stereotype has become an essential part of the vocabulary of women's history.[60]

In the South, the image of women was shaped and re-shaped by the effort of Southern male society to perpetuate a conservative social order. Southern womanhood became the symbolic manifestation of the purity and sanctity of the one institution that seemed to best defend social stability: the family. Many whites, of both sexes, supported lynching and the disfranchisement of African American voters on the throroughly irrational grounds that they helped to safeguard the family and the purity of white womanhood.[61] With African American voters disfranchised and the supposed racial threat removed, the way was clear for Southern white women themselves to enter the political arena as advocates of reform.

It is ironic that the "new woman" of the New South came to embody the highest values of Southern culture as a defender of family, domesticity, and purity, but, at the same time, she still was considered "no class" or, at least, a class without civil rights. The "new woman" was a product of a changing society and the efforts of a number of churches, particularly the Methodist Church South, which were able to respond to the social needs arising out of the region's economic transformation.

58. Quoted in Tipton, p. 151.

59. John C. Ruoff, "Southern Womanhood, 1865–1920. An Intellectual and Cultural History," Ph.D. Dissertation, University of Illinois, 1976, p. 7.

60. Barbara Welter, "The Cult of True Womanhood: 1820–1860," *American Quarterly*, vol. 18, 1966, pp. 151–174.

61. On the growing unreasonable fear of African-Americans after emancipation, see Forrest G. Wood, *Black Scare: The Racist Response to Emancipation and Reconstruction*, Berkeley, 1968, pp. 143–55.

Women were encouraged to try to ameliorate society, working beyond the confines of the household through organizations such as the WCTU.

Anne Firor Scott makes it clear that "the new women were asking not only for rights, but also for responsibilities, and there were plenty of women who found the older system perfectly comfortable and satisfactory."[62] Any generalization is, therefore, misleading, because the "new women" were a small minority. "Like the Lady," Scott argues, "the new woman represented only a small minority of all women in the South. Unlike the Lady, she did not become the universal ideal."[63] At any rate, after women's suffrage became a reality for American women, many white middle-class women in the South asserted their newly acquired rights and enthusiastically entered the political arena. They evolved "a new conception of the proper role of women"[64] without, as some noted, losing the traditional attributes of grace and femininity. In an article in the *St. Louis Star* entitled "Does suffrage unsex women?" it was acknowledged that Southern ladies did not turn their backs on the elegance and grace associated with the plantation tradition even in the midst of a political campaign.[65]

In many ways, members of the middle-class elite were only the tip of the iceberg of female public activity in the South, where many "invisible" women, white and black, with roles as artisans, managers, teachers, factory workers, farmers, and heads of families, worked to improve social conditions during the later nineteenth century and Progressive era.[66] But Southern middle-class women had their role. Many entered the public arena to become social and political reformers. Abandoning nostalgia for courage, they moved from myth to history.

62. Anne Firor Scott, "The 'New Woman' in the New South," *South Atlantic Quarterly*, vol. 61, 1962, reprinted in *Making the Invisible Women Visable*, Urbaha, Illinois, 1984, p. 219.

63. Scott, *Making the Invisible Women Visible*, p. 220.

64. Ibid.

65. *St. Louis Star*, 25 March 1919.

66. See Scott, *The Southern Lady* and "Historians Construct the Southern Woman." On the activity of Southern women as social reformers and protagonists of the welfare movement in the Progressive Era, with a new focus on black women, see Nancy Hewitt, "Beyond the Search for Sisterhood: American Women's History in the 1980's," *Journal of Social History*, vol. 10, 1985, pp. 299–321; and Linda Gordon, "Black and White Visions of Welfare: Women's Welfare Activism, 1890–1945," *Journal of American History*, vol. 78, 1991, pp. 559–90. On the centrality of women to progressivism, see Noralee Frankel and Nancy S. Dye, eds., *Gender, Class, and Race in the Progressive Era*, Lexington, 1991.

7

Black Social Science and Black Politics in the Understanding of the South: DuBois, the Atlanta University Studies and *The Crisis*, 1897–1920

David Turley

The Atlanta University studies, deriving from the annual conferences and under W.E.B. DuBois's direction from his appointment in 1897, constitute, in combination with *The Philadelphia Negro: A Social Study* (1899) and a cluster of sociological papers separately published in the same period, DuBois's main claim to have "singlehandedly initiated serious research in blacks in America." Though they have had their later critics, the studies were nonetheless received at the time by perceptive students of racial questions, both within and beyond the United States, as marking a substantial scientific advance in the understanding of the lives and circumstances of southern blacks. And their reputation has remained as "classic statements about black conditions at the turn of the century."[1] Since their publication they have been quarried by scholars looking for material on the racial and class arrangements of the South in the period. By contrast, *The Crisis*, in its early years under DuBois's editorship from 1910, has been seen as plainly reflecting the growing militancy over the position of African Americans that had led to the formation of the NAACP. It therefore appears as a crucial historical source that registered the changing temper and forms of anti-racist politics in a period in which the relations of black and white, especially in the South,

---

1. Elliot Rudwick, quoted in Nancy Leys Stepan and Sander L. Gilman, "Appropriating the Idioms of Science: The Rejection of Scientific Racism" in *The Bounds of Race. Perspectives on Hegemony and Resistance*, ed. with intro. Dominick LaCapra, Ithaca and London, 1991, p. 96, note 44; Dan S. Green and Edwin D. Driver, "Introduction" in *W.E.B. DuBois on Sociology and the Black Community*, ed. Green and Driver, Chicago and London, 1978, p. 31; W.E.B. DuBois, ed. *Economic Cooperation among Negro Americans*, Atlanta, 1907, p. 5.

provoked – as the very title of the periodical suggested – growing alarm.[2]

Understood in this way, the sociological studies and the magazine appear as quite distinct enterprises with very different purposes: the search for scientific truth and the agitation for social reform respectively. Their main link would seem to be as two phases in the career of DuBois. This paper argues, however, that if the Atlanta University studies and *The Crisis* are approached through the different styles of thought they embody and with due attention paid to their form as texts and their various rhetorical strategies, they assume additional significant meanings. These meanings have to do with the different but overlapping stages of *intellectual* resistance to racism in the Progressive era. This approach also underlines the self-conscious social role educated African Americans proposed for themselves and hints at changes over the period in their sense of their relation to the mass of southern blacks. It should also become apparent that, given the dominance of DuBois in both these publishing activities, his own evolving sense of the nature and manifestations of racial oppression, as well as of the resources available to an African American intellectual to combat them, make his personal experiences closely intertwined with the more general intellectual and cultural significance of the two forms of publication. Evolution in personal consciousness and shifts in the public discourse about race had a mutual development. According to this perspective, the story of the studies and the first decade of *The Crisis* is a continuous one rather than one having two distinct phases.

There was initially no doubt in DuBois's mind as to the purpose of the annual Atlanta conferences and subsequent studies. The object was "a careful search for truth conducted as thoroughly, broadly and honestly as the material resources and mental equipment at command will allow." But however disinterested the search for truth may have been it was likely to have substantial non-academic implications when, as DuBois himself admitted in 1898,

2. John Hope Franklin. *From Slavery to Freedom. A History of Negro Americans*, 3rd ed., New York, 1969, pp. 387, 402, 409; August Meier and Elliott Rudwick, *From Plantation to Ghetto*, rev. ed., New York, 1970, ch. 5 and p. 313. A recent monographic use of the Atlanta studies is Linda Gordon, "Black and White Visions of Welfare: Women's Welfare Activism, 1890–1945," *Journal of American History*, vol. 78, no. 2, Sept. 1991, pp. 559–90. On the relation of *The Crisis* to militancy, Franklin, op. cit., pp. 447, 478–79, 487, 502; Meier and Rudwick, op. cit., pp. 209–10.

... we possess endless final judgements as to the American Negro emanating from men of influence and learning, in the very face of the fact known to every accurate student, that there exists today no sufficient material of proven reliability, upon which any scientist can base definite and final conclusions as to the present condition and tendencies of the eight million American Negroes.[3]

Yet, ironically, many of those "men of influence and learning" were claiming the sanction of science for their final conclusions about African Americans and it is within the context of the intellectual predominance of these conclusions, cumulatively termed "scientific racism," and of the prestige of the idea of "science," that it is necessary to begin to read the additional intellectual and cultural meanings of the Atlanta studies.

By the 1890s, "scientific racism" in the eyes of even many educated Americans gave intellectual legitimacy to widespread attitudes in society as to the appropriateness – because of the "naturalness" – of racially-structured hierarchy. "Race science," however, was not simply reflective of prejudice. It claimed to draw on a mass of detailed information accumulated by travelers and other observers to abstract general ideas about races cast as conclusions about racial types. Behind any particular individual lurked the notion of the type to which he or she belonged. In pursuit of closer definition of such racial types, scientists studied comparative anatomy and physiology and placed particular emphasis on measurement as a procedure. They took skull measurements with particular frequency on the assumption that skull size indicated mental capacity. Such procedures, some of which went back decades, by the end of the century were adapted to the triumphant Darwinian intellectual framework of the "survival of the fittest" in the necessary "struggle for existence" between races. This led to supposed "conclusions" about the physical and mental distinctiveness and inferiority of African Americans that confined them to a lower place in nature than caucasians and therefore to a subordinate place in society.

In the second half of the nineteenth century, science came to be perhaps the most prestigious of all forms of knowledge, requiring intellectual standards and such specialized training as to be extremely exclusive in regard to those who were to be recognized as members of the scientific community and able to speak authoritatively on scientific matters. As Stepan and Gilman have argued, science's prestige grew

---

3. W.E.B. DuBois, *Dusk of Dawn* in *W.E.B. DuBois: Writings*, ed. Nathan Huggins, New York, 1986, p. 600; DuBois, "The Study of the Negro Problems" in *W.E.B. DuBois on Sociology and the Black Community*, p. 79.

from its supposed characteristics of "factuality" and neutrality in relation to values and thus greater certainty in conclusions. Scientific racism
drew on these characteristics and this prestige, particularly through biology, physical anthropology, and medicine, to conclude that African
Americans were racially distinct and inferior. These scientific investigations characteristically presented their conclusions through diagrams,
quantification in tabular form, and impersonal formulations.[4] By definition, the subjects of these studies were marginal to the scientific
community and thus unable to challenge these conclusions in terms to
which scientists would pay attention. There were two debilitating implications of this situation for African Americans who wished to challenge
this predominant tendency: once racial distinctiveness had been apparently demonstrated in ways that pointed to the inherent inferiority of
blacks the assumption too easily followed that they were entitled to no
more than inferior conditions, opportunities, and freedom. Second, this
way of dealing with race appeared to make illegitimate arguments in
favor of rights and equality based on moral, religious, and political
considerations, thus dismissing as irrelevant the substance of the tradition of racial egalitarianism of earlier decades.

There were some scattered efforts by African Americans to argue
different conclusions from the scientific racists within the framework
of contemporary work in biology and medicine, including an early
paper by DuBois on "The Conservation of Races" (1897), but these
had little apparent effect.[5] It was instead through the development of a
black *social* science, pioneered by the Atlanta University studies, that
some educated African Americans began to deal with the intellectual
dominance of scientific racism. As will be seen, moreover, the intellectual underpinnings of the detailed Atlanta investigations were
appropriately adapted to handling a major prop of scientific racism in
the strand of Social Darwinism that stressed the significance of heredity in shaping character and the mechanism of natural selection in
determining the superior position of one group rather than another.
This was an outlook that easily led to an emphasis on the differential
rates of evolution of different racial groups as "natural" and even,
sometimes, anticipation of the disappearance of the less evolved race
from a society in which it was in direct competition with a more highly
evolved one.[6]

4. Stepan and Gilman, "Appropriating the Idioms of Science," pp. 72–80.

5. DuBois, "The Conservation of Races" in *W.E.B. DuBois: Writings*, pp. 815–26.

6. James M. McPherson, *The Abolitionist Legacy. From Reconstruction to the NAACP*, Princeton, 1975, p. 118; George M. Fredrickson, *The Black Image in the White Mind. The Debate on Afro-American Character and Destiny, 1817–1914*, New York, 1971, pp. 322, 324.

By the time of his appointment to the Atlanta faculty to act as secretary to the third and subsequent conferences and to edit the studies, DuBois had for years been consciously preparing himself for conducting social investigations on African Americans through his studies at Harvard, in Germany, and in his first venture into large-scale sociological investigation in Philadelphia in 1896/97. His study at the University of Pennsylvania of "the social condition of the Colored People of the Seventh Ward of Philadelphia" built on graduate courses in political and social science and, in Berlin, statistical work on the American agricultural economy. He was now in a much better position to achieve his stated ambitions of 1893 that included getting "a position in one of the Negro universities and to seek to build up there a department of history and social science ... to study scientifically the Negro question past and present with a view to its best solution."[7]

The pursuit of truth through social science had a number of advantages for an African American intellectual at that date. It was not explicitly dependent on moral, religious, or political considerations and could draw authority for conclusions from the prestige of science, provided the investigations met certain criteria in their procedures and the results were presented in a proper form. Here was an implicit admission of the irrelevance of the language of morality and religion in the treatment of race intellectually. But at the same time it was an assertion of African American capacity to treat race scientifically in a wider context and in more detail than the scientific racists, even without any specific invocation to reform. On the contrary, it is noteworthy how the explicit rhetoric of social reform and moral uplift present in some degree in the first two studies substantially disappeared after DuBois took over. The annual volumes came to contain quite full accounts of the methods and procedures by which the investigation had been carried out. After a topic was chosen, schedules of questions and points on which information was required were prepared and sent out to correspondents – "mostly graduates of this and other Negro institutions of higher training" – who filled out the schedules after local inquiry. Other relevant sources of information were trawled and then followed the conference with discussion by speakers familiar with the topic. At the end of a year a report emerged that met the requirements of scientific form through summarizing and exemplifying the materials upon which the study was based, using statistical tabulations and "enlarged by the addition of historical and other

---

7. DuBois to Academic Council, Harvard University, April (?) 1890; DuBois to Educational Committee, John F. Slater Fund, 10 March 1893; DuBois to Trustees, John F. Slater Fund, 6 December 1893; C. C. Harrison [Provost, University of Pennsylvania] to Whom It May Concern, 15 August 1896, all in Herbert Aptheker, ed., *The Correspondence of W.E.B. DuBois*, vol. 1, Amherst, 1973, pp. 1, 7, 23, 25, 26, 40.

material." In addition, after a decade of the studies, eight of which had been under his supervision, DuBois instituted a second cycle of studies, producing new reports on the same topics ten years after the originals to aid measurement of change through comparison. Consequently there exist, to give two examples, studies of *The College-Bred Negro* in 1900 and 1910, and of *The Negro Artisan* in 1902 and 1912.[8]

As this account of the methods and materials of the studies suggests, there was a second virtue for African Americans in the social science approach within the context of a dominant scientific racism. "Difference" between whites and blacks could be accepted, indeed one side of it was documented by the studies, but without any need, or justification scientifically, for accepting as explanation the closed certainty of racial inferiority. This was because materials on the history of blacks, their social and economic environment, their limited and blocked opportunities, could be brought to bear and given explanatory weighting in the impersonal prose framework constructed by DuBois for the detailed information collected. Finally, more fundamentally, the perspective with which DuBois informed the studies was one of social and cultural evolution whose implications will be treated in more detail later. It is sufficient to note here that this is plain from the first report for which he was responsible, *Some Efforts of Negroes for Social Betterment* (1898)[9], that such evolution drew in part from distinctive African social and cultural experience, and that it was implicitly open-ended. The approach to race through social science thus potentially challenged conclusions as inadequate if they were cast in the terms purely or primarily of biological or medical science and the evolutionary emphasis challenged the *finality* of any scientific conclusions.

There are two other features of DuBois's project of the Atlanta studies that are significant for understanding later developments. Although he initially insisted that the pursuit of truth should not become mixed up with the aim of social reform, even before he began to withdraw from his "ivory tower" position the findings of the studies were essentially *corrective* of the conclusions of scientific racism and could clearly have policy implications. By the time of some of the later reports this is quite explicit: "We wish not only to make the Truth clear but to present it in such shape as will encourage and help social reform."[10]

8. George Bradford, ed., *Mortality Among Negroes in Cities*, Atlanta 1896, pp. 20–29; George Bradford, ed., *Social and Physical Conditions of Negroes in Cities*, Atlanta, 1897, pp. 26–28; DuBois, "The Laboratory in Sociology at Atlanta University" in *DuBois on Sociology and the Black Community*, pp. 63–64.

9. DuBois, ed., *Some Efforts of Negroes for Social Betterment*, Atlanta, 1898, pp. 43–44.

10. DuBois, "The Study of the Negro Problems," p. 80; DuBois, ed., *The Negro American Family*, Atlanta, 1909, p. 5.

The other crucial feature of the project was that it was mounted by and was largely dependent upon the efforts of the class of educated African Americans. DuBois invited other African American intellectuals to take part in the conferences and the contributions of blacks such as Kelly Miller and Monroe Work were printed in the studies alongside those of whites interested in southern problems, such as Frank Sanborn, Franz Boas, and Jane Addams. More important was the educated network through which the schedules of questions were completed. The reports were built upon returns and "statistical investigations" from students and graduates of Atlanta University and through similar work year after year from graduates of other black colleges such as Fisk, Spelman, and Howard. Partly, this was an economical way of proceeding when resources were so scarce, but it also consciously carried through DuBois's early intention "to collect capable young Negro students and to see how far they are capable of furthering by independent study and research, the best scientific work of the day." It was also linked to the explicit intention in DuBois's first report of training "talented members of this race to be leaders of thought and missionaries of culture" among the mass of the black population in the South. Therefore, in addition to offering a form of intellectual resistance to scientific racism in the way in which they were executed, the studies were perceived as an achievement of the expanding educated black elite of the South and were proposed as foreshadowing a larger set of responsibilities on the part of this elite towards the majority of the black population.[11]

The content of the studies makes it clear how, within the perspective of social and cultural evolution amongst African Americans, a number of sub-themes emerged that refined the idea of evolution as it applied to the mass of southern blacks. Under DuBois's direction, the annual reports on different facets of black life assumed that evolution towards a more civilized or "advanced" society was always most notably manifested in a growing commitment to the idea of division of labor and to increased differentiation of function in social and economic institutions. So far as southern blacks were concerned the broad pattern of evolution had been significantly influenced in two ways. First, blacks retained through the whole process some social and cultural baggage from Africa in the form of habits, assumptions, and ideas, but these were fragmentary as a result of the impact of the slave trade compared with what they might have been. "The ideas", of which some elements remained, "were

---

11. DuBois, ed., *Some Notes on Negro Crime, Particularly in Georgia* Atlanta, 1904, V; DuBois, *Dusk of Dawn*, p. 602; DuBois to Educational Committee, John F. Slater Fund, 10 March 1893 in Aptheker, ed., *Correspondence*, I, p. 25; DuBois, ed., *Some Efforts of American Negroes for Social Betterment*, p. 3.

not the highest, measured by modern standards, but they were far from the lowest, measured by the standards of primitive man." Second, the transplantation to America and the "unremitting toil" of slavery in most respects had marked a backward movement. However, it could not be concluded, DuBois wrote in *The Negro Church* (1903), that "every vestige of spontaneous social movement" was destroyed. The continuing role of the priest and preacher, for example, had led to the rapid spread of the church, especially after the Civil War, thus producing "the first distinctively Negro American social institution ... Christian ... but with many of the old customs still clinging to the services."[12]

This evolution with distinctive features had occurred, DuBois also emphasized, amongst a group that had not reached the economic development of the surrounding nation "and which perhaps never will surrender itself entirely to the ideas of the surrounding group." In other words, the conception of social and cultural evolution underlying the studies did not envisage that reaching an advanced state required complete assimilation of white American patterns and standards.[13] However, it is also likely that implicit awareness of the dominance of scientific racism was relevant to the particular attention the studies devoted to areas of southern black life in which evidence of evolution was plainly to be found. One other consequence of this focus, considering the studies as a whole, was the *relative* neglect of features of black life prevalent amongst the majority in rural areas and working on the land. Even on topics that seemingly comprehended rural blacks, such as *Notes on Negro Crime, Particularly in Georgia* (1904) most of the evidence collected and analyzed dealt with urban populations.

Much emerged nonetheless about developments in religion and the sort of institutional differentiation derived initially from church activity within black communities. The growth and vitality of the church, it was argued, arose from its being "the sole surviving institution of the African fatherland" and in the circumstances of slavery and the more recent situation "it assumed many functions which the other harshly suppressed social organs had to surrender; the Church became the center of amusements, of what little spontaneous economic activity remained, of education and of all social intercourse."[14] It was possible to distinguish easily between less and more advanced styles of religion within the black church. It was clear in rural Thomas County, Georgia, that "standards of slavery time and directly after still prevail" in the lack of any educated religious leaders and the style of worship that attracted the loyalty of the local black population. Regeneration in their eyes, it was

12. DuBois, ed., *The Negro Church*, Atlanta, 1903, pp. 1–5.
13. DuBois, ed., *Economic Cooperation among Negro Americans*, pp. 10–12.
14. DuBois, ed., *The Negro Church*, p. 5.

suggested, was most likely to arise from "the shout-producing discourse ... accompanied with weird cries and shrieks and contortions." Such was the competition to keep congregations that although changes for the better, in the emergence of slightly better educated younger ministers and "more intelligent worship" amongst newer denominations were discernible, many were still in "the old ruts." By contrast, Atlanta churches, reported a group of undergraduate social science students, had pastors of excellent character and high educational attainments. A mark of their standing and of the business- and professional-class character of their congregations was that "there is no emotionalism in the churches." They were also at the center of a proliferation of church groups indicative of "ability to organize and systematize, arrange a regular income and spend it effectively," a true measure of social and cultural advance. In the longer run the distinctive African heritage of "African churches in America" had contributed to their continuing, progressive disentanglement from white patronage and provided through their history "one of the most important examples of the meaning and working of Social Heredity as distinguished from Physical Heredity."[15]

The 1898 study on efforts at social betterment had shown earlier that some church-related groups were becoming "centers of systematic relief and reformatory work." Alongside them, however, were secret societies that were more socially selective because they required higher intelligence and "more quiet business-like persistence" for their specialized operations. They generated authoritative elites amongst the competent who were effectively able to direct regular resources to life and sickness insurance, even if in a social form that largely did away with "the democratic freedom of the church." Although some loss was equally involved, black insurance societies with separate boards of directors even more obviously represented "the saving, banking spirit among the Negroes and are the germ of commercial enterprise of a purer type."[16] Economic progress for the race was in the first instance assumed to aim at meeting and developing the market amongst blacks themselves for goods and services through small-scale, independently black-financed workshops, stores, and service industries. For that reason the experience of running community social betterment organizations was considered invaluable.

The real reason individual black business enterprise had not developed further, DuBois argued, was the effect of slavery that had "robbed the slaves of all thought of economic initiative." Lack of capital, moreover, because of a relative lack of opportunities for saving for invest-

---

15. Ibid., pp. 57–61, 73, 79, 153–54.
16. DuBois, ed., *Some Efforts of American Negroes for Social Betterment*, p. 17.

ment, was likely to remain a difficulty for many aspirant African American businessmen. Nevertheless, a beginning had been made by the end of the nineteenth century. It was perhaps inevitable that the categories of business occupation in which African Americans initially engaged grew out of the different occupations under slavery. By the time of *The Negro in Business* (1899), however, a new kind of business activity more suited to the historical experience, social environment, and economic circumstances of blacks was being documented and, with the publication of *Economic Cooperation among Negro Americans* (1907), given emphatic endorsement. This was cooperative business activity, particularly of the sort that brought it together with semi-social functions in the black community – funeral parlors, doctors linked to sick-benefit societies and druggists to both, private cemeteries, newspapers and publishing often connected to religious denominations or even individual congregations. Many of these were initially making a business virtue out of the necessity enforced by segregation. By 1907 they were represented as a distinctive departure in that "the new Negro business man caters to the colored trade" rather than to whites and often through cooperative efforts. The rhetoric is unmistakeable: this was an advance especially in the black urban areas "representing at least 300,000 persons" in which "the group economy approaches a complete system." The cooperative principle was in fact presented as a powerful force linking many facets of black life in the South and beyond and was able to be published in properly scientific diagrammatic form.[17]

Within the broad evolutionary schema of the studies, DuBois and his associates, sometimes explicitly and sometimes implicitly targeting the conclusions of scientific racism, were able to demonstrate the superiority of *their* brand of science to that of the scientific establishment. Their main method was to criticize the inadequacy of the evidence offered as the basis for some conclusion and provide superior evidence pointing to a different conclusion. In *Health and Physique of the Negro American* (1906), DuBois attacked evidence collected to support conclusions on the low brain-weights of African Americans as based on an inadequate sample and uncontrolled for the variables of age, stature, social class, occupation, nutrition, and cause of death. He had a thousand students at the Hampton Institute measured in a variety of ways and also produced additional new data from the United States Census to overturn accepted conclusions. Similarly, when the less than scientific James K. Vardaman nonetheless used census materials to charge that blacks constituted the most criminal element in the population, DuBois published detailed

17. Ibid., pp. 21–22; DuBois, ed., *The Negro in Business*, Atlanta 1899, pp. 6–9, 11–15; DuBois ed., *Economic Cooperation among Negro Americans*, pp. 179, 24–55, 73–92.

analyses in the 1904 report demonstrating the inadequacy of the census as a source of statistics on crime. He concluded that Roland P. Falkner's work, which criticized the 1890 census returns, "reduces the responsibility of the Negro for crime in this land from 30% to 19%." In addition, as Monroe Work's contribution to the volume on crime indicated, any surplus of criminal activity by African Americans above their proportion of the population could plausibly be accounted for by features of their social and economic environment rather than racial degeneracy.[18]

The sensitive question of black criminality makes it appropriate to add one qualification to the preceding argument. There remained some limited overlap within the studies of "old" and "new" discourses about race even under DuBois's direction. It is striking how prominent is the language of moral deficiency as explanation, and moral uplift as solution, in the 1896 and 1897 studies for which DuBois had no responsibility. A great deal of reliance is placed on the ability to choose, the will, and the moral restraint of African Americans to bring about improvement. Yet both in the report on crime and in *The Negro American Family* (1908) "moral uplift and inspiration among Negroes" find a prominent place in reducing crime and strengthening the family. The language of science and environment was predominant but did not exclude the older language of morality and individual effort. Neither of these rhetorics, however, sanctioned a conception of fixed racial difference, let alone innate black inferiority.[19]

The corrective content of the Atlanta University studies, even before the increasingly overt commitment to social reform in the later volumes, prompts inquiry as to what instruments of change were envisaged, to what extent they distinguished DuBois and his associates from others, and what effect the studies themselves had on the possibilities of change. Some of the remedies to encourage African American betterment had to lie with government. The taxation system in the southern states was perceived as carrying much of the blame for squeezing the position of a respectable and potentially exemplary black middle class. According to *The Negro Common School* (1901), much of the ignorance of the black population came from the fact that schools for African American children were inadequate in number and grossly underfunded, with only one million of three million children regularly attending school. Even those who could go to school had much shorter sessions than their white counterparts. Southern state governments, however,

18. Stepan and Gilman, "Appropriating the Idioms of Science," p. 96; DuBois, ed., *Some Notes on Negro Crime*, pp. 9–12, 15–16, 8–9, 32.

19. Bradford, ed., *Mortality of Negroes in Cities*, p. 9; Bradford, ed., *Social and Physical Conditions of Negroes in Cities*, pp. 4, 14–17, 21; DuBois, ed., *Notes on Negro Crime*, p. 65; DuBois, ed., *The Negro American Family*, pp. 36–37.

were unlikely to act, the same report recognized, when "the white rank and file" had not accepted the fundamental idea that a public school system for blacks was "a wise measure of self-defense to guard the State against the errors and crimes of sheer ignorance" and not a charitable gesture.[20]

Far from southern states being responsive, the studies recognized that public authorities actively contributed in several ways to the plight of African Americans. Ensuring residential segregation and refusing to maintain black neighborhoods damaged even the "better class" of blacks. Disproportionately heavy sentences on blacks and the convict-lease system constituted "the slavery in private hands of persons convicted of crimes and misdemeanours in the courts." The Atlanta studies themselves revealed that the political and judicial processes were much less likely to be channels for beneficial change than obstacles to it.[21]

As has already been suggested in the context of overlapping discourses, stress on self-help remained significant even though the language of moral uplift ceased to permeate discussion of the various topics. Not only in their personal moral conduct but, for example, in taking extra trouble to patronize the business establishments of members of their race, African Americans would ultimately be helping themselves. This had something in common with Booker T. Washington's outlook, but the differences were apparent from Washington's address to the 1902 conference printed in *The Negro Artisan*. Country life and work had to be the main concern of blacks, Washington declared, and only knowledge "harnessed to the real things of life" was worthwhile. Domestic service by blacks in the homes of southern whites was also important. "If we are wise and patient," he argued, "we can use all forms of service in a way not only to lift ourselves up, but to bind us eternally in fellowship and good will to the Southern white man by whose side we must live for all time." The strictures on appropriate education, the absence from Washington's picture of the growing, college-educated black elite and their relation to the rest of the black community, and his assumption of continued dependence on southern whites indicate major differences of outlook from that of the Atlanta studies despite a superficially common concern with self-help.[22]

If the studies revealed the difficulties of influencing the political process – even as they made clear its necessity – they still offered clear

---

20. Ibid., pp. 67–68; DuBois, ed., *The Negro Common School*, Atlanta, 1901, pp. ii, 93–95.

21. DuBois, ed., *Notes on Negro Crime*, pp. 5–8.

22. DuBois, ed., *Some Efforts of Negroes for Social Betterment*, pp. 47–48; DuBois, ed., *The Negro in Business*, p. 50; DuBois, ed. *The Negro Artisan*, Atlanta, 1902, pp. 6–7.

guidelines for activity by the new black educated, professional class and the emerging business class. Their functions were to advance understanding of black life, and use their professional skills to lift the race where possible and encourage "progressive" developments in the black community generally. By 1910, however, at least for DuBois, that was not enough. His disagreements with Washington became public from 1903 onwards as such factors as the extent of lynching of blacks in the South, the Atlanta riot of 1906, and the Brownsville incident of the same year combined to increase skepticism about the gradualist approach associated with Washington. DuBois began to move away from self-identification primarily as an academic social scientist when he assumed a leading role from 1905 on in the Niagara Movement. The program he and his associates articulated was much more militant in demanding voting rights, equal educational opportunities, and "the abolition of all caste distinctions." By the end of the decade, he indicated later, he realized that "not simply knowledge, not simply direct repression of evil, will reform the world ... the actions of men which are not due to lack of knowledge nor to evil intent, must be changed by influencing folkways, habits, customs and sub-conscious deeds." In 1910, resigning from Atlanta, he chose founder membership of the NAACP and editorship of *The Crisis* as the way to attempt this.[23]

From its first issue, DuBois's paper claimed to stand for the rights of men, irrespective of race, for the ideals of American democracy, and for "reasonable but earnest and persistent" efforts to achieve them. Although *The Crisis* was the official organ of the NAACP, an alliance of white liberals and some of the more militant members of the rising black middle class, DuBois from the start ran it in his own way and raised the question of what kind of voice or voices the paper should develop to make its impact. DuBois and other African American intellectuals had discussed the possibility of running a serious journal for several years and he had edited two short-lived periodicals while still at Atlanta. But was it to be a medium "through which he [the African American] presents his case to thinking white people, who after all are the arbiters of our destiny?" Or, should it attempt, when the race was "in a critical condition" to bring about "united, concerted effort" amongst blacks "which will save us from being crushed" by telling of "the deeds of themselves and their neighbors, interpreting the news of the world to them and inspiring them towards definite ideals?"[24]

23. James M. McPherson, *The Abolitionist Legacy*, pp. 368–93; DuBois, *Dusk of Dawn*, pp. 618, 716.

24. *The Crisis*, Nov. 1910, p. 10; Chas W. Chestnutt to DuBois, 27 June 1903, *Correspondence*, ed. Aptheker, I, p. 25; DuBois to Jacob Schiff, 14 April 1905, ibid., pp. 108–9.

In practice, from its earliest issues, at one level *The Crisis* built on what had been achieved at Atlanta by way of scientific analysis. DuBois published a paper by Franz Boas arguing against the supposed scientific evidence indicating black inferiority as well as later pieces by the German-born physiologist Jacques Loeb. These papers were used editorially to draw out argument that popularized some of the terms of intellectual resistance to racism. The language of science in dealing with race was extended into a quasi-political argument that claimed greater weight than that of mere opinion. This kind of discussion was supported by sharply phrased editorial paragraphs on the verbal and expressive forms that race prejudice characteristically took, DuBois relating the comment to some expression of prejudice in a popular publication. In both their popular and more formal expressions, claims to white racial superiority were taken apart, examined, and found wanting. Such education of consciousness DuBois saw as the first stage in a much larger role for *The Crisis* in "the freeing of ten million ... that means power and organization on a tremendous scale." Those who were necessary to the organization would be trained by the paper "not simply in its words, but in its manner, its pictures, its conception of life."[25]

The African Americans most likely to work actively for racial equality and most likely to be reached by the paper were those already rising in the world. Discrimination did not fall simply on those "who do not feel it and who by their position naturally fall outside the lines of discrimination [the underclass] but it comes with crushing weight upon those other Negroes to whom the reasons for discrimination do not apply in the slightest respect and they are thus made to bear a double burden." Even if they were to accept segregation wholesale "the White South does not want Separation but Subordination" so that African American political, economic, and social independence as the price of segregation would not be permitted by the South. What was happening there constituted the death of the democratic ideal.[26]

DuBois was relentless not only in arguing against this but in documenting the process in different areas of southern black life: the difficulties of acquiring land, the invasion of existing property, the degradation of black schools, and political exclusion. This kind of voice emerging from *The Crisis* was acceptable to white liberal elements in the NAACP alliance. It culminated logically, through the language of racial reconciliation in pursuit of justice, with hopes for joint activity in American communities. Hard though it was, DuBois acknowledged, for

25. *The Crisis*, Dec. 1910, pp. 22–25; ibid., June 1914, pp. 83–84; ibid., Dec. 1914, pp. 92–93; ibid., Nov. 1911, p. 26; ibid., Feb. 1915, pp. 182–83; DuBois to Joel Springarn, 28 October 1914, *Correspondence*, ed. Aptheker, I, p. 204.
26. *The Crisis*, Nov. 1910, p. 11; ibid., Feb. 1911, pp. 20–21.

African Americans to put aside their distrust of whites, he insisted "it is indeed the only way by which the burden shall fall and its former bearer led into the large upper chamber that looks toward the sunrise and that is named Peace."[27]

Coming from *The Crisis* at the same time, however, and interwoven with the analytical argument against prejudice and discrimination and its tireless exposure, was another kind of voice. This provoked unease and criticism amongst both blacks and whites who were themselves opposed in some measure to the caste system of the South. Amongst blacks it was expressed by those who were reluctant to abandon both the conciliatory tone and gradualist approach of Booker T. Washington. The caste system, DuBois editorialized, had advanced "under the silence, the absence of criticism, the kindly sentiments and widespread complacency" resulting from the dominance of Washington as a spokesman for African Americans. Prejudice had intensified with the growth of "numbers of intelligent and forceful black folk." DuBois's paper was there to contest the idea that only encouraging facts about the racial situation should be put forward; its job was to tell the truth and assert the right of an African American "to appear as a man among men."[28]

In that sense it spoke for the NAACP as "the new abolition society" committed to "agitation" against "the crying evil of race prejudice.... It is Pain; Pain is not good but Pain is necessary. Pain does not aggravate Disease – Disease causes Pain. Agitation does not mean Aggravation – Aggravation calls for Agitation in order that Remedy may be found." Blacks had to refuse to be silenced by protesting against the degradation of democracy produced by the caste system of the South. The tone was often Garrisonian. DuBois insisted, nonetheless, that the voice of the agitator and the voice of the scientific analyst could be combined. The cry of protest would be the more effective the greater amount of scientific truth it drew upon and the more sharply defined were the agitators' demands.[29]

The voice of agitation and the language of outrage became more prominent as *The Crisis* grew in size and in circulation during its first decade. DuBois's intense consciousness of the "color line" especially focuses upon its most unambiguous expression in the South – lynching. Lynching provoked his most passionate outbursts, his most biting irony, and an attempt to summon all the possibilities of the paper to bring

27. Ibid., Jan. 1911, p. 17; ibid., May, 1911, pp. 28–32; ibid., Feb. 1915, pp. 181–82; ibid., Jan. 1912, p. 121; ibid., July 1913, p. 130.

28. Ibid., June 1911, pp. 62–64; ibid., Dec. 1912, pp. 76–77.

29. Ibid., Dec. 1913, p. 88; ibid., Nov. 1910, p. 11; ibid., Jan. 1913, p. 129; ibid., Dec. 1910, pp. 16–17.

home the realities of the crime. Eventually, as will be argued below, lynching appeared to be the best key to understanding the nature of the South and rendered hollow any claims to American moral leadership in the world in the Wilson years. When a mentally disturbed black woman servant was lynched in Georgia in 1912 after killing her mistress, DuBois commented "with that progressive form of local government which constitutes every man his own sheriff, there seems to be no doubt that the colored woman is to have equal rights, privileges and protection with the colored man. There is to be no discrimination on the grounds of sex. Pinehurst has advanced ideas."[30] In July 1916 the paper published, not for the only time, a supplement detailing a lynching that had occurred in Waco, accompanied by horrifying photographs and a dismissal of any charge of bad taste as coming from people "who so hate the evil of the world that they are unwilling to be disturbed by it." This was the context in which DuBois chose to put America's posture in the international situation: "any talk of the moral leadership of this country in the world; any talk of the triumph of Christianity, or the spread of human cultures is ideal twaddle so long as the Waco lynching is possible."[31]

DuBois's developing inclination to see lynching as defining the essential nature of the white South was connected to what he concluded was the weakening of forces for progress in the region. The clearer this tendency became, the more distant the section was from fulfilling "the meaning of the twentieth century" as "the freeing of the individual soul." The South was "whirling in a back eddy, damming progress." In substantiating the weakness of progressive forces in *The Crisis*, DuBois drew on magazine writings by southerners to satirize the modern white inhabitant's presentation of himself as "a man who has assembled no new ideas as to democracy and social classes since 1863; he must be 'haughty,' intolerant and snobbish. His ancestors must have been 'aristocrats' and he must have had a black nanny whom he loved and as evidence of this love he now and then lynches her grandchildren." Southerners who were different, such as Walter Hines Page, had in effect been repudiated by the South that was more accurately represented by Vardaman, Blease, and Tillman. One factor in the changing tenor of DuBois's writing was precisely the need to respond to the race-baiting demagogues.[32]

Disenchantment with the possibilities of progress under any southern political leader, even "a scholar and a gentleman" like Woodrow Wilson, was the consequence of this conviction about the balance of

---

30. Ibid., Feb. 1912, p. 153; ibid., Aug. 1912, p. 196.
31. Ibid., July 1916, pp. 1–8, 135.
32. Ibid., Nov. 1915, p. 30; ibid., Nov. 1911, p. 25; ibid., Nov. 1913, p. 337.

forces in the South. Wilson had brought to Washington with him "in his closest counsels all the Negro-hating, disfranchising, lynching South." By the end of 1914, *The Crisis* concluded that, despite his high ideals, it was simply beyond Wilson's conception that black men should be treated as "independent human beings." His public declarations of concern for African Americans could only be insincere, as when he spoke in the South "as a Southerner" telling his audience they must know the needs of the Negro and sympathetically help him in every way but did no more while "lynching bees" proceeded across the South. By the time of the 1916 campaign, *The Crisis* expected nothing from Wilson, and DuBois indicated personally that he preferred Hughes.[33]

In the final years of DuBois's first decade as editor of *The Crisis*, the South was presented not merely as retarded in comparison with other regions of the country but as lacking in virtually any redeeming features, especially in those that it claimed for itself: "Does the thing which the South calls culture ... represent really a modern, civilized community? Is it not rather true that the former slave states stand today at least three hundred years behind the civilized world in all essential social and economic thought?" The South had become the quintessence of barbarism whose prime claim to civilization was the "modern forward-looking class [of] the educated Negro." The binary opposition that was thus posed between the white South and civilization not only underlay the repeated insistence thereafter on its lawlessness, wretched education system, exploitation of labor and the political unrepresentativeness of its spokesmen considering the southern population as a whole – all measures of its barbarism – but its use as an antithetical "other" in a variety of ways by DuBois and *The Crisis*.[34]

In conceptual, moral, and sometimes visual contrast, through photographs displayed in the paper, was placed the lynching, burning white South and the decorous, respectable black bourgeoisie about its social activities and intellectual, professional, and even athletic achievements. Here was a plain reversal and recontextualizing of the terms employed by white racists, broadly parallel to the reversals earlier attempted through social scientific research. Moreover, the South as the hateful "other" was a place literally to get as far away from as possible. When DuBois began to pay considerable attention to black migrations northward in the monthly issues of 1916 and 1917 his encouragement was passionate to the escapee "who wishes to be in close touch with civilization." It was his business to get out of the South as soon as possi-

---

33. Ibid., Dec. 1912, p. 75; ibid., Dec. 1914, p. 82; ibid., Feb. 1915, pp. 173–74; DuBois [for NAACP] to President Wilson, 10 October 1916, *Correspondence*, ed. Aptheker, I, pp. 217–19.
34. *The Crisis*, Mar. 1917, p. 216; ibid., Dec. 1918, p. 77; ibid., Feb. 1920, p. 171.

ble. Only months *after* his espousal of migration did DuBois turn to serious analysis of the actual causes of migration and the opportunities, but
also significant difficulties, in relocating to other parts of the country.
Social analysis followed slowly on passionate rejection of the South and
even then, in part at least, took the form of dubious distinctions between
northern and southern violence.[35]

This movement in DuBois's handling of the racial question provoked
unease amongst even some sympathetic whites because it was combined
with elements of what George Fredrickson has termed "romantic racialism" and DuBois's determination to maintain the editorial independence
of the paper. Romantic racialists recognized blacks as different from
whites and were inclined to believe that to a degree they always would
be.[36] In earlier years in the Atlanta studies, DuBois had given some
historical and cultural reasons to explain this. More immediately, some
reformers feared that these differences might be understood within a
fixed hierarchy and give comfort to white supremacists. DuBois, of
course, never understood the idea of separate black qualities in that way
in "The Conservation of Races," *The Souls of Black Folk*, or later. Yet
even without offering an opening to white supremacists, the idea of
distinct characteristics was in tension with the racial equalitarianism of
white members of the NAACP and conceivably made some whites feel
they were in danger of being outsiders. Mary White Ovington may have
meant this in her correspondence with DuBois in April 1914 about his
editorial conduct, when she defined her unease: "The magazine is the
organ of two races but its psychology is the psychology of the colored
race." DuBois, however, saw pressures upon his editorial independence
as evidence of the "color line" even within the NAACP. As he told Joel
Springarn, he believed that the only way to overcome the historical
inability of whites and blacks to work together in equality was "to see if
we could not have two branches of the same work one with a white head
and one with a colored."[37]

These tensions died down, though they did not entirely die away, in
part because on the foundations of his romantic racialism DuBois began,
without completing, an ideological structure that aimed at presenting not
merely some blacks as more civilized than most southern whites, but
some features of the "black ethos" as foreshadowing a higher form of
civilization that would be exemplary for southern and other whites. In

35. Ibid., Oct. 1916, p. 270; ibid., June 1917, pp. 63–66; ibid., Sep. 1917, p. 216; ibid.,
Jan. 1920, p. 105.

36. Frederickson, *The Black Image in the White Mind*, pp. 101–2; DuBois to Oswald
Garrison Villard, 18 March 1913, *Correspondence*, ed. Aptheker, I, p. 181.

37. James M. McPherson, *The Abolitionist Legacy*, p. 344; Mary White Ovington to
DuBois, 11 April 1914, *Correspondence*, ed. Aptheker, I, pp. 191–93; DuBois to Joel
Springarn, 28 October 1914, ibid., pp. 203, 206–7.

respect to both motherhood and sexual appetite, DuBois had suggested in the Atlanta studies that the black attitude was superior. Similarly, the cooperative economic inclinations of African Americans that pointed to "the wide distribution of capital and a more general equality of wealth and comfort" offered a superior ideal to individual acquisition. In the publication of stories and poetry by African American writers and reports on black artistic and musical creation, *The Crisis* hinted at "ideals higher than the world has realized in art and industry and social life."[38]

One other experience, widely shared by many southern blacks at the end of the first decade of *The Crisis*, linked the usage of the South as a barbarous region to the paper's outspokenness in racial politics. From his own trip to Europe at the end of the war and the editorial correspondence he received from black troops, DuBois recognized the enhanced determination of many of them to stand for their democratic rights on their return to the South. And he received reports of resistance to white mobs. His editorials in favor of the use of force in self-defence no longer chided or instructed his readers (and there were many more of them) but spoke directly on behalf of the militant amongst them. This way of handling white racism was far removed from the reliance on scientific truth in the studies and indicated, at least momentarily in the violent days of 1919, a very different relation to the mass of southern blacks.[39]

This essay has analyzed the personal evolution of DuBois through different kinds of intellectual activity and writing with rather different rationales. Yet the development is both continuous and more than individual. The terms in which DuBois dealt with race and racial difference changed, but also overlapped and combined from one phase to another in this period. They did so because he was responding to and helping to constitute the various and conflicting terms in which race was publicly discussed. His shifts also bore a broad relation to his assessments of the changing types and balance of forces in the South and the nation. Looked at in this way the evidence provided by the forms and substance of the studies and *The Crisis* under DuBois offers both a window on the South and a mirror held up to the man himself.

38. DuBois, ed., *The Negro American Family*, p. 42; DuBois, ed., *Economic Cooperation among Negro Americans*, p. 4; *The Crisis*, Dec. 1913, an extrapolation from accounts of black cultural activity typical of this phase of the magazine.

39. Wm. A. Hewlett to DuBois, 26 August 1919, *Correspondence*, ed. Aptheker, I, pp. 234–35; Rev. Dr. James Arthur Martin to DuBois, 30 May 1919, ibid., pp. 233–34; *The Crisis*, Oct. 1916, pp. 270–71; ibid., Sept. 1919, p. 231; ibid., Nov. 1919, p. 335.

8

The Role of Intellectual History in the Histories of the Civil Rights Movement

Richard King

Neither the influence of ideas *on* or *in* the civil rights movement has been significantly dealt with in its otherwise rich historiography. This is all the more surprising since the figure now most identified with the movement, Martin Luther King, Jr., held a Ph.D. in philosophical theology, and the "S" in SNCC stood for "Student." Indeed, SNCC's spiritual leader was Robert Moses, an M.A. in philosophy who had done work on Albert Camus, while the college students – white and African American – who made up the SNCC cadres read and argued about Gandhi, Thoreau, Camus, Sartre, Baldwin, and Niebuhr in those early years. Without a fuller account of how ideas and experience related to one another in the movement, we can hardly do justice to its full complexity, particularly in the areas of political thought and culture. As Clayborne Carson has written: "Although the literature of the black struggle has traditionally paid little attention to the intellectual content of black politics, movement activists of the 1960s made a profound, often ignored, contribution to political thinking."[1]

I would like to explore in this essay some of the possible explanations for this inadequacy, briefly sketch in a way of understanding the movement as an intellectual phenomenon, and then discuss two instances in which the intellectual historian can aid our understanding of the movement. The first is by determining the meaning(s) of "freedom," a crucial term in movement rhetoric, and hence for movement goals. The second is through an analysis of Keith Miller's recent claims about the sources of Martin Luther King's thought and rhetoric, King being the one movement figure who has been treated as a serious thinker. Miller has argued that the dominant influence on King's life was southern black culture, what he refers to in *Voice of Deliverance* (1992) as

---

1. Clayborne Carson, "Charismatic Leadership in the Mass Struggle," *Journal of American History*, vol. 74, 1987, pp. 448–54.

"folk religion" rather than the thoughts of "Great White Thinkers."[2] This interpretation of King is likely to become the wave of the historiographical future. It is consequently important that it should be carefully examined.

Some early critics of the movement did maintain that it was too dependent on "white" political, social, or cultural thought. It is only necessary to read Addison Gayle's *The Black Aesthetic* (1971) to hear early, full-throated protests against understanding a "black" movement, or the black experience generally, in "white" terms, and to detect the coincidence of intellectual assessment with skin color. According to Larry Neal, for instance: "It is the opinion of many Black writers, I among them, that the Western aesthetic has run its course." He went on to quote Don L. Lee's argument that "We must destroy Faulkner, dick, jane, and other perpetrators of evil. It's time for DuBois, Nat Turner and Kwame Nkrumah. As Frantz Fanon points out: destroy the culture and you destroy the people." John O'Neal sounded a variation on this theme when he asserted that "Western culture is simply decadent."[3]

This line of reasoning suggested that the intellectual and cultural heritage of the West was the wrong resource for African Americans to have exploited in their struggle for liberation. Moreover, it encouraged the dubious claim that to rediscover the African and Afro-American sources of black insurgency required a jettisoning of the western intellectual tradition of political and cultural thought. Indeed, inasmuch as it drew upon ideas of white/western bourgeois provenance, the civil rights movement itself was perceived not as a solution but as part of the problem. The difficulty with this approach is that, as well as assuming that intellectual achievement is a characteristic of Western white – rather than Afro-American or African – culture, it also ignores the degree to which black thinkers such as Fanon or DuBois were the products of high European culture. One univocal source of intellectual sustenance is simply replaced by another. Stark oppositions replace interaction and mutual enrichment.

2. Keith Miller, *Voice of Deliverance: The Language of Martin Luther King Jr. and Its Sources*, New York, 1992, p. 7. Miller's "Composing Martin Luther King, Jr.," *PMLA*, vol. 105, 1990, pp. 70–82, is a compressed version of the book, but with more attention to King's authorship of his books than to his writings as a graduate student. See also Cornel West, "The Religious Foundations of the Thought of Martin Luther King, Jr." in *We Shall Overcome: Martin Luther King, Jr. and the Black Freedom Struggle*, ed. Peter J. Albert and Ronald Hoffman, New York, 1990, pp. 113–29, for a more balanced version of the kind of argument Miller is presenting. This essay represents an attempt to summarize my approach to the civil rights movement in *Civil Rights and the Idea of Freedom*, New York, 1992. I have incorporated some material from the book, but though I dealt briefly with Miller's *PMLA* article there, *Voice of Deliverance* appeared too late for me to include a response to it.

3. Addison Gayle, ed., *The Black Aesthetic*, Garden City, N.Y., 1971, pp. 58, 47.

Such a view also forgets that the necessity for the movement's intellectual and theoretical replenishment had become clear for civil rights leaders such as SNCC's James Forman even by the mid–1960s. Forman, at that time, was reading, and urging others to read, Malcolm X, Mao, Che, Nkrumah, and Fanon among others.[4] None of these activist/intellectuals had a metropolitan, white, bourgeois background. Nevertheless, western ideas of liberation and revolution deriving from Hegel, Marx, Freud, and Sartre among others were essential, sometimes central, components in their vision. The influence of Fanon among radical sectors of the movement associated with SNCC and then the Black Panthers was particularly strong. As one observer was told during the urban rioting of the 1960s: "No one of them [the rioters] hasn't read the Bible ... Fanon ... you'd better get this book. Every brother on a rooftop can quote Fanon."[5] Finally, one would have to be deaf to miss the significance of the political self-education of black radicals such as Eldridge Cleaver, Huey Newton, Bobby Seale, and George Jackson while they were in prison, a fact that led one observer to liken these figures to "Bigger Thomas with a reading list."[6] The sources of their political *Bildung* were, needless to say, not just non-Western, as any reading of their texts will quickly reveal.

In addition, the civil rights movement itself was of paramount importance in the rediscovery of the Afro-American intellectual and cultural tradition and the political importance of the concept of black culture in the post-movement years. This is the area where the movement's greatest energizing effect on the intellectual life of Afro-Americans can be detected. As August Meier and Elliott Rudwick observe in *Black History and the History Profession, 1915–1980* (1986), by the "middle of the decade [1950s] ... sales of Franklin's survey reached a vanishing point." But there were "beginnings of curriculum revisions" between 1963 and 1965, and they were "one of the significant by-products of the current Civil Rights Revolution."[7] Meier and Rudwick have suggested, therefore, that it was the movement that revitalized black intellectual and cultural traditions rather than itself being an outgrowth of an African American intellectual renaissance. With the effects of the movement fully registered, the intellectual and historiographical contours of Afro-American – and American – history have never been the same.

---

4. James Forman, *The Making of Black Revolutionaries*, New York, 1972.

5. Don Watts quoted in Aristide and Vera Zolberg, "The Americanization of Frantz Fanon," *The Public Interest*, vol. 9, 1967, p. 50.

6. I have not been able to verify the source of this quotation.

7. August Meier and Elliott Rudwick, *Black History and the History Profession, 1915–1980*, Urbana, 1986, p. 176.

Another possible explanation for the neglect of the intellectual dimensions of the movement builds on the assumption that the civil rights movement was political and social rather than intellectual in character. It was a mass movement rather than the movement of an elite that took ideas seriously. There is a certain cogency to this position. It would be hard to find a single master intellect – a Marx or Rousseau – or theoretical vision that shaped or permeated the whole movement. Yet the movement itself was suffused with a rhetoric of freedom, and also with that of equality, rights, justice, democracy, and citizenship. If we are not to dismiss all this as "mere" rhetoric, then these concepts that were so central to the political discourse of the movement must be interrogated and an effort made to recapture their meaning.[8] Because grassroots participants were not intellectuals does not mean they remained uninterested in "big" conceptual issues. It is a banality worth repeating that ordinary people articulate intellectual and spiritual concerns beyond their own immediate self-interest and worries about survival. To think otherwise is to condescend to rather than understand them.

Moreover, to say that the movement was primarily concerned with political action does not begin to reveal what "political" meant in that context. A narrow view that the movement was essentially concerned with the destruction of Jim Crow has been succinctly expressed by J. Mills Thornton: "From the perspective of the ideal of individual liberty, the Civil Rights Movement ended because, with the Civil Rights Act of 1964, the Voting Rights Act of 1965 and finally the Fair Housing Act of 1968, the movement had achieved its goal."[9] To accomplish this end, however, it should not be forgotten that the cadre of lawyers, trained at Howard Law School under the guidance of Charles Hamilton Houston and led in their long march through the nation's legal institutions by Thurgood Marshall, were highly trained constitutional lawyers, what Gramsci called "organic intellectuals," without whose work the civil rights movement in its activist phase would have been unimaginable. Their political action took the form of legal/ constitutional thinking and

8. Among the oral histories of the movement, Howell Raines, *My Soul is Rested: Movement Days in the Deep South Remembered*, New York, 1978, is particularly useful, while the Civil Rights Documentation Project in the Morland-Spingarn Collection at Howard University in Washington, D.C. includes a great number of yet unpublished interviews with movement participants conducted in the late 1960s. Two valuable studies of the language of politics are William Connolly, *The Terms of Political Discourse*, 2nd ed., Oxford, 1983, and Daniel T. Rodgers, *Contested Truths: Keywords in American Politics Since Independence*, New York, 1987. In general, the work in the history of political thought of Quentin Skinner and J.G.A. Pocock has emphasized the need to pay close attention to political language and the context of its utterance.

9. J. Mills Thornton, in *The Civil Rights Movement in America*, ed. Charles Eagles, Jackson, Miss., 1986, p. 149.

argumentation amongst themselves, in legal journals, and, of course, in the courts between the early 1930s and the 1960s.[10]

The main objectives of the classic civil rights movement were, in fact, far from exhausted by the eradication of Jim Crow in all its manifestations. Pervading the history of the movement was another major *leitmotif*: the reconstitution of Afro-American identity. Part of Fanon's great appeal was that he offered a vocabulary, however inadequate, for describing and explaining how the older "slave" or "colonised" self could be destroyed and how a new, free self could be created. For this project the civil rights movement, as well as the black consciousness movement, needed all the intellectual help it could find. A major tragedy of the movement was its failure to find, or the Western as well as African and Afro-American traditions' failure to supply, appropriate theoretical models for understanding or achieving collective self-respect or "somebodyness." Even now we have no adequate theoretical account of how – or if – participation in political struggles permanently transforms identity.

Another type of explanation cuts closer to the historiographical bone, but is also more ambiguous. It relates to the dominance throughout the 1970s and into the 1980s of the by now not so "new" social history. This type of history attempts to recapture the historical reality of common people, rather than concentrating on the thought and action of elites. It is written "from the bottom up." It attempts a "depiction of traditions, experiences and struggles," while stressing, according to T.J. Jackson Lears, the "autonomy and vitality of subordinate cultures."[11] Its practitioners make extensive use of "non-literary" (in the conventional sense) sources, including, to quote Ira Berlin, "census rolls, tax lists, and voting registers." Finally, fields such as statistics, and emerging subdisciplines such as demography and anthropology, supply new models for understanding social structure and the operations of power. Family and community rather than the larger society and polity generally receive most attention.[12]

10. See Genna Rae McNeil, *Groundwork: Charles Hamilton Houston and the Struggle for Civil Rights*, Philadelphia, 1983; Mark Tushnet, *The NAACP's Legal Strategy vs Segregated Education 1925–1950*, Chapel Hill, 1987, and his "In Constitutional Law: The Equal Protection Clause, Dr. DuBois, and Charles Hamilton Houston," *Journal of American History*, vol. 74, 1987, pp. 884–903. Tushnet's work shows the way that unpacking and analyzing political-legal concepts, in this case "equality," can enrich our understanding of the pre-history of the movement.

11. For a descriptive analysis of the new social history, see James Henretta, "Social History as Lived and Written," *American Historical Review*, vol. 84, 1979, pp. 1293–1322; T.J. Jackson Lears, "The Concept of Cultural Hegemony: Problems and Possibilities," *American Historical Review*, vol. 90, 1985, p. 573.

12. Ira Berlin, *Slaves Without Masters: The Free Negro in the Antebellum South*, New York, 1974, xix–xx.

All this seems unexceptionable and its effects can readily be seen in the most recent work done on the movement. The historiographical tendency has been to shift attention from the national level to the politics of and within the movement, to downplay the importance of movement elites, especially leaders such as King, and to emphasize the crucial role of grassroots participants. David Garrow used a quotation from Ella Baker to clinch his argument along these lines in *Bearing the Cross* (1986): "The movement made Martin rather than Martin making the movement."[13] But though their purposes are more polemical and their argumentative context different from mine, Eugene Genovese and Elizabeth Fox-Genovese have identified the neglect of intellectual history as a major shortcoming of the new social history. "The withdrawal from intellectual and political history," they insist, "constitutes an indefensible denial of the centrality of formal political power and of elite culture in the development of society."[14] In essence, the new social history deploys sophisticated social science models and methods to show the unimportance of specialized intellectual life, as opposed to describing daily cultural life and crucial transformations in popular consciousness or *mentalité*.

Despite or because of the suspicion with which social and intellectual historians view one another, the writing of American intellectual history has been affected both by the new social history and theoretical developments in Europe and America. "It is now uncontroversial," according to James Kloppenberg, "to conclude that the non-historical study of the history of ideas is dead.... Just as social historians have turned increasingly to reconstructing the past as it was lived, so intellectual historians have tried to reconstruct ideas as they were thought." T.J. Jackson Lears has also noted the pressure of the new social history on intellectual and cultural history by claiming that Gramsci's work gives intellectual historians "an opportunity to connect ideas with the 'social matrix' that they are constantly being urged to locate."[15] Although it is important for the intellectual historian to maintain a tension between historicizing past ideas and paying close attention to their internal logic, between contex-

13. Quoted in David Garrow, *Bearing the Cross: Martin Luther King, Jr. and the Southern Christian Leadership Conference*, New York, 1986, p. 625.

14. Elizabeth Fox-Genovese and Eugene D. Genovese, "The Political Crisis of Social History: Class Struggle as Subject and Object," *The Fruits of Merchant Capital: Slavery and Bourgeois Property in the Rise and Expansion of Capital*, New York, 1983, pp. 179–212.

15. James Kloppenberg, "The Virtues of Liberalism: Christianity, Republicanism and Ethics in Early American Political Discourse," *Journal of American History*, vol. 74, 1987, pp. 10, 11; Lears, "Concept of Cultural Hegemony," p. 572. For the relationship of the new social history to intellectual history, see Laurence Veysey, "Intellectual History and the New Social History," in *New Directions in American Intellectual History*, ed. John Higham and Paul Conkin, Baltimore, 1979, pp. 3–26.

tualizing and contesting them, and to emphasize the way in which ideas can move across historical divides and affect new historical contexts, the impact of social history upon intellectual history has been generally beneficial.

Several theoretical conclusions accompany this newly emerging consensus in the human sciences, however. In the first place, the metaphysical dualism between Idealism and Materialism, between ideology and reality, no longer has any significant theoretical importance for doing history. The assumption that consciousness precedes society – or the opposite – is a metaphysical not an empirical claim. Specifically, to refer to the theme of "Race and Class in the American South," it is a *theoretical* choice that allows someone to privilege class over race or race over class in understanding the modern South. Barbara Jean Fields, for example, is correct when she argues that racism can never be the only explanation for anything, that racism assumes many different forms, and that racial antipathy can be suspended and alliances formed across racial lines. Thus race as a theoretical or historical concept is thoroughly ideological. But so is class, at least if it is defined as Fields does, by having it "refer to a material circumstance: the inequality of human beings from the standpoint of social power." Another way of saying this would be to accept that class, i.e., inequality of power, needs explaining and is mediated by all sorts of other factors such as economic structures, religion, region, culture – and racial consciousness. In sum, both race and class are "imaginary" constructs producing real effects.[16]

Second, it follows from the abandonment of the Idealism-Materialism dualism that the dichotomy drawn between the historian's effort to understand the *reasons* historical agents have for acting as opposed to identifying the structural *causes* underlying those actions is just as otiose. This does not mean that there are no strategic reasons for emphasizing the one over the other in a specific context. The important point is that reasons or causes do not refer to separate ontological areas whose boundaries are somehow inviolate. For instance, someone might want to write the history of the civil rights movement in terms of the long-range historical, institutional, and economic causes that set the stage for its success – and its limitations. Another person might want to chart the developing consciousness of southern blacks and the role that

---

16. Barbara Fields, "Ideology and Race in American History," in *Region, Race and Reconstruction*, ed. Morgan Kousser and James M. McPherson, New York, 1982, p. 150. Fields does admit that class is also a mediated term, yet finally treats it in the way she claims race has been treated, as having "transcendent, almost metaphysical status" (p. 144). Another problem is that her definition of class in terms of power differential is not sufficient to distinguish it from other sorts of power differentials: that is, to define class in such a general way strips it of most of its content.

ideas played in creating awareness that significant social and political change was possible after 1954 within the South. These two approaches could even be combined. But no one approach reflects reality or the nature of things more accurately than any other one.

An individual example might make the point clearer: why did Rosa Parks refuse to vacate her seat on the Montgomery bus that fateful 1 December 1955? One type of account would suggest that Parks's action was a function of her physical and emotional weariness arising from the constant wear and tear of her job as a seamstress in which she was, as an African American woman, undoubtedly underpaid and over-worked. Her action derived from her experience that was, in turn, the product of the common experience of an oppressed social group or groups. Clearly, race, class, and gender are relevant categories of analysis here. Yet once we have located certain social and economic determinants producing inequalities of power, there is little or nothing else to say about the action arising from that experience. Certainly, no intellectual history or history of black consciousness could be very informative on this matter.

And yet, Rosa Parks was also the secretary of the local NAACP, and was thus already involved in the fight against Jim Crow. There was certainly no economic advantage to her action, while thousands in her situation and worse accepted the basic conditions of segregated exis-tence. Even more revealing is the fact that Mrs. Parks had attended the Highlander Folk School in Monteagle, Tennessee in the summer of 1953. There, she and other potential civil rights activists of both races learned about the theory and practice of non-violence and engaged in group work, resulting in her political education. Without such prior intellectual/political education, it is unlikely that Parks would ever have acted. As Adam Fairclough has written, Parks's action in Montgomery was "the purposeful act of a politically aware person."[17] From this perspective, the historian does, after all, have something to explain, reasons and motivations to explore, intellectual and cultural influences to reconstruct. The mere fact of exploitation or discrimination is inade-quate by itself to explain action taken to correct it.

Which is the best explanation? Which dimension of reality – reasons or causes, consciousness or structures – should be privileged? This seems in many ways an undecidable issue. The crucial thing is that the focus should fall on an actor and an action in a certain historical context or set of contexts, the relevance of which will vary with the purpose of the historian's inquiry.

---

17. Adam Fairclough, *To Redeem the Soul of America: The Southern Christian Leadership Conference and Martin Luther King, Jr.*, Athens, Ga., 1987, p. 16.

There may well be other, more clear-cut cases where the intellectual historian can help promote understanding of the civil rights movement. For those who have been convinced by the claims of the new social history and/or are wary of attributing too much, if any, influence to the dominant white, elitist culture, the proper level at which to analyze the forms of political and ethical consciousness present in the movement and its intellectual leaders such as Dr. King is southern black culture. Here the emphasis falls primarily upon what Keith Miller calls the "black folk religion" of the South, both as a social institution and as cultural discourse permeated by biblical Christianity in general, and by the historical experience of slavery and segregation specifically. In this way, imagery and narratives, themes and ideas will be grounded in the daily life and accessible forms of life shared by Afro-Americans in the South.

On the other hand, the bias of the intellectual historian would be toward analyzing those intellectual elites, white and black, and those institutions of learning, again white and black, where people were trained in the specialized analysis, manipulation and articulation of written texts and complex systems of thought. Intellectual history's claim would be that without understanding this intellectual and cultural context, one just as socially and institutionally "real" as the culture of everyday life of southern blacks, the civil rights movement itself cannot be properly understood.[18]

If we turn to the rhetoric of the movement, the major weight placed upon "freedom" seems undeniable. But such a ubiquitous term surely deserves analysis in terms of the possible contexts of use, and hence meaning, associated with it. Since the concept of freedom can be found in such widely disparate contexts, past and present, it is imperative to go inside some of those contexts. But the intellectual historian does not assume *a priori* that freedom has one fixed meaning in Western or American or Southern or Afro-American political discourse. To establish the meaning(s) of a term such as freedom does not depend on there being a core "real" meaning of the term, against which its variants are measured.[19] That said, the striking thing about most accounts of the movement is that they are largely silent on the issue of what freedom meant.[20]

18. As David Harlan has observed in "Intellectual History and the Return of Literature," *American Historical Review*, vol. 34, 1989, pp. 581–609, one major difficulty facing intellectual historians – and social historians – is to decide what the proper context for understanding the effects of theories or ideas is.

19. Here I depart from Orlando Patterson's *Freedom: Freedom in the Making of Western Culture*, New York, 1991. He sees freedom as having one historically determined meaning, though he grants that the general concept/value of freedom is composed of a "chordal triad" of sovereignal, personal, and civic freedom.

20. An exception here is Robert Penn Warren, *Who Speaks for the Negro?*, New York, 1965, in which one of the questions Warren posed those he interviewed concerned the meaning of freedom. Unfortunately, the answers were rarely interesting.

The historian of Afro-American experience might begin by arguing that to understand the way freedom was used in the movement, it is necessary to focus on the centrality of the "Exodus" story or narrative in the history of Judaism and Christianity, in the history of Protestant Christianity in North America going back to the Puritans, and especially in the history of Afro-American Christianity. That story is understood as a figural prophecy of the liberation of Afro-Americans, as God's chosen people, from bondage in the United States. The central importance of this narrative of collective liberation from actual slavery, as well as spiritual liberation from the bondage of sin, made it all but inevitable that freedom would become one of the main values – and perhaps the prime value – in Afro-American self-understanding.[21] It was hardly surprising, therefore, that Martin Luther King in that last address in Memphis thundered that (like Moses) "I've been to the mountain top," or that his audience responded as it did. Where slavery had been, emancipation had come. Where the Civil War had led to black emancipation, there would be the movement and Dr. King to lead the exodus from Jim Crow.

In spite of the importance of Afro-American Christianity in imparting to freedom a narrative meaning with biblical and historical resonances, this comes nowhere near exhausting the meaning of freedom. For the ambience of the movement was secular as well as sacred: not only spirituals but also secularized "freedom songs" were mainstays of movement morale and group action. If a literal collective exodus from America's "Egypt" back to the "promised land" of Africa was impossible, or not even a universally desired goal, freedom could still assume a psychological meaning in a culture accustomed to talking about and experiencing spiritual transformations, i.e., being saved. In secular terms, consequently, another meaning of freedom in the movement was the achievement of some sort of new sense of self, what Dr. King called "somebodyness" and what a black newspaper man in Albany, Georgia identified as "self-respect." Another movement participant, Edward Brown, the brother of H. Rap Brown, suggested that the ideology of the movement had to "do with freedom and breaking dependency; dependency of any kind." SNCC's John Lewis talked of a new feeling of being "the free agent."[22] Other terms associated with "positive" freedom such as "autonomy" and "self-determination" were also used to refer to a new psychological state of being.

21. Strangely, Patterson does not include collective liberation among the core components of freedom, an omission reflected in his neglect of the biblical narrative of Exodus in the history of the value and idea of freedom. See Patterson, *Freedom*, pp. 33–34.
22. A.D. Searles in Pat Watters, *Down to Now: Reflections on the Southern Civil Rights Movement*, New York, 1971, p. 158; Edward Brown interview, Civil Rights Documentation Project, p. 62; John Lewis in William Beardslee, *The Way Out Must Lead In*, Westport, Conn., 1983, p. 8.

All of this echoed a coherent line of essentially secular black thinking stretching back through Henry Highland Garnet and Frederick Douglass to David Walker that stressed the idea that "To be dependent is to be degraded."[23] Indeed, Frantz Fanon's therapeutics of violence had in certain ways been anticipated by Douglass's argument during the Civil War that the only way to win manhood was to take up arms.

It is worth noting that not only have several varieties of modern nationalism (and racial-ethnic exceptionalism in Protestant countries) taken the Exodus study of chosenness and deliverance as paradigmatic, but also that the notion of spiritual transformation has been secularized into a psychological, as well as an ethical and political theoretical, concept of autonomy and self-determination. This is not to say that civil rights leaders or followers were avid students of Kant. But black philosophers such as Bernard Boxill and Lawrence Thomas have explored the links between movement concerns with freedom as a form of self-respect and contemporary ethical and political theory's concern with autonomy and self-respect. "If we are self-respecting," Thomas claims, we feel we deserve "full moral status" and "the basic rights of that status" by virtue of being a person.[24]

The civil rights movement also operated within a profoundly liberal political and legal culture. This conceived of freedom as the removal of obstacles to choices and actions within a framework of equal access to and applicability of the laws. In fact, "freedom of choice," one way of expressing this liberal form of "negative" freedom, became a slogan used by whites to preserve predominantly white schools in the South. The concept of negative freedom, however, was also the basis of the constitutional challenge to segregation, not just as a restriction on this or that liberty or violation of this or that right, but as an unfair restraint on action and as an outrage to freedom as equal status before the law.

Moreover, although Martin Luther King's vision of a "beloved community" went beyond the liberal notion of a society of equals with-out, what John Rawls calls, a "comprehensive notion of the good," it is worth emphasizing that the idea of civil disobedience is central to radical liberalism of the American variety.[25] In civil disobedience, the actor temporarily gives up her or his freedom in order to illuminate the profounder restriction upon freedom that, for instance, is exemplified by segregation laws. In agreeing to suffer the consequences of disobedience,

23. Henry Highland Garnet in John Bracey, August Meier, and Elliott Rudwick eds., *Black Nationalism in America*, Indianapolis, 1970, p. 43.

24. Lawrence Thomas, "Self-Respect: Theory and Practice," *Philosophy Born of Struggle*, ed. Leonard Harris, Dubuque, Iowa, 1983, p. 176.

25. See John Rawls, "The Priority of Right and Ideas of the Good," *Philosophy and Public Affairs*, vol. 17, 1988, pp. 251–76.

therefore, figures like King showed their devotion, not hostility, to the American constitutional system. Moreover, though the abolition of Jim Crow affected black Southerners as a whole, the constitutional language emphasized the protection or retrieval of individual constitutional (and for King, God-given) rights. This appeal to rights has generally been at the center of American liberalism, particularly in its radical manifestations. From this perspective, rights are particular specifications upon freedom and generally, though not always, concerned with removing restrictions or protecting against their imposition rather than enjoining positive or substantive commitments. In other words, rights generally specify what may not be done rather than what one should do.[26]

A fourth idea of freedom at work in the civil rights movement is much harder to pin down. It has to do with the identification of freedom with speaking and acting in public on matters having to do with the common or public interest. As Edward Brown observed about the ideology of the SNCC wing of the movement, the "ideology has to do with freedom, it has to do with democracy, in terms of people participating in decisions – it has to do with the whole rebuilding of the sense of community."[27] No trace of religious sentiment nor any expression of "folk religion" appears in this passage. If we look back to the history of republicanism/civic humanism or forward to a contemporary thinker such as Hannah Arendt, we find a similar emphasis upon freedom as the specific capacity, duty and, most importantly, privilege of the citizen. Though it entails freedom as equal status, political freedom also assumes a certain commitment of subordinate individual interests to the common good. At this point participatory freedom begins to intersect freedom as self-transformation, as involving a change in character, and departs from the spirit of liberal or negative freedom. Nevertheless, King's idea of *agape*, derived from Christian theology but turned to political effect, was one virtue term that the religious sector of the movement sought to inculcate in its participants, while racial solidarity came to define political virtue among movement radicals after the mid–1960s.

Arendt also emphasizes the virtuosity and courage required to speak and act in public, qualities that not only King but any number of civil rights leaders and followers displayed in abundance.[28] The power of

26. For this idea of rights as specifications on freedom, see Rodgers, *Contested Truths*, p. 219; and Agnes Heller, "Freedom as a Value Idea and the Interpretation of Human Rights," *Eastern Left, Western Left*, Atlantic Highlands, N.J., pp. 146–60. See Edward Andrew, *Shylock's Rights*, Toronto, 1988, pp. 3–22, for the distinction between "rights" and "right."

27. Edward Brown, Civil Rights Documentation Project, p. 64.

28. See Arendt, "What is Freedom?" *Between Past and Future*, Cleveland, Ohio, 1961, pp. 143–72, for an introduction to her ideas of politics, action, and freedom.

collective public speech and action to illuminate the nature of the public realm and to extend the literal and virtual space of public appearance, indeed, is nowhere better exemplified than in the civil rights movement. As King wrote, "It [the power structure of Birmingham, Alabama] was imprisoned in a luminous glare revealing the naked truth to the whole world."[29] Where liberal freedom emphasizes the protection of individual and private interests by asserting rights, the participatory idea of freedom sees freedom most importantly as public action. Where the individual is a rights-bearer in the liberal ethos, he or she is primarily a citizen in the participatory tradition of freedom. No one reading the oral histories of the movement can miss the importance of the rhetoric of citizenship nor the sense of release that came from participating in the movement and in becoming political beings. Nor can anyone overlook the willingness of participants to risk their lives for the good of the group and the nation.

Undoubtedly, these four types or discourses of freedom do not exhaust the dimensions of freedom expressed in the movement.[30] But delineating them does convey something of the sheer variety of meanings of "freedom." It also conveys something of the rich, complex, and sometimes contradictory weave of political traditions – European, American, Afro-American, even Southern; liberal and republican; radical and religious – at work in the thought and rhetoric of the movement. It is not possible to fathom the meaning of freedom in the movement without considering the influence of African American Christianity. But to assume, on the basis of this alone, that we have understood everything about the meaning and deployment of the rhetoric of freedom is naive. Most importantly, to widen the focus beyond southern black culture implies that *both* the rhetoric of freedom at the grassroots level of movement activity and the ideas of freedom in formal political thought are relevant to any effort to capture the multifaceted nature of the movement.

This leads on to the question of Martin Luther King's authorship and ultimately the source of his ideas and of his vision. In discussing these matters, it will be assumed – and accepted as undeniable – that, by any common understanding of the term, King was guilty of plagiarism in his dissertation (and some of his papers written in divinity school), and that swatches of his books and articles were not only ghost-written but taken sometimes word-for-word, often thought-for-thought, from other texts

29. Martin Luther King, *Why We Can't Wait*, p. 39.
30. Sovereignal freedom, freedom as domination of others, would be another species of freedom that might play a role in the political culture of the movement and that of its white southern opposition. See Patterson, *Freedom*, pp. 3–4.

without attribution.[31] As to the authentic source of King's vision, Keith Miller has succinctly expressed the view that will be examined here:

> King learned about slave religion from his father, a folk preacher, and adopted its vision of deliverance as the foundation of his thought and oratory. Indeed, the worldview of slaves proved far more important for King than anything he learned at Morehouse College, where he earned an AB degree; Crozier Theological Seminary, where he obtained a Bachelor of Divinity; and Boston University, where he received a Ph.D.[32]

In light of Miller's work, although its research antedates the revelations about King's plagiarism, and of his own research, David Garrow suggests a new consensus in the making: "King was far more deeply and extensively shaped by the black church tradition" than by his formal academic studies, and "the emergence and development of the black freedom movement was in no way the simple product of individual leaders and national organizations."[33]

As expressed, Garrow's second claim is unexceptionable, although it is a rather anodyne version of the more insistent thesis, as expressed by Ella Baker in *Bearing the Cross*, about the relationship between King and the movement. It is also possible to question whether Garrow's statement about the relative importance of black leaders and national organizations has any essential connection with his claim about the shaping influence on King of the black church.

But it is to Miller's starkly expressed position that I want to turn, since it is a prime example of the way the positive importance of ideas for political and social action can be misconstrued. Miller's analysis of King's relationship to southern black religion, as expressed in his sermons and major addresses, is often extremely stimulating and convincing. The central place he reserves for biblical narratives such as the Exodus story seems entirely appropriate, while his analysis of the generic conventions of the sermon is of great importance. Indeed, I would happily concur with Miller's judgement that King's "successful theology consists of his sermons, speeches, civil rights essays, and political career – not his formal theological work."[34] What is unconvincing is

---

31. The most thorough recent discussion of the plagiarism issue can be found in "Becoming Martin Luther King, Jr. – Plagiarism and Originality," *Journal of American History*, vol. 78, 1991, pp. 11–12. See also Keith Miller "Composing Martin Luther King, Jr.."

32. Miller, *Voice of Deliverance*, p. 17.

33. David Garrow, "King's Plagiarism: Imitation, Insecurity, and Transformation," *Journal of American History*, vol. 78, 1991, p. 86.

34. Miller, *Voice*, p. 162.

his dismissal of other influences on King as nugatory, even non-existent. There is a contemptuous undertone to Miller's polemics, the best example of which is his repeated reference to major figures in American and European intellectual history as "Great White Thinkers," the upper-case letters serving as an orthographic sneer. It is not easy to imagine how Fanon or DuBois would have reacted to such a claim.

In order to analyze Miller's position more closely, it is necessary to state it in full, if schematic, form. The argument runs as follows: the influence, as already said, of "Great White Thinkers" on King was minimal. Where they are discussed in his work, the sources are rarely the texts of the thinkers themselves but of popularizers.[35] Furthermore, King studded his sermons and essays (and by extension his books) with references to Hegel and Tillich, Buber and Niebuhr to attract an educated, white liberal audience, and earlier to impress his white teachers in seminary. Such philosophical name-dropping was a labor of "necessity" rather than "conviction."[36] Ironically, Miller's claims seem bizarrely to imply that only whites would or could respond to high cultural reference.

In reality, Miller claims, the proper context for understanding King's visionary rhetoric is the "Protestant homiletic tradition," specifically "two sermonic traditions" derived from popular white preachers such as Harry Emerson Fosdick, and, of course, from the traditional "black folk pulpit."[37] In Miller's opinion, the traditional sermon has its own generic structures that bear little resemblance to the generic requirements of philosophical argumentation. Only in an occasional piece, such as "Letter from Birmingham Jail," did King meld the two genres into one. Finally, in both the white and black homiletic traditions, the habit of "voice merging," or the borrowing of anecdotes and phraseology without acknowledgement, was common, though Miller admits that the white Protestant side of the tradition worried about borrowing, while "African American folk preachers never felt ambivalent about borrowing sermons."[38]

Finally, as already stated, Miller's bedrock claim is that the essence of King's values and vision derived from the "worldview of the slaves" that he learned from his father, himself the son of a slave. Furthermore, he contends that black folk Christianity, along with the influence of the two sermonic traditions, "have been systematically patronized, distorted, obscured, scorned, ignored, and dismissed by many King scholars and most other students of religion."[39] Though this is quite a

35. Miller devotes more space to this in his article than in his book.
36. Miller, *Voice*, p. 65.
37. Ibid, p. 83; p. 187.
38. Ibid., p. 128.
39. Ibid, pp. 7–8.

strong claim, it is backed by no evidence, no citations from, or analysis of, passages composed by miscreant scholars. Black folk religion may have been "ignored" for too long, but the other claims are so overstated as to lack credibility.

What, aside from the overheated rhetoric, are the problems? First, though Miller analyzes the conventions as well as the content of black folk sermons, there is very little historiographical, sociological, or anthropological discussion of what a "folk" religion is. "Folk" as opposed to what – "elite" or "modern"? Or is "folk" a euphemism for "black" or "rural"? Is there Southern white folk religion and are its homiletic conventions and visionary message different from the black version? Has Miller compared King's use of voice merging and unattributed intertextual linkages with other southern black educator-intellectuals such as Benjamin Mays or Howard Thurman whose roots were presumably also in the folk traditions? Whatever the intellectual viability of "folk religion" as a concept, Miller reifies it into an invariant sent of characteristics, lacking much historical specificity at all.

More importantly, what Miller does to King the man gives pause. By tying him so exclusively to black folk religion, Miller runs the risk of calling into question the importance of King's example and his vision today. To contextualize King in this way threatens to make King all but (politically) inaccessible. Second, to make his case Miller must be selective about those portions of King's own writings he [Miller] credits. For instance, in discussing King's attraction to the theological position called Personalism, Miller claims that "despite King's statement to the contrary, slave religion – not Personalism – was always his 'basic philosophical position.'"[40] In general, Miller accepts King's testimony as to the great influence of his family and of southern black religion, but rejects his account of more formal intellectual influences as either misjudged or as dissembling for a white audience.

Finally, the ultimate effect of Miller's analysis is to present a disturbing character profile of King as *either* incapable of learning the conventions of "white" academic life, such as attribution via footnotes, even though he underwent several years of academic training, *or* as deeply cynical about the white world, particularly about white academics and their favorite thinkers, all of which led him merely to go through the motions in his college and seminary training. Miller claims, and several other historians seem to agree, that familiarity with the King papers shows that the "dissertation did not deeply engage his intellectual interests. Neither did several of his term papers."[41] This

40. Ibid., p. 63.
41. Miller, "Martin Luther King, Jr. and the Black Folk Pulpit," *Journal of American History*, vol. 78, 1991, p. 120.

may be true. But based on this view, one would have to attribute diabolical cleverness to King for asking his wife to send him two volumes of Paul Tillich's *Systematic Theology* when he was sent to jail in Georgia in late October 1960, or when he read, or at least, had with him, DuBois's *Souls of Black Folk* and Ralph McGill's *The South and the Southerner* while in jail in Birmingham in 1963.[42] Was it all only about "Puttin on Ole Massa," whether Ole Massa was King's dissertation supervisor, Mark DeWolfe Howe, or white liberal and radical audiences generally?

But it is Miller's reductionism that is most bothersome and most relevant for a discussion of the pertinence of intellectual history. His understanding of the relationship of ideas to experience is one-dimensional and inadequate. In passage after passage, he succeeds in reducing King's mature thought to what King had experienced in early childhood, or on Sunday morning (and Wednesday evening) at church.

1. On the Social Gospel:

> Indeed, King's awareness of the social gospel did not stem primarily from reading Fosdick or Rauschenbusch or anyone else. Nor did it develop from his professor's tutelage. Plainly his initial and most pivotal instruction in the social gospel occurred at Ebenezer Church.[43]

Never mind that discussion of social problems and denunciation of injustice hardly exhaust the meaning of the social gospel. Miller thinks that expressions of social concern in his father's sermons were tantamount to education in a theological position.

2. On Reinhold Niebuhr and the problem of evil:

> Listening to his father's fervent preaching, King had little choice but to develop a well-ingrained sense of sin as a deep, pervasive reality. Had he lacked the benefit of his father's sermonizing, he would hardly have needed to read Niebuhr to grasp the immense potential of human evil. As a child, all he had to do was glance at the system of segregation.[44]

Here there is a double reduction: not Niebuhr's ideas, but his father's sermons; if not the sermons, then King, Jr.'s own experience.

42. Taylor Branch, *Parting the Waters*, New York, 1988, pp. 363, 747.
43. Miller, *Voice*, p. 58.
44. Ibid., p. 59.

But such claims ignore the kinds of questions that Niebuhr raised about sin and social injustice – the source of sin, what we can expect from struggle with it as Christians, and particularly the way in which the oppressed are also sinners, caught up in structures that require chastened recognition of, not merely withdrawal from, an unjust social reality.

3. On Christian love:

> Undoubtedly, Fosdick and three other writers helped refine King's conception of love.... But King's first lessons about love came earlier.[45]

Here Miller grants what is often the case with ideas and theories: they refine and clarify experiences. He then undermines his own point, however, by implying that all King really needed to know was acquired in the bosom of his family and the church. It is hard to imagine that the sophisticated distinction between *agape*, *eros*, and *philia* could be arrived at through the experience of family love.

4. On Hegel and "growth through struggle":

> In reality, Hegel reinforced King's earlier instruction in dissent.... Even if the elder King had somehow failed to pass on that lesson, King, Jr. was not required to read Hegel to learn that social change comes from struggle.... Early in the new century, without citing Hegel, the founders of the NAACP built their organization on the premise that struggle ... would lead to justice.[46]

Here Miller repeats the double reduction but also flirts with demagoguery: "Unschooled in Hegel, Rosa Parks accepted the necessity for struggle."[47] Moreover, what is at issue in Hegel and King is not just struggle, but recognition from the other in struggle and that struggle is not dualistically, but rather, dialectically structured and ultimately resolvable. Ironically, DuBois, the one black member of the original NAACP board, was profoundly influenced by Hegel's thought, although he too had encountered struggle before he went to Harvard or studied in Berlin.

45. Ibid., p. 60.
46. Ibid., p. 63.
47. Ibid., p. 63.

5. On Gandhi and non-violent civil disobedience:

> But when King first met the American Gandhians, he heard nothing terribly surprising. Instead, advanced lessons in Gandhi served mainly to confirm and elaborate what he was always taught as a child and adolescent. One older member of Ebenezer Church observes that he originally "learned nonviolence from his mother."[48]

On this issue, Miller's clarifications seem to me quite valuable, except that American Gandhian, Bayard Rustin might have been taken aback, had he been alive to read such a claim, since Rustin reported that King kept a gun in his home during the Montgomery crisis.

By now the point should be clear: Miller's basic assumption is that to identify the origin of an idea in an early experience is to explain it in all its complexity as it emerged at a later time. On one level, he is passing on banalities as iconoclastic blows for truth. Presumably, personal experiences at an early age, as internalized and processed unconsciously, predispose us to this or that view of the way to deal with the world as adults and as political actors. But to pretend that the origin just is the essence, specifically that black folk religion provided all King needed to deal with the world as he found it in college, seminary, the churches he pastored, or the movement he led, not to mention the white world of politicians, enemies, and allies, is scarcely credible. To be sure, Miller gives lip service to the idea that complex theories or systems of ideas do perform a function, but, although he uses the appropriate words – "confirm and elaborate," "reinforced," "helped retain" – the subtextual message, when not explicit, is that everything other than the basic experience is persiflage, camouflage, excess, or superfluous baggage.

Finally, it is not clear if Miller's reductionist "originology" applies to King alone, or whether it implies a general account of how ideas and experience are brought into confluence. In either case, it is an extremely impoverished view of these processes, if for no other reason than that his account assumes a monolithic and univocal original experience. As already mentioned, Miller never fully develops the concept of folk religion. But monolithic and univocal, black southern life certainly was not. If King learned love in the family, he undoubtedly learned about anger and exertions of the will from his father and his siblings. If the pulpits of the black church rang with denunciations of social injustice at times, they were just as often silent on the great issues of their day affecting black southerners. They were hardly bastions of radical politics. Nor

48. Ibid., p. 99.

were they the source of anything approaching the proto-socialist utopian vision of Rauschenbusch and the social gospel. Sin and evil were existential realities for young King. But so was the theological strain in Afro-American Christianity that de-emphasized doctrines of personal depravity, while stressing God's care for, not his judgment upon, his people.[49]

Nor, as I have tried to indicate, was the social gospel just about social reform, Niebuhr just about evil, Hegel just about struggle, Gandhi just about nonviolence. Even popularizations, from which King's knowledge of these figures allegedly derive, would have told him that. If it was so manifestly the case that King lived in a world of evil and was himself a sinner, what was he to do about it? Deny these "facts"? Accept them but await an eternal reward? Struggle against their implications and try to meliorate them? Fight violence with violence, coercion with coercion? Gandhi had one answer; Niebuhr another. Hegel may have taught about struggle, but how did that comport with King's experience of love in his own family and his community? The point here is that just as the black folk culture of the South was not an undifferentiated whole, from which one could read off straightforward lessons about the nature of things, so were King's intellectual precursors far from agreement with one another.

Indeed, the surprising thing about King is not the fit between what he became and where he came from, but what a difference there was. During adolescence he rebelled against the hyper-emotionality of black folk religion. At this stage ideas and theories were perhaps for him what fiction can be for other young people – both a way out of the given world and a way of exploring alternative ways of being in the world. But ideas were also instruments for political education in his own life and as he introduced them to his followers. They were not tools of manipulation, but ways of illuminating the world and suggesting the possibilities of action. That is, ideas had a utopian, liberating function and implied hope, reconciliation, and community. Ideas could also reflect the hard realities of sin and evil, injustice and oppression; but they sharpened and refined the ways he chose to confront these realities. Finally, King probably did use ideas, at times, to impress educated white people and to make black people proud of his erudition.

Whatever the case, when he returned, *sartor resartus*, to assume the ministry in Montgomery, he was equipped in a quite different way from when he left. One can maintain that it was all unnecessary window-dressing. But that would be to miss the drama of the self-

49. See Eugene D. Genovese, *Roll, Jordan, Roll*, New York, 1974, pp. 159–284.

formation of a man and a people, a return to where he began but at a level of greater complexity. Miller is correct in this: King's message was his total existence not in his writing or thinking alone. But King could not have moved from being "Mike" or "M.L." to "Martin Luther King, Jr." if he had left, never to return, or if he had never left home at all.

What then do we learn about the civil rights movement when we approach it through intellectual history and vice versa? Historians of the movement might find that a closer examination of the rhetoric and the basic political ideas enunciated in the movement would enrich their understanding of what the movement was about. For instance, the liberal idea of freedom and freedom as self-respect are not entirely compatible, and the tension between them may help explain and/or reflect divisions within the movement and the shift from nonviolence to violence. Indeed, by focusing on the centrality of recasting black identity, we can see the links, as well as the differences, between the civil rights movement and the black power/black consciousness movement that succeeded it. Moreover, how the movement tended to view the purpose of politics sheds light on the limited, parochial conception of politics still held by political historians of the movement as well as political scientists. If the movement showed anything, it was that conceiving of politics as the pursuit of self-interest is simply inadequate as a way of understanding politics in general, or the kind of politics the movement pursued in particular.

For the historian of political thought and political culture, the movement also presents a unique opportunity, a laboratory as it were, for examining the way ideas such as freedom are articulated and embodied in specific political and social movements. Specifically, it reminds the student of political thought that the classical and secular modern traditions of political discourse should be augmented by the study of forms of political self-consciousness informed by biblical traditions. It still needs repeating that religion is a vital part of political thought; and it is, moreover, not always a tool of political reaction. In addition, the civil rights movement was clearly a catalyst, along with the anti-war movement of the 1960s, for the resurgence of rights talk in political theory and political consciousness generally, a resurgence that has found global resonance in the years since then.

Finally, a task remaining for both historians and political theorists is to explore the similarities between the civil rights movement and the movements of political rejuvenation of the 1980s and early 1990s in South Africa, China, Eastern Europe, and the former Soviet Union. Neither a liberal/social democratic reform movement nor a proletarian uprising led by a vanguard party, the civil rights movement was a movement of potential citizens who sought to regain or recreate a public space for political talk and action. It brought religion into politics in a "progressive" form for a time, and also was faced with, and perhaps foundered on, the seemingly insoluble problem of racial and ethnic differences. In this the successes and failures of the civil rights move-ment prefigured in many important ways the successes and failures of the revolutions of 1989 and beyond.

–9–

Racial Politics, Culture and the Cole Incident of 1956[1]

Brian Ward

Historian Pete Daniel has written of the South that, "By 1960, there was more integration in music and in the sports world than in schools or in society at large."[2] Certainly, as the southern civil rights movement gathered momentum and white resistance to desegregation intensified, popular culture provided an important arena within which diverse black and white agendas were articulated and tested. This was particularly true in the field of popular music which, as a result of the commodification and dissemination of black popular music by an exploitative industry and a deeply penetrative mass media, became one of the areas of southern life in which racial barriers were first eroded and then breached. Consequently, popular music became the focus of intense scrutiny from both those who welcomed and those who deplored such developments as portents of a new era of race relations in the region. This essay employs the assault upon black singer-pianist Nat King Cole as a means to explore the evolving politics and ideology of white Alabama resistance and the changing configuration of black political consciousness at a particular moment in the development of the southern civil rights movement.

Cole was attacked by members of the White Citizens' Council on 10 April 1956 as he performed before a white audience at the Municipal Auditorium in Birmingham, Alabama. Although rarely described in any detail, let alone convincingly explained, this incident has become a regular footnote to the historiography of southern race relations and the civil rights movement. On occasions, it has even crept into the main text, where it has fulfilled a number of historical functions.

1. The author would like to thank the following for their help with the preparation of this paper: Jim Murray, Genette McLauren, Dan Carter, Bruce Crowther, Tony Badger and John White.
2. Pete Daniel, *Standing at the Crossroads: Southern Life in the Twentieth Century*, New York, 1986, p. 194.

The Cole incident appears, for example, in Michael Belknap's *Federal Law and Southern Order*, cited as a rare example of southern justice operating to convict white men who had perpetrated a violent crime against a black man.[3] It can be found in Neil McMillen's history of the Citizens' Council movement, where it illustrates the tactical differences between Asa Carter's North Alabama Citizens' Council – whose members carried out the assault – and other, more moderate branches, of the Council movement in Alabama.[4] In two biographies of Alabama's Governor, James Folsom, the incident is used to illustrate the eclipse of Folsom's brand of racial liberalism and the rise of racial extremism in Alabama in early 1956.[5] Further references to the assault can be found in both biographies of Cole and histories of early rock and roll, where it exemplifies the opposition of adult white America, in this instance, southern adult white America, to the spread of rock and roll music.[6]

These interpretations of the Cole incident are neither wrong nor mutually exclusive. Indeed, one aim of this essay is to reconcile and synthesize them: to create a more comprehensive version of what happened in the Municipal Auditorium on the night of 10 April 1956, and to offer some tentative conclusions about the real significance of those events. Certainly, there are too many loose ends and yawning gaps in the existing accounts; too many apparent paradoxes that have not even been explored, let alone resolved. Belknap, for instance, simply settles for calling the incident, "inexplicable."[7] It is easy to understand, if not endorse, this assessment, since the Cole incident poses a number of interpretive challenges. The most obvious concerns the fact that, while perpetrators, contemporary public and subsequent commentators alike have perceived the assault as an attack against rock and roll, Cole, a stylish jazz pianist turned cool balladeer, never sang in that style.

This apparent paradox raises other questions central to this essay. Why, if rock and roll was really the object of white anger, was there no comparable attack before April 1956? A black rock and roll show had played the Municipal Auditorium just a month earlier. An integrated

3. Michael R. Belknap, *Federal Law and Southern Order*, Athens, 1987, pp. 31–32.

4. Neil McMillen, *The Citizens' Council: Organized Resistance to the Second Reconstruction*, Urbana, 1971, pp. 41–58.

5. George E. Sims, *The Little Man's Big Friend*, Tuscaloosa, 1985, pp. 176–77; Carl Grafton and Anne Permaloff, *Big Mules and Branchheads*, Athens, 1985, pp. 201–2.

6. James Haskins (with Kathleen Benson), *Nat King Cole: The Man and his Music*, London, 1986; 1991 ed., pp. 137–43; Maria Cole (with Louie Robinson), *Nat King Cole: An Intimate Biography*, London, 1982, pp. 122–29; Charlie Gillett, *The Sound of the City*, London, 1970; rev. ed. 1983, pp. 17–18; Nick Tosches, *Unsung Heroes of Rock and Roll*, New York, 1984, p. 32; *Rolling Stone Rock Almanac*, London, 1984, p. 21.

7. Belknap, *Federal Law*, p. 31.

rock and roll show, with Bill Haley performing alongside black artists like Joe Turner, LaVern Baker and Smiley Lewis had played in January. Not only was there no violence at these concerts, but there was no adverse mainstream press comment and none of the sort of vehement public condemnations of rock and roll that had become commonplace by the late spring of 1956.[8]

Furthermore, if white outrage against rock and roll suddenly intensified during the spring of 1956, some eighteen months after the music began to gain mass popularity with white youths, how is that intensification to be explained? What were the racial, social, and psychological co-ordinates of mounting southern opposition to rock and roll? Where does the music industry fit into the picture? How did the black community, north and south, respond to the affair? These are the puzzles this essay addresses and hopes to unravel.

Cole's appearance, on the evening of 10 April 1956, was as the headliner on the "Record Star Parade of 1956" package tour, which also featured white acts such as singer June Christy, the Four Freshman vocal group, dancer Patty Thomas, and comedian Gary Morton. Ted Heath's "Famous British Orchestra" provided the musical accompaniment for these performers.

Before arriving in Birmingham, the tour had played under a variety of racial arrangements in the South. On 9 April, Cole had performed before a mixed, but segregated, audience at Mobile, Alabama. Similar arrangements applied in Fort Worth and Houston. In San Antonio and Winston-Salem, audiences were completely integrated. In Birmingham, local Jim Crow laws dictated that shows must be completely segregated. Even tickets for the two scheduled performances – one for whites, starting at 7:00 pm, one for "coloreds" commencing at 9:30 pm – were sold through separate outlets. Whites bought theirs from E.E. Forbes on North 20th Street, blacks from the Temple Pharmacy.

In its advance publicity for the concerts, the *Birmingham News* boasted, the "biggest colored show yet to hit the Municipal Auditorium stage."[9] This was curious, given that Cole was the sole black performer on the program and that just a month earlier a huge "Rhythm and Blues, Rock 'n' Roll Show" had taken place in the Municipal Auditorium, featuring only black acts, among them bluesman B.B. King, shouter Roy Brown, and vocal groups the Midnighters and Five Royales.[10]

In part, this claim can be explained in terms of routine publicity hyperbole and the fact that Cole was the most eminent name on the bill. Moreover, the local press made much of the fact that Cole was returning

8. *Birmingham News*, 11 March and 15 January 1956.
9. *Birmingham News*, 1 April 1956.
10. *Birmingham News*, 11 March 1956.

to his native Alabama, where he had been born on St. Patrick's Day, 1919, the second son of the Reverend Edward James Coles – pastor of Montgomery's First Baptist Church.[11] "Nat King Cole is the Montgomery boy who has really hit the top in race records," reported the *Birmingham News*, carefully noting the fact that Cole was a "race records" star, although, in fact, he had enjoyed great success with white audiences around the country for a number of years.[12] In 1955 alone, Cole had secured seven top thirty hit records on *Billboard's* national pop charts at a time when black penetration of the mass white market for popular music was still very limited.[13] Indeed, prior to the spring of 1956 Cole had played dates in the South and in Birmingham itself on six or seven occasions with no problems.[14]

At the first, whites-only, show on the evening of 10 April 1956, Cole was assaulted. He was midway through his third song, a rendering of the Tin Pan Alley ballad, "Little Girl," which he had first recorded with his Trio in 1947.[15] Someone shouted "Let's go get that coon" and four men sprinted down the center aisle towards Cole. One turned back and was never apprehended, but the other three, Willis Vinson, his older brother, E.R. Vinson, and Kenneth Adams vaulted over the footlights and onto the stage. Cole was hit in the face by a falling microphone and wrenched his back as Adams wrestled him over the piano stool onto the floor.[16]

There was a touch of grim farce amid the confusion as plain clothes policemen, tipped-off about possible trouble, rushed to protect Cole, only to clash briefly with uniformed officers who thought the plain clothes men were the second wave of attack. Meanwhile, the Ted Heath Orchestra, with whom Cole was sharing the stage, stayed at its post in time-honored "dance-band on the Titanic" tradition and, at a loss to play anything more appropriate, launched into "God Save the Queen" as the curtain was brought down and Cole rescued.

11. For Cole's early life and career, see Haskins, *The Man and his Music*, pp. 13–27.

12. *Birmingham News*, 1 April 1956.

13. See Joel Whitburn, ed., *The Billboard Book of U.S. Top Forty Hits, 1955 to Present*, London, 1983, p. 68.

14. *Birmingham News*, 11 April 1956.

15. Nat King Cole Trio, "Little Girl," Capitol Record 15165 (1947).

16. *Birmingham News*, 11 April 1956. This account of the attack and its immediate aftermath has been drawn from the following sources: The Schomburg Center for Research in Black Culture, Clipping File: "Cole" (hereafter cited as SC-File: "Cole"), which contains extracts on the incident from the *Philadelphia Evening Bulletin*; *New York Post*, *Christian Science Monitor*; *Daily Worker*; *Atlanta Journal*; *Greensboro Daily News*, and *New York Herald Tribune*. Also, *Birmingham News*, 11, 12, 16, 17, 18, 21 April 1956; *Birmingham World*, 13, 17, 24 April 1956; *New Orleans Times-Picayune*, 11, 21 April 1956; *Atlanta Constitution*, 11 April 1956; *Raleigh News and Observer*, 11–13 April 1956, *Baltimore Afro-American*, 11, 21 April 1956; Cole, *Nat King Cole*, pp. 122–29; Haskins, *The Man and his Music*, pp. 137–43.

Shortly after the attack Cole returned to the stage to a rousing reception from what appears to have been a genuinely apologetic and chagrined white audience. "I just came here to entertain you," Cole announced from the stage. "I thought that was what you wanted. I was born here. Those folks have hurt my back. I cannot continue, because I have to go to a doctor." Cole appeared later that evening for the black show at the Auditorium, but then cancelled scheduled performances in Greenville, South Carolina, and Charlotte, North Carolina, while he recuperated in Chicago. He eventually resumed his tour on 13 April in Raleigh, North Carolina.[17]

Under the auspices of Public Safety Commissioner Robert Lindbergh and with the support of Birmingham's acting Police Chief Jamie Moore, Detective C.B. Golden, and Detective Sergeant M.H. House led the investigation into the attack with a thoroughness and alacrity not always associated with southern police departments in cases of white violence against blacks. They quickly uncovered the full extent of the plot against Cole. Hatched four days before the attack in Kenneth Adams' Anniston filling station, the plan called for more than one hundred white men to storm the stage on Adams' command. "Our information," reported House, "is that they had planned to infiltrate the audience, overpower the band, the police, and anyone else who interfered with them. But the expected mob of 150 failed to show." It is certainly possible, as Maria Cole has suggested, that the intention was to kidnap her husband, although the defendants claimed that they just wished to make a statement from the stage.[18]

Six men were arrested in connection with the attack: Jesse Mabry, Mike Fox, and Orliss Clevenger, in addition to Adams and the two Vinson brothers. All, except Jesse Mabry, came from Anniston, a hotbed of Klan and segregationist activity located sixty miles east of Birmingham, which, in May 1961, etched itself into the national consciousness as the scene of a firebomb attack upon an interracial group of Freedom Riders. Mabry was from Birmingham itself. Originally, all the men were charged with assault with intent to murder, but ultimately only Kenneth Adams and Willis Vinson were indicted on that count.

Birmingham justice moved remarkably quickly and the four men facing lesser charges first appeared before Judge Ralph Parker of the

17. *Birmingham News*, 14 April 1956; Cole, *Nat King Cole*, p. 124; *Greensboro Daily News*, 11 April 1956 (SC-File: "Cole"); *Raleigh News and Observer*, 13, 14 April 1956. Haskins incorrectly claims that Cole cancelled the Raleigh date and spent a week in Chicago. Haskins, *The Man and His Music*, p. 139.

18. *Birmingham News*, 12 April 1956; *Baltimore Afro-American*, 21 April 1956; *Atlanta Journal*, 12 April 1956 (SC-File: "Cole"); Cole, *Nat King Cole*, p. 123, 14 April 1956; Cole, *Nat King Cole*, p. 123.

Birmingham Recorder's Court on 13 April. Charged under various sections of the 1944 General City Code of Birmingham with disturbing the peace, conspiracy to commit a breach of the peace, and conspiracy to commit assault and battery, all four were found guilty and sentenced four days later. Jesse Mabry was given six months in jail and fined a total of 110 dollars for disorderly conduct and failing to comply with the lawful order of a police officer. According to testimony from officers G.F. Faulkner and G.R. Jones, Mabry had tried to harass the lawmen defending Cole, commenting that, "You ought to have that damn negro out here instead of those white folks," and demanding that the police stop beating up "white boys" and turn their batons on Cole.[19]

Mabry's penalty was the maximum available to Judge Parker, who was similarly severe with the other defendants. They also received six month sentences, 100 dollar fines for conspiracy to commit assault and battery, and were ordered to pay five dollars costs. In addition, Clevenger was fined twenty-eight dollars for possession of a concealed weapon. Fox and Clevenger had been arrested outside the Auditorium, waiting in Clevenger's car, which at the time resembled a mobile arsenal. The weaponry found inside included brass knuckles, a blackjack, and two .22 calibre rifles – equipment for a turkey shoot, according to the two men.[20]

White Southern opinion appears to have been generally sympathetic to Cole and condemnatory of the culprits. James W. Morgan, head of the Birmingham City Commission, delivered a personal apology to Cole, while the *Birmingham News* called for the rapid and severe dispensation of justice and denounced the "deplorable incident" as a "very disturbing example of the grave dangers involved in extremist passions and actions in the troubled field of race relations."[21] The *Raleigh News and Observer*, published in the city where, on 13 April, Cole resumed his tour, termed the Birmingham attack, "reprehensible and wholly unprovoked," and printed a statement from the city's Chief of Police Tom Davis to the effect that, "I can't believe the citizens of Raleigh and vicinity would stoop to, or condone any mis-conduct."[22]

Much of the southern condemnation was directed specifically against the maverick North Alabama Citizens Council led by the rabidly anti-

19. *Birmingham News*, 16 April 1956; General City Code of Birmingham of 1944, sections 311, 831, 1231, 1521. The appearance Bonds for Mabry (case nos. 65376/65377/65378), Clevenger (case nos. 65398/65399), and E.L. Vinson (case nos. 65359/65360/65361) can be found in the Birmingham Public Library Archives (BPLA). Fox's appearance bond could not be located, but according to the Recorder's Court No. 1 Docket (BPLA), his charges were consolidated as case no. 65368.

20. *Birmingham News*, 16 April 1956.

21. *Birmingham News*, 11 April 1956.

22. *Raleigh News and Observer*, 13 April 1956; *Birmingham News*, 11 April 1956.

semitic, anti-communist, anti-negro, segregationist Asa "Ace" Carter. Certainly the attackers all belonged to Carter's co-ordinating organiza- tion, the Alabama Citizens' Council (ACC). Jesse Mabry was editor of Carter's newspaper, *The Southerner*, and Kenneth Adams was on the board of directors of the affiliated Anniston Council. Other branches of the Alabama Council movement, although like Carter resolutely commit- ted to the defence of segregation, also quickly condemned the use of violence. Carter's great rival within the Alabama Council movement, state senator Sam Englehardt, stressed that his organization advocated, "peaceful and legal means of settling the segregation question," and pledged that, "If we find any members like these in the Citizen's Council of Alabama (CCA), they will be thrown out."[23] Expressions of disap- proval came from other pro-segregation organizations across the South, such as the Georgia States' Rights Council, the South Carolina Association of Citizens' Councils, and a Citizens' Council in New Orleans.[24]

The peculiar factionalism and rivalry within the Alabama Citizens' Council movement, characterized by one contemporary observer as, "part of the old feud between the Bourbon and the Redneck," provided an important context for the attack on the hapless Cole.[25] Equally impor- tant was the marked intensification of Massive Resistance in Alabama, indeed throughout the South, during early 1956.

When, in May 1954, the United States Supreme Court delivered its epochal verdict in *Brown v. Board of Education of Topeka*, declaring segregated schools "inherently unequal" and undermining the intellec- tual and constitutional basis upon which Jim Crow had been established in the South since the *Plessy v. Ferguson* decision of 1896, the white South was naturally alarmed. Nevertheless, faced by this portentous threat to its peculiar racial arrangements and the whole way of life pred- icated upon those arrangements, the reaction of the white South to the *Brown* decision was generally calm and restrained. After years of litiga- tion sponsored by the National Association for the Advancement of Colored People (NAACP), the decision was hardly unexpected and most whites trusted a variety of political, economic, and legalistic strate- gies to preserve the racial *status quo*.[26]

In May 1955, the Supreme Court's second ruling on *Brown*, which called for desegregation with "all deliberate speed," undoubtedly

23. *Birmingham News*, 12 April 1956.

24. *Birmingham News*, 12 April 1956; McMillen, *The Citizens' Council*, p. 5, fn. 37.

25. Douglas Cater, "Civil War in Alabama's Citizens' Councils," *The Reporter*, 17 May 1956, p. 20.

26. For overviews of the tactics of Massive Resistance in the South, see Numan Bartley, *The Rise of Massive Resistance*, Baton Rouge, 1969; Francis M. Wilhoit, *The Politics of Massive Resistance*, New York, 1973.

intensified white anxieties. Nevertheless, the timetable was still vague enough to prevent a major southern panic. Moreover, by referring to local school boards the responsibility for implementing desegregation, the court, as Aldon Morris suggests, "in effect gave the very groups that adamantly opposed school desegregation the responsibility to desegregate the schools."[27] Consequently, even after May 1955, the South still found the court's rulings relatively easy to ignore or circumvent in the localities. As Francis Wilhoit notes, "though southern resistance perceptively hardened after Brown II, the resistance had not yet taken on the form of overt violence that would be so much a part of the South's backlash in later years."[28]

This general pattern was clearly evident in Alabama.[29] Immediately after the first *Brown* decision, Sam Engelhardt pledged himself to "keep every brick in our segregation wall intact," while the Birmingham City Commissioners declared themselves "unalterably opposed" to the desegregation of schools in the city.[30] Yet, while there was intense concern about the decision and its implications for the future of race relations in the South, and a freely expressed determination to resist the court's rulings, there was no real panic and little doubt that an evasion of desegregation would be possible for the foreseeable future.

Alabama Senator John Sparkman, "deplored" the *Brown* decision, but drew comfort from the fact that "it may be years before school segregation ends in the South."[31] An editorial in the *Birmingham News* admitted the Supreme Court's decision heralded the eventual end of school segregation, but noted that, "It may be months before the ground rules are established for carrying out the court's findings," adding that, "It could be years if legal snags crop up."[32] The same newspaper reported that, "some southerners predict a `century of litigation' before any major admission of Negroes to white schoolrooms."[33] The resounding victory of racial moderate Jim Folsom in the gubernatorial election of 1954 also suggested that Alabama was still some way from making

27. Aldon Morris, *The Origins of the Civil Rights Movement*, New York, 1984, p. 29.
28. Wilhoit, *Politics of Massive Resistance*, p. 45.
29. Numan Bartley has actually contended that Alabama was unique among Deep South states in its initial moderation after *Brown*; see, Bartley, *Massive Resistance*, p. 77. While a convincing case can certainly be made for Alabama being more restrained than her neighbors prior to 1956, Bartley's claims for an instantaneous "hysterical" response to *Brown* throughout the remainder of the Deep South needs qualification.
30. *Birmingham News*, 17, 18 May 1954.
31. *Birmingham News*, 17 May 1954.
32. *Birmingham News*, 18 May 1954.
33. *Birmingham News*, 24 May 1954.

overt opposition to *Brown* and strict racial orthodoxy the only criteria for election to political office.[34]

This relative calm disintegrated in late 1955 and early 1956, as southern blacks increasingly took the initiative in the struggle for desegregation, not just in schools, but in a whole range of public amenities. At the end of 1955 and beginning of 1956, a series of black protests and boycotts in the South not only galvanized the black community, but dramatically radicalized the southern white mood and brought forth the full force of Massive Resistance.

In August 1955, Alabama blacks began to directly petition education officers in Alabama to implement the immediate desegregation of public schools. In December 1955, the year-long Montgomery Bus Boycott began, heralding the rise of mass non-violent protest by southern blacks and the emergence of an exceptional black leader in Martin Luther King, Jr. In February 1956, Autherine Lucy won her three-year battle to be admitted to the previously white University of Alabama at Tuscaloosa and duly sought to attend classes. Moreover, a series of pro-desegregation decisions emanating from the Fourth and Fifth Circuit Appellate Courts, based in Richmond and New Orleans respectively, further raised southern anxieties. The racially partisan workings of southern justice had previously been viewed as a trusty bulwark against the horrors of desegregation.

By early 1956, white Alabamians felt that the entire edifice of Jim Crow was under immediate and direct assault from both within and without the state. In this newly intensified, embattled situation, the stakes for white southerners were dramatically raised and they responded forcefully at a number of levels: political, economic, legal, and extra-legal.

In January 1956, the Alabama state legislature became the first during the existing crisis to implement the states' rights tactic of interposition, declaring the Supreme Court's ruling "null, void and of no effect," and interposing state power between what was perceived as a hostile, unjust law and the people. Also in early 1956, Alabama state senator Albert Boutwell introduced a "freedom of choice" school bill, designed specifically to avoid compliance with the Supreme Court's desegregation ruling. In March 1956, Alabama senators and representatives were among those who signed the Southern Manifesto, declaring their implacable opposition

34. For the initially measured response of Alabama to the *Brown* decisions, see James Tyra Harris, "Alabama's Reaction to the Brown Decision, 1954–56: A Case Study in Early Massive Resistance," unpublished Doctor of Arts Thesis, Middle Tennessee State University, 1978; Robert Corley, "The Quest for Racial Harmony: Race Relations in Birmingham, Alabama, 1947–1963," unpublished Ph.D Thesis, University of Virginia, 1979, pp. 79–114; McMillen, *The Citizens' Council*, pp. 41–42; Bartley, *Massive Resistance*, p. 77.

to enforced integration. The first months of 1956 also saw concerted efforts to destroy the NAACP in the state, lead by Alabama's attorney-general and future governor, John Patterson. In April 1956, Birmingham's Interracial Council, for several years a major point of contact between the races, finally collapsed, unable to reconcile the demands of anxious whites with those of an increasingly activist black community.[35]

Meanwhile, the racial liberal, "Big Jim" Folsom, suddenly found his moderation a major political burden. An archetypal New Dealer with Populist leanings, Folsom had welded together an alliance of Alabama's back-country whites and fifty thousand enfranchised blacks, using this "Branchhead" constituency to secure office against the power of the "Big Mules" of Birmingham and the agrarian conservatives of the Black Belt counties. By late 1955, however, the tentative bi-racialism of Folsom's "vigorous if sometimes chaotic rural liberalism," had made him vulnerable to attack from Alabama's segregationist leaders.[36] Folsom's November 1955 meeting to discuss civil rights with the flamboyant Harlem congressmen Adam Clayton Powell was especially condemned as an act of racial treachery. In early March 1956, Asa Carter called for the impeachment of Folsom "for failure to uphold our constitution."[37] Even more temperate segregationists, such as Englehardt, denounced Folsom for supporting the programs of the hated NAACP.[38] By the time of the Nat King Cole attack, Folsom's position with the white community had become so perilous that he dared not issue a public apology to the singer, but quietly sent a message of regret through A.G. Gaston, the black businessman who served as Folsom's main conduit to the black community.[39]

As spring turned to summer, even the relatively moderate *Birmingham News* conceded that Folsom's defeat by Charles McKay in an election for the Democratic National Committee, "points plainly to acute dissatisfaction with his record in office and his position on the segregation issue."[40] Folsom himself recognized that the rise of the

35. For the eclipse of Alabama's racial moderates and the rise of Massive Resistance, see Corley, "Race Relations in Birmingham"; Harris, "Alabama's Reaction to the Brown Decision"; Bartley, *Massive Resistance*, pp. 87–90, 131–35, 201–6, 215–16, 220–21, 279–86; McMillen, *The Citizens' Council*, pp. 41–58; Wilhoit, *Politics of Massive Resistance*, pp. 46, 105–7, 111–12, 137, 171–74, 196–98.

36. Numan V. Bartley and Hugh D. Graham, *Southern Politics and the Second Reconstruction*, Baltimore, 1975, pp. 25–26. See also Grafton and Permaloff, *Big Mules and Branchheads*; Sims, *The Little Man's Big Friend*; Robert J. Norrell, *Reaping the Whirlwind: The Civil Rights Movement in Tuskegee*, New York, 1985, pp. 64–65, 70–73, 87–92, for Folsom's role in the Tuskegee gerrymandering controversy.

37. *Birmingham News*, 10 March 1956.

38. *Birmingham News*, 2 May 1956.

39. Sims, *The Little Man's Big Friend*, p. 176.

40. *Birmingham News*, 2 May 1956.

Solid South had rendered his style of racial liberalism obsolete and bemoaned the fact that now he, "couldn't be elected dogcatcher" in Alabama.[41] In 1958, he was replaced as governor by arch-resister John Patterson in a very conspicuous rejection of the racial heresy that had become (un)popularly known in Alabama as "Folsomism."

White Alabama's growing anxiety was also reflected in the escalation of mob action, violence, intimidation, and vicious racial demagoguery. Lucy Autherine's brave attempt to integrate the University of Alabama ended, after three days of white mob action, with her suspension from classes. Some whites turned to systematic terrorism to supplement the political and legal machinations of Massive Resistance. The Ku Klux Klan re-emerged to intimidate and brutalize blacks who challenged segregation and their liberal white supporters. By 1957, there were at least seven distinct Klan groups operating in Alabama alongside a plethora of other hate organizations.[42]

Although supposedly disavowing the violence of the Klans, since they liked to boast that they drew support from the "active middle and upper class of businessmen," the White Citizens' Councils also prospered, waging their own shadowy campaign of organized resistance.[43] Able to attract only scattered support before the end of 1955, the various Alabama Councils claimed, no doubt with some creative accounting, membership of around 40,000 in February 1956, including an impressive collection of the state's leading white politicians, businessmen, and professionals.[44]

In that same month, Alabama's Council leaders organized the first statewide association. Individual Councils became affiliated to one of four regional bodies, all centrally co-ordinated by the Alabama Association of Citizens' Councils (AACC), with Englehardt as its executive secretary and Dr. John Whitley, a drugstore manager from the Tarrant City suburb of Birmingham, as chairman. Asa Carter, a former radio commentator, sometime soft-drink salesman and secret member of the savage Ensley Klan Klavern No. 31, dominated the North Alabama Citizens' Council (NAAC).[45] Centered in Birmingham, the NAAC

41. *Birmingham News*, 1 May 1956.

42. For the revival of the Ku Klux Klan in Alabama, see Wyn Craig Wade, *The Fiery Cross*, New York, 1987, 1988 ed., pp. 302–3; Bartley, *Massive Resistance*, pp. 201–6.

43. John Bartlow Martin, *The Deep South Says Never*, New York, 1957, p. 7.

44. *Birmingham News*, 19 February 1956; McMillen, *The Citizens' Council*, pp. 43–44.

45. Dan T. Carter has recently described the remarkable transformation of Asa Carter from the Citizens' Councils and the Klan, via at least one murder, to employment as a speech writer for George Wallace and finally, with a change of identity ("Forrest Carter"), to a career as western novelist. See Dan T. Carter, "The Transformation of a Klansman," *New York Times*, 4 October 1991.

became increasingly divorced from the statewide organization. While the vaguely patrician Macon County planter, merchant, and cotton-gin owner Englehardt tried to preserve an aura of respectability concerning the Council's legal and political resistance to segregation, Carter, a rough-hewn product of the North Alabama upcountry, courted the blue-collar workers of Birmingham with a much more vigorously populist, anti-semitic as well as anti-black, and occasionally violent approach to the preservation of Jim Crow. While the advertisements in the pages of *The Southerner* suggest that Carter's organization attracted its share of small, independent businessmen, its rhetoric was aimed resolutely at the white workers of the Black Belt, whose interests, Carter claimed, were being betrayed by a self-serving, political, and economic elite, personified by Englehardt, with a worrying tendency towards equivocation on racial matters.[46]

While Englehardt and Carter recognized each other's ability to reach different elements within white Alabama, their relationship was always strained. Significantly, in terms of the events at the Municipal Auditorium on 10 April, the rift between Carter and the AACC widened dramatically in the spring of 1956. In addition to a general unease about Carter's radical rhetoric and tactics, a particular source of friction was his relentless anti-semitism, as reflected in the ruling that members of his NACC must pledge their faith in the divinity of Jesus Christ. Sam Englehardt countered with an assurance that the AACC generally was, "not interested in religious bias or prejudice ... only in maintaining segregation and in preserving our Southern traditions and Southern way of life."[47]

The growing tensions within the Alabama Council movement came to a head over the appropriate response to the Autherine Lucy affair. Carter angrily demanded the dismissal of President O.C. Carmichael of the University of Alabama for allowing even temporary desegregation when Lucy had spent her three nightmarish days at the institution. When the rest of the AACC refused to support Carter's proposal, thus sanctioning in his mind a treacherous breach in the solid wall of white resis-

---

46. Among the advertisements alongside those for grocery stores, heating companies, restaurants, refrigeration, and television services featured in *The Southerner* was one for Kenneth Adams' Anniston Service Station, bearing the legend, "As Good As The Best For Less Than The Rest," *The Southerner*, August 1956. For an example of Carter's anti-elitist, anti-Englehardt, anti-AACC line, see *The Southerner*, vol. 1, no. 1, March 1956, in which he promised that, "If the power of control of the councils is left in the hands of the people and not in the hands of men who say they are for segregation but will allow themselves to be 'bought off,' then we will defeat the forces of integration for all time."

47. See, *Birmingham News*, 4 March 1956; Cater, "Civil War in Alabama's Councils," p. 21.

tance, Carter left and established his own independent umbrella organization, the Alabama Citizens' Council (ACC), to co-ordinate a more vigorous, uncompromising response to the gathering threats to the southern way of life. To avoid confusion with Carter's new organization, the old AACC changed its name to the Citizen's Council of Alabama (CCA).[48]

Despite Carter's potent rhetoric and a series of impressive rallies held during the spring, he struggled to match the popularity of Englehardt's more subtle, though no less determined, brand of Council activity. Moreover, in March 1956, Carter's ambitions were dealt a severe blow when two thousand members from the eastern section of his ACC defected to Englehardt's group, denouncing both Carter's extremism and his dictatorial running of the organization.[49]

By March 1956, then, Asa Carter desperately needed something – an issue or an event – with which to maintain the profile and credibility of his organization and raise his own personal stock as a leader of Alabamian resistance. One of the issues with which Carter hoped to revive his fortunes and invigorate his campaign was rock and roll. It was Carter who orchestrated the outcry against the spread of that black-derived music style, emphasizing the pernicious influence it was having on the morals of southern white youth. In rock and roll, a music that drew on black rhythm and blues, white pop and the white South's own beloved country music for its inspiration and techniques, and that boasted black and white performers and fans, Carter located a powerful metaphor for the horrors of integration. Ultimately, he skillfully used the specter of rock and roll to tap into all manner of social, political, generational, as well as racial, anxieties afflicting adult white America – particularly in the South – at mid-century.

Consequently, the apparent paradox inherent in interpreting the Cole incident as an attack upon rock and roll – the fact that Cole was in no way a rock and roll singer – turns out to be just a paradox. It is simply impossible to begin to understand the attack, without taking cognisance of Carter's new, very public preoccupation with the perils of rock and roll in the spring of 1956. Certainly, contemporary opinion was in no doubt that rock and roll was the real target of the attack and that Cole was just an unfortunate, but at a crucial moment in the evolution of Carter's ideas and strategies, accessible surrogate. The initial coverage of the incident in the *Birmingham News* set it firmly in the context of

48. For the conflict and schism within the Alabama Councils, see Cater, "Civil War in Alabama's Councils," pp. 19–21; *Birmingham News*, 4, 7 March 1956; McMillen, *The Citizens' Council*, pp. 50–58.

49. McMillen, *The Citizens' Council*, pp. 53–54; Harris, "Alabama's Reaction to the Brown Decision," pp. 290–94.

Carter's recent outbursts against rock and roll, while carefully noting that Cole did not perform in that style.[50]

Carter, not a particularly sophisticated thinker on matters of musical differentiation, was not in the least concerned about applying the correct musical terminology to the style he was attacking. Like many other critics of rock and roll, he used that term interchangeably with "be-bop," "blues," "congo rhythms," "jungle music," and a whole host of other choice epithets. It is reasonable to suppose that his supporters were similarly untroubled by the manifold musical differences between Cole and genuine black rock and rollers like Chuck Berry when they plotted their attack. In any case, Carter argued, it was, "only a short step ... from the sly, night club technique vulgarity of Cole, to the openly animalistic obscenity of the horde of Negro rock `n' rollers."[51]

Indeed, Carter, whose personal complicity in the planning of the Cole attack remains a moot point, confirmed that the men had gone to the Auditorium as part of what the press characterized as, "the Council studies of be-bop and rock-and-roll music."[52] There had, Carter insisted, been no planned violence. He blamed the assault on a black man in the rear of the Auditorium who had deliberately knocked a camera held by one of the Council men. "The incident," Carter explained, "made him mad, and he ran down the aisle towards Cole, who was just another Negro to him."[53] Just what the "Negro" was doing attending a strictly segregated, whites-only, performance was never explained.

Carter's first formal statement on the evils of rock and roll appeared in the pages of his newspaper, *The Southerner*, in March 1956.[54] After a relatively calm, even indifferent, response to the spread of the music before early 1956, Carter helped to make rock and roll part of what the historian Francis Wilhoit has termed, the South's "demonology" of Massive Resistance. Although Wilhoit himself is silent on the southern campaign against rock and roll, his proposition that, "Massive Resistance included not only a pantheon of saints and martyrs and verbalized propositions such as white supremacy and states' rights federalism, but also a vast panoply of symbols, icons, emblems, totems, taboos, scapegoats, and stylized rituals," provides an extremely useful context within which to place the rise of opposition to rock and roll music.[55]

50. *Birmingham News*, 11 April 1956.
51. *The Southerner*, vol. 1, nos. 2/3, May 1956.
52. *The Southerner*, 12 April 1956.
53. *The Southerner*, 12 April 1956.
54. *The Southerner*, vol. 1, March 1956.
55. Wilhoit, *Politics of Massive Resistance*, p. 122.

By early 1956, the intensification of southern anxieties manifested itself, not just in political and violent resistance, but in the widespread, vigorous affirmation – one might argue, reaffirmation – of a sectional ideology based essentially upon the twin doctrines of states' rights and white racial supremacy, with its correlate of black inferiority. This southern ideology, of which active participation in Massive Resistance was merely the most conspicuous expression, contained a number of key themes or propositions, some of which were by no means unique to the South.

Paramount in the white southern mind was the notion that racial integration would compromise the spurious purity of the white race. Taking white supremacy and black moral, cultural, and intellectual inferiority, as a *sine qua non*, this oft-repeated fear was inextricably linked to the longstanding dread of miscegenation and the specter of mongrelization. State representative Charles McKay appeared before a meeting of 2,000 Council members in the same auditorium that witnessed the Cole attack to denounce those who were "scheming to tear down our segregation and bring about mongrelization of the races."[56]

A second co-ordinate of the southern ideology at this time was the idea that greater exposure to blacks and their culture would increase the incidence of juvenile delinquency among white youth. It is clear that the problem of juvenile delinquency had reached the level of a major obsession throughout adult America in the 1950s. There was what James Gilbert terms a "cycle of outrage," in which new patterns of teenage behavior coupled with, and in many instances shaped by, the extended influence of the mass media created the impression that, "society was coming apart, that pernicious outside influences could now breach the walls of community and family institutions."[57]

The fear of rampant juvenile delinquency was apparent from the extensive news coverage given to teenage crime and impropriety in the southern press: "Teenage gangs festering in Birmingham"; "Teen-age pair admits hold-up, vicious beating"; "Teenage beer party raided." Two days after the Cole incident, it was reported that in Jefferson County, where Birmingham is located, delinquency rates had increased by 14.3 percent between 1948 and 1954.[58] The popular connection between inte-

---

56. *Birmingham News*, 17 May 1956.

57. James Gilbert, *A Cycle of Outrage*, New York, 1986, p. 76. See also J. Ronald Oakley, *God's Country: America in the Fifties*, New York, 1986, pp. 268–71; John P. Diggins, *The Proud Decades*, New York, 1988, pp. 198–207.

58. *Birmingham News*, 4, 11 January 1956, 27 September 1956. The national average increase in the juvenile crime rate was actually higher than in Jefferson County at fifty-four per cent. *Birmingham News*, 12 April 1956.

gration and juvenile crime and sexual impropriety was made explicit in the comments of a white Birmingham parent who explained "some of the reasons why I will never willingly send my children to a mixed school," by offering a catalogue of statistics about the higher incidence of homicides, venereal disease, and illegitimate births among the black community. "I would no more expose my children to this condition than I would deliberately expose them to the bubonic plague or any other dreadful disease."[59]

Another key aspect of the southern demonology was the dread of outside interference with racial affairs that were rightly the business of the South. At its most politically coherent, as in the various interposition bills and the Southern Manifesto, opposition to outside interference took the form of a vigorous championing of states' rights against the allegedly unconstitutional encroachment of federal power. More often, it took the form of a regional xenophobia, involving the reification of something implicitly understood and cherished as, "the southern way of life."

The defence of the South's peculiar institutions was often expressed in a language that starkly revealed the persistence of antebellum racial stereotypes of docile, contented blacks and benevolent, paternalistic whites. Just prior to the attack on Cole, J. Melancon, a self-professed Birmingham moderate, wrote that, "speaking generally the Southern position is a feeling of friendship and kindly regard for the Negro. He is with us in large numbers, good natured and carefree, happy-go-lucky and easy to get along with when not swayed by extraneous influences." Describing the 1896 *Plessy* decision as the catalyst for "phenomenal progress both in education and the assumption of civil rights," Melancon argued, "it is in the best interests of both races that segregation be maintained at least for the forseeable future."[60]

Frequently, southern fears of outside intervention and agitation mingled with the anti-communism so prevalent throughout America in the mid–1950s. One commentator, Lois Crick from Hueytown, Alabama, insisted that, "If the northerner, the politician and the Communist will let us alone with our way of life we will handle such situations as we are now confronted with in the usual diplomatic manner which must be agreeable to all concerned, certainly to the negro, otherwise we wouldn't have so many of them."[60] The Supreme Court, Martin Luther King, and the NAACP were repeatedly accused of being communist agents or, at best, unwitting communist dupes. H.B. Inzer, a Council supporter from Margaret, Alabama was "fully convinced that it

59. *Birmingham News*, 11 March 1956.
60. *Birmingham News*, 7 March 1956.
61. *Birmingham News*, 5 March 1956.

is not the Negroes of Alabama who want integration, but they are being pushed by the agents of communism."[62]

These crucial icons and demons, ideals and fears, of Massive Resistance were not discrete phenomena, but were fused together in a sensational and emotive legitimation of the southern way of life and a bold affirmation of the moral rectitude of trying to preserve it. In a single speech in January 1956, state senator and Council activist Walter Givhan was able to condemn "outside agitators" like the NAACP ("champions of mongrelization"), synthesize gnawing fears of communism and miscegenation ("The communists know that if they can mongrelize the Anglo-Saxon southern white, they can destroy us") and warn against the corruption of white youth, all in a heartfelt plea for organized resistance to desegregation. "The reason we're here and the reason we've fought these battles is your little boy and your little girl," explained Givhan. "That's who we're fighting for. We're going to keep these little white boys and these little white girls pure."[63]

While it is impossible to be certain, the fact that ideas of racial purity and the horror of black defilement of white youth and womanhood were so central to the ideology of Massive Resistance may help explain the actual timing of the assault on Nat King Cole. It was only when Cole began to sing "Little Girl" – his third song of the evening – that his assailants rushed the stage. It is conceivable that the sight of a black singer crooning to his "little girl" conjured up the mythical black rapist of the white psyche and acted as the immediate trigger for the attack.

Certainly, Carter repeatedly stressed the threat to white womanhood posed by black music. *The Southerner* frequently featured pictures of inter-racial couples, often at dances or concerts. Invariably, these scandalous images were accompanied by suitably outraged captions, such as "THIS, IN ALABAMA!"[64] Cole himself was featured several times in such damning photographs. One picture depicted "COLE AND HIS WHITE WOMEN," another showed the singer signing autographs for a group of female white fans and bore the legend, "COLE AND YOUR DAUGHTER." "More than once," Carter noted, Cole has, "publicly degraded that which the white man holds most dear as the protector of his race – white womanhood."[65]

62. *Birmingham News*, 1 April 1956. In a curious inversion, which emphasizes the pervasiveness of the communist issue in mid–1950s America, Charlotte Wing Johnson, in condemning the attack on Cole, wondered if the white extremists responsible were themselves operating on orders from Moscow. "How pleased the Kremlin must be that some ignorant people make it so easy for them to keep turning Americans against each other. Are these people blind, dumb – or willing dupes." *Birmingham News*, 13 April 1956.

63. *Birmingham News*, 17 January 1956.

64. *The Southerner*, May 1956. See also *The Southerner*, March 1956; *The Southerner*, August 1956.

65. *The Southerner*, May 1956.

In August 1956, *The Southerner* also printed a publicity photograph featuring Cole seated at a piano, while white singer June Christy stood close behind, with her hands resting on his shoulders.[66] Regardless of the dangerous proximity of a white woman to a black man, this particular pose – the black man seated with a white woman standing behind in attendance – visually challenged the very core of southern sexual and racial etiquette. "How close are the Cole's and the innumerable negro entertainers bringing the white girl to the negro male?" Carter asked in the article accompanying the Christy-Cole photograph. "How many negroes have been encouraged to make advances to white girls and women, by the constant drumming of such propaganda into their minds?... You have seen it, the fleeting leer, the look that stays an instant longer ... the savagery, now, almost to the surface."[67]

Carter and other opponents of rock and roll employed precisely the same rhetoric and terms of emotional reference in their condemnations of the music that massive resisters used to decry integration. Horrified by what he had witnessed at the 11 March, "Rhythm and Blues, Rock and Roll" show at the Municipal Auditorium, Carter denounced rock and roll as, "sensuous negro music," which, "as the utter beast is brought to the surface," eroded, "the entire moral structure of man, Christianity, of spirituality in Holy marriage ... all the white man has built through his devotion to God: all this, was crumbled and snatched away, as the white girls and boys were turned to the level of animal." Rock and roll represented a physical and moral threat to white children, exposing them to "coarse negro phrases" and luring them into the dark world of black sexual depravity.[68]

Resorting to the sort of conspiracy theory so important to southern resisters, Carter accused the "communistic" NAACP of deliberately seeking to corrupt white teenagers with rock and roll music – remarks that prompted NAACP secretary, Roy Wilkins, to comment that, "Some people in the south are blaming us for everything from measles to atomic fallout."[69]

The day before the assault on Cole, the Woodlawn Citizens' Council, claiming the support of another seventy-three local Councils in Alabama, announced that they had "declared war on b-bop and Negro music," believing that, "it contributes to the moral degradation of children and serves the cause of integration." Ralph Edwards, chairman of the Woodlawn Committee, announced the intention of the Councils to

66. *The Southerner*, August 1956.
67. *The Southerner*, August 1956.
68. *The Southerner*, March 1956; Cater, "Civil War in Alabama's Councils," p. 19; McMillen, *The Citizens' Council*, pp. 54–55.
69. *New York Times*, 30 March 1956; also *Baltimore Afro-American*, 7 April 1956.

visit those in Birmingham responsible for playing the sort of music that "promotes integration of races and demoralizes children" and to protest the use of such music on the radio and at public gatherings.[70]

Denunciations of rock and roll increased after the attack on Cole. In late April, Carter gave an interview to Newsweek in which he explained, this time for the benefit of a national audience already anxious about the latest dating rituals associated with youth culture and bewildered by the staggering success of Elvis Presley, the intimate links between black-derived music and sexual abandon. "[Rock And Roll] is the basic heavy beat of Negroes," said Carter. "It appeals to the very base of man, brings out the animalism and vulgarity."[71]

On 8 May 1956, Carter and Ralph Edwards wrote to Mayor James Morgan to protest the continued use of the Municipal Auditorium "for indecent and vulgar performances by Africans before our white children." Urging the Birmingham City Commission to ignore the "left-wing, integration press, and integration pressure groups," the NACC demanded that Morgan and his colleagues, "make use of your offices and power to help maintain our standards of decency; our Anglo-Saxon heritage; our race and our Nation."[72]

This was not the first time that the use of the Municipal Auditorium provided a rallying point for segregationists. In 1938, Eugene "Bull" Connor insisted that the first meeting of the bi-racial Southern Conference for Human Welfare at the Auditorium observe strict segregation, while a city-wide referendum in the early 1950s rejected the idea of allowing integrated professional sports in that civic facility. Once again, in May 1956, concerned Birmingham whites looked to the Municipal Audiitorium and, more specifically, its policy concerning the staging of integrated rock and roll concerts, for signs of offical commitment to the preservation of Jim Crow.

Anxious citizens wrote to Mayor Morgan, Public Safety Commissioner Lindbergh and Fred McCallum, the manager of the Auditorium, demanding that civic authorities take the lead in resistance to integration. "The City of Birmingham does not need money badly enough to rent the Auditorium to negroes to entertain white people," insisted one petition, adding that, "There is not a negro singer nor a negro musician anywhere who does not at some time during his or her program sing or play 'suggestive' songs or music and become vulgar."[73]

70. *Birmingham News*, 9 April 1956.

71. *Newsweek*, 23 April 1956.

72. Ralph Edwards and Ace Carter, letter to Commissioner James Morgan, 8 May 1956, James W. Morgan, Mayoral Papers, Folder 3.27 (BPLA).

73. Mrs Mary B. Anderson *et al.*, letter to Mr James W. Morgan, 7 May 1956, James W. Morgan, Mayoral Papers, Folder 3.27 (BPLA).

One of the signatories of this petition, a self-professed "white American and a true Southerner," also wrote a separate letter to Morgan noting with horror that a "rock `n' roll show" was scheduled to play at the Auditorium on the 20 May. "It would be better to tear the Auditorium down than to use it for such purposes ... after one of these so-called shows the whole City of Birmingham needs a good disinfectant. Who is responsible? Will your conscience be clear? Do you sleep well at night?"[74]

Despite these protests, on 20 May two rock and roll concerts – one for blacks and one for whites – did take place at the Auditorium. Moreover, it was an integrated bill, featuring the Platters, LaVern Baker, Bo Diddley, Clyde McPhatter, and the kiss-curled white rock and roller Bill Haley. This time the organizers were careful to ensure that "the negro stars ... appeared first and were all off stage before the white groups came on," reflecting the widespread view that it was Cole's presence on stage with white artists that in part provoked the April assault.[75] By the end of 1956, however, the City Commissioners, while still resisting extreme demands to outlaw black performances for white audiences entirely, further tightened the regulations concerning events at the Auditorium to prevent exactly this sort of maneuver. In December, Fred McCallum was advised,

> not to book any shows, basketball games, or any other type of event that had mixed races in the personnel. However, if the personnel of the show, basketball game, or other event were all colored, including referees, officials, between game and between half performers, that this show, basketball game or other event could be presented to an all white audience at one performance and to an all Negro audience at a separate performance.[76]

NACC members were out in force on 20 May, picketing the afternoon, whites-only performance at the Auditorium and hoping once more to "call to the attention of white parents everywhere, that rock `n' roll, negroid animalistic music is being used to drive the white youth to the level of the negro."[77] The banners held by the demonstrators and the slogans chanted again illustrate the common ground between the attack

74. Barnes (first name illegible), letter to James W. Morgan, 11 May 1956, James W. Morgan, Mayoral Papers, Folder 3.27 (BPLA).

75. *Birmingham News*, 21 May 1956.

76. Fred McCallum, letter to Jack House, 4 December 1956, James W. Morgan, Mayoral Papers, Folder 3.27 (BPLA).

77. *The Southerner*, August 1956.

on rock and roll and the dominant themes in the southern ideology of Massive Resistance: "NAACP says integration, rock & roll, rock & roll"; "Jungle music aids delinquency"; "Churches must speak out against these anti-Christ forces."[78] Intriguingly, one of the pickets was none other than Carter's editor, Jesse Mabry, whose jail sentence for his part in the Cole assault, like those of his confederates, had apparently been commuted upon appeal to the fine that Michael Belknap mentions.

Another particularly revealing index to the rising tide of popular adult opposition to rock and roll in Alabama was the columns of Roger Thames, entertainment writer on the Birmingham News. In January 1956, Thames had even given Elvis Presley, later the epicenter of the national storm over rock and roll, a favorable review. Commenting on Presley's "I Forgot to Remember to Forget," Thames confessed he "was pleasantly surprised; he's got a good voice." Certainly, there was no hint of moral outrage in Thames' pronouncement that, "I don't Dig that type of music, which is not to say I don't think he's good."[79] By the spring of 1956, however, Thames' column regularly featured readers' letters that lamented that, "the air is filled with be-bop, blues, congo rhythms – all disgusting ... in my day this was considered `red light' music as it was supposed to excite the passion."[80]

Thames himself dismissed rhythm and blues and rock and roll as "an abomination" and described Presley's singing voice as "unintelligible – which is all right because the words he sings don't make sense."[81] Nevertheless, he actually avoided the most hysterical excesses of rock and roll's opponents and never personally succumbed to explicitly racist condemnations of the music. Instead, he did his bit for the preservation of civilized values by championing Doris Day's "Whatever Will Be Will Be" against the cacophony of Presley's "Hound Dog" and "Don't Be Cruel." The Day song, he insisted, was "a mighty pretty tune, and its heartening to see such a rose in a virtual field of thorns."[82] Thames continued the good fight by virtually deifying Perry Como. In a piece that speculated that Elvis Presley and Carl Perkins might be the same person, Thames was positively rhapsodic about Como's version of the "Lord's Prayer": "Listening to a number like that, you wonder what moves people to listen to rock and roll."[83]

78. *The Southerner*, August 1956. Jesse Mabry next come to public prominence for his part in the ritual castration of a black painter and decorator, Edward "Judge" Aaron, by Klan members in September 1957.

79. *Birmingham News*, 13 January 1956. See also *Birmingham News*, 2 January 1956.

80. *Birmingham News*, 4 March 1956.

81. *Birmingham News*, 6 May 1956.

82. *Birmingham News*, 25 September 1956.

83. *Birmingham News*, 4 April 1956.

This essay has sought to locate the outcry against rock and roll, of which the Cole attack was a paradoxical expression, within the context of a Massive Resistance campaign and its attendant ideology, which only really assumed major proportions in Alabama in early 1956. There were, however, other factors that help to explain the increasing concern about rock and roll in early 1956.

Perhaps the most crucial factor was the dramatic emergence of Elvis Presley as a national star of unprecedented proportions. Following his first national pop hit with "Heartbreak Hotel" in January 1956, Presley secured eleven chart hits, including five number ones, before the end of the year.[84] More crucially, he appeared, amidst much controversy, on a succession of prestigious, national network television shows, beginning with the Dorsey Brothers' Stage Show on 28 January. By the end of 1956, he had also appeared on the Steve Allen Show, the Milton Berle Show, and the Ed Sullivan Show, arousing adult anger and disgust with every swivel of his hips and curl of his lip. One television critic described Presley as "an unspeakably untalented and vulgar young entertainer," while *Look* magazine called Presley, "mostly nightmare. On stage his gyrations, his nose wiping, his leers are vulgar." Presley very soon became the most conspicuous target for those opposed to rock and roll. *Life* magazine, which had been able to report the new rock and roll craze with relative calm and equanimity in April 1955, had by the following summer branded Elvis "a disturbing kind of idol."[85] For many southern adults, the flagrant sexuality of his style seemed to confirm the debasing effects on a good, God-fearing, mother-loving country boy of over-exposure to black culture.

Presley's phenomenal success coincided with Senator Estes Kefauver's energetic chairmanship of the Senate Sub-Committee on Juvenile Delinquency, which excited public concern about youth, media, and morality to new heights. The connection between rock and delinquency, first suggested by the use of Bill Haley's "Rock Around the Clock" as the theme for the 1955 film *Blackboard Jungle*, became quite explicit. One troubled parent wrote to the Kefauver Committee, "His [Presley's] strip-tease antics threaten to `rock `n' roll' the juvenile world into open revolt against society. The gangster of tomorrow is the Elvis Presley type of today."[86]

Another important development in the rise of opposition to rock and roll, particularly relevant in a racial context, was the fact that whereas between mid–1954 and the beginning of 1956 anodyne cover versions

84. Whitburn, *Billboard U.S. Top Forty*, p. 217.
85. Quoted in Arnold Shaw, *The Rockin' 50s*, New York, 1974, p. 151; *Look*, 7 August 1956; *Life*, 18 April 1955; *Life*, 24 August 1956.
86. Cited in Gilbert, *Cycle of Outrage*, p. 18.

of black rhythm and blues hits sung by white artists such as Pat Boone, the McGuire Sisters, Gale Storm, Georgia Gibbs and their ilk had routinely outsold the black originals, from the spring of 1956, young whites increasingly rejected these white covers in favor of the black originals. In May 1956, *Billboard* noted that, "it certainly looks as though the public is beginning to show a decided preference for the originals – regardless of their origin" – which actually meant regardless of their racial origin.[87] Thus, Pat Boone's version of "Tutti Frutti" easily outsold little Richard's original in the winter of 1955/1956. The following May, however, Boone's version of "Long Tall Sally" failed to match the popularity of Richards' original with white audiences.

Ever since the first sustained crossover of black rhythm and blues records into the white popular music charts began with the Chords' "Sh-Boom" in the summer of 1954, most adult Americans had assumed – indeed, prayed – that rock and roll was but a passing fad. Alongside the rampant success of Presley and his many imitators, the growing acceptance of the original black recordings suggested that far from disappearing, the rock and roll aberration was actually gaining momentum. Moreover, the growing young white audience for black artists such as Chuck Berry, the Coasters, Fats Domino, and Little Richard merely emphasized the music's racial roots and intensified adult white concerns about its possible effects, particularly, if by no means exclusively, in the South.

One other phenomenon contributed to adult white opposition to rock and roll in the South. This was the rapid expansion of black-oriented broadcasting in the region after 1947, when WDIA in Memphis became the first American station geared exclusively to a black market. By 1956 there were twenty-two southern radio stations programmed entirely for a black audience and a further twenty-four in the region that broadcast more than thirty hours a week of black-oriented programming. Many more offered at least some black music.[88] Moreover, by 1956 it was clear that many young southern whites were also listening extensively, if often covertly, to these black-oriented programs. Radio had breached the walls of segregation, creating a huge prospective market for rhythm and blues and rock and roll, among white teenagers. For the remainder of the decade, opponents of rock and roll channeled much of their energy into various local and national attempts to purge the airwaves of the rock and roll nightmare.

---

87. *Billboard*, 5 May 1956; see also Jonathan Kamin, "The White Rhythm and Blues Audience and the Music Industry, 1952–56," *Popular Music and Society*, vol. 6, no. 2, 1978, pp. 150–67; Kamin, "Taking the Roll out of Rock and Roll: Reverse Acculturation," *Popular Music and Society*, vol. 2, no. 1, 1972, pp. 1–17.

88. *Broadcasting Yearbook*, vol. 52, February 1957, pp. 324–25 .

The attack on Nat King Cole represented a dramatic and extreme expression of the anxieties that afflicted white America in the mid–1950s and that fueled the campaign against rock and roll. More specifically, the Cole incident symbolized a particularly sensitive moment in Alabama's racial, political, and cultural affairs as whites groped for an acceptable and effective response to the desegregation crisis. If few condoned Carter's violence and extremism, many sought alternative means to similar ends.

It is similarly possible to interpret the black response to the affair as symptomatic of a quite specific moment in the development of the civil rights movement and its attendant consciousness. Once the immediate condemnations of redneck southern racism and violence had abated, black reaction to the Cole incident was generally one of anger and indignation directed against the singer himself. His attitude towards the whole affair had been resolutely conciliatory. "I can't understand it," he said. "I have not taken part in any protests. I haven't said anything about civil rights. Nor have I joined an organization fighting segregation. Why should they attack me?"[89]

Cole appeared eager to forgive and forget the whole incident, assuring the South that he bore no grudges and denouncing those trouble-making activists who sought to make political mileage from the incident. "There will be a few agitators who will keep it going a while but I'd just like to forget about the whole thing."[90] He defended his decision to play segregated dates, insisting that he, "was not intending to become a politician," but was, "crusading in my own way ... I don't condone segregation. But I can't change the situation in a day."[91]

Cole's moderation, self-professed political indifference, and continued willingness to play segregated shows drew sharply divergent responses from the white South and civil rights activists. White southerners applauded Cole as a black man who knew his place; one who had no intention of challenging the racial norms of the segregated South and who even echoed its deep concerns about outside agitators stirring up racial antagonism. This helps to explain southern eagerness to side with the hapless Cole and condemn his attackers. Blacks like Cole were not the problem and, in an age of burgeoning black militancy, were to be encouraged. "The conduct of Cole himself has been most commendable," noted the *Greensboro Daily News*. "He behaved himself throughout as a gentleman, refused to be made a martyr or to become the principal in a cause celebre."[92]

89. *Baltimore Afro-American*, 21 April 1956.
90. *Christian Science Monitor*, 12 April 1956 (SC-file: "Cole").
91. *Birmingham News*, 14 April 1956; *Raleigh News and Observer*, 14 April 1956.
92. *Greensboro Daily News*, 15 April 1956 (SC-File: "Cole").

Judge Ralph Parker, in sentencing Cole's attackers, reiterated those sentiments, portraying Cole as a model black southerner. "He has displayed an understanding of our customs and our traditions. He was born in Alabama. And he has conducted himself in a manner as to win the respect of his white friends in the South. He didn't violate any of our customs and our traditions, or any of our laws."[93]

Black activists, militant editors, and some white liberals meanwhile dismissed Cole's moderation as either culpable naivete or "Uncle Tomism" belonging to a by-gone era of black compliance and docility. An angry Thurgood Marshall, the NAACP's leading lawyer, reputedly commented that all Cole lacked was a banjo to complete his Uncle Tom role.[94] *The Chicago Defender* commented,

> The "King" was dead wrong for going into Birmingham under an arrangement whereby he played first to a white audience and then a Negro audience. It was an insult to his race and he should have known better. If he couldn't have played to a group of American citizens on an integrated basis, he just should have stayed out of Birmingham.[95]

The *Amsterdam News* was similarly scathing, commenting that Cole, "in a purely selfish desire to add to the money he already has, agreed to humiliate himself and his race and sell his talents under Jim Crow conditions."[96]

Further south, black press reaction was more measured, perhaps indicating a genuine fear of white reprisals should the papers try to use the Cole incident to stir up popular black activism against Jim Crow. The *Birmingham World*, for example, treated the affair very cautiously and avoided any direct censure of Cole's apoliticism or his appearance at a segregated date. Instead, the paper tried to draw encouragement from the aftermath of the attack, emphasizing the "commendable and fearless way the local police met the challenge to law," and the widespread white condemnation of the attack: "Significantly, an overwhelming majority at the affair exhibited their disapproval of the unwarranted, unprovoked attack on the entertainer. It happened in Birmingham, Alabama to the shame and regret of most of the citizens we believe."[97] Alabama journalist Joe Sewell, however, summed up black surprise that

---

93. Judge Ralph E. Parker, "Statement prior to sentencing defendants in Cole case," 18 April 1956, James W. Morgan, Mayoral Papers, 23.17: "Recorder's Court" (BPLA).
94. Cole, *Nat King Cole*, p. 125; Haskins, *The Man and His Music*, p. 140.
95. *Chicago Defender*, 21 April 1956.
96. *Amsterdam News*, 21 April 1956.
97. *Birmingham World*, 17 April 1956.

someone of Cole's stature was still playing segregated gigs in the Deep South and tacitly endorsing the Jim Crow system. "I could see it if he was struggling," Sewell commented, "but not for someone of Cole's eminence.[98]

In the radical, Chicago-based *Daily Worker*, black columnist Abner Berry articulated a similar sense of betrayal at Cole's appearance before a segregated audience, particularly in Alabama, which the Montgomery bus boycott and the Autherine Lucy case had made the most conspicuous battleground in the fight against Jim Crow. "For nearly five months now the 100,000 marching feet of Montgomery Negroes (two feet to a citizen) have been tapping a message to the world: `No compromise with the evil of segregation...,'But the famous Negro singer Nat `King' Cole, a native of Montgomery, seems not to have got the message." Berry charged that Cole's success with white audiences had made him indifferent to the plight of other blacks and the ravages of segregation: "he never worried about jimcrow laws or jimcrow customs. That was for the other guys." But, Berry urged, "There is no middle ground. Every Negro is part of the struggle, indeed every American is part of it – even one called Nat `King' Cole."[99]

Liberal white columnist Barry Gray of the *New York Post* and Roy Wilkins agreed with Berry on this point. Gray held that "When Cole said he `wasn't in politics' but was merely `an entertainer' he indulged in fanciful thinking. Everyone's `in politics,' particularly an entertainer who is a member of a minority group." Wilkins, meanwhile, wrote to Cole, urging him to join the civil rights movement. "Racism is one fight none of us can escape," he insisted.[100]

Cole was in an invidious position as criticism of his apolitical stance mounted. He had no desire to jeopardize his existing white record-buying and concert-going audience by adopting a conspicuously militant posture on the race issue. Moreover, in the spring of 1956 he was already campaigning for the network television show that he finally secured on NBC in November. It was clearly not in Cole's best commercial interests to court controversy. In any case, his natural tendency towards moderation and compromise made him an unlikely supporter of racial militancy.[101]

If personality and economic interests partly explain Cole's attitude after his attack, he and his subsequent apologists have offered another

98. *Baltimore Afro-American*, 21 April 1956.

99. *Daily Worker*, 29 April 1956 (SC-File:"Cole").

100. *New York Post*, 19 April 1956 (SC-File:"Cole"); *Birmingham News*, 14 April 1956.

101. Haskins, *The Man and His Music*, pp. 143–45; Cole, *Nat King Cole*, pp. 113–17. Bruce Crowther, "Jazz Life and Times: Nat King Cole," unpublished manuscript in possession of the author, pp. 83–89.

explanation for his muted public response to the Birmingham incident and to the race issue more generally. This explanation takes seriously Cole's own contention that he was campaigning in his own way against racial prejudice. In a May 1956 letter to *Downbeat* magazine, he hoped to clarify his position on civil rights. He insisted that, "I am, have been and will continue to be dedicated to the complete elimination of all forms of discrimination, segregation and bigotry." Written in response to the personal abuse that followed Birmingham, it is difficult to disentangle Cole's retrospective rationalizations from a genuine strategic commitment to challenging discrimination in particular way. Nevertheless, Cole insisted that he had, "fought, in what I considered an effective manner, against the evil of race bigotry through the years. I had hoped that through the medium of my music I had made many new friends and changed many opinions regarding racial equality."[102]

And, indeed, Cole could boast a genuine record of support for civil rights action. In his *Downbeat* letter, he proudly noted that he had performed a number of benefit concerts for the NAACP, contributed financially to several chapters of that organization, and donated to the Montgomery bus boycott.[103] While these were relatively anonymous expressions of support, in the late 1940s and early 1950s Cole had also taken very public stands against discrimination at several hotels and nightclubs where he had been scheduled to perform but was forbidden to use the establishment's facilities on account of his color. In September 1951, for example, he sued the owners of the Hotel Fort Armstrong in Rock Island for 62,000 dollars when he was refused a room. Moreover, in 1948, when Cole had moved into a new home in the all-white Hancock Park area of Beverly Hills, he bravely stood up to legal and extra-legal attempts by local whites to remove him.[104]

Carter was certainly aware of Cole's civil rights record and, in fact, tended to exaggerate it for his own purposes. Carter caricatured Cole as an uppity, militant, black agitator: "Nat `King' Cole has donated thousands of dollars over a period of years to the NAACP ... he is a `blockbuster'... forcing his way into a white neighborhood ... he once instituted a suit against a white hotel, forcing it to admit Negroes."[105]

Significantly, however, Cole's acts of conspicuous defiance to racial discrimination, all took place outside the South – in Los Angeles, Chicago, Rock Island, Las Vegas, and Pittsburgh. It was as if he was

102. Cole letter, *Downbeat*, 30 May 1956.
103. Ibid.
104. Haskins, *The Man and his Music*, pp. 77–83; Cole, *Nat King Cole*, pp. 105–12; Crowther, "Life and Times," pp. 69–71. Cole's move into Hancock Park provided the first real opportunity for Los Angeles whites to test the Supreme Court's 1948 ruling in *Shelley v. Kramer* forbidding federal and state courts to enforce restrictive covenants.
105. *The Southerner*, May 1956.

willing to challenge Jim Crow when it appeared beyond its "natural" boundaries and encroached upon the "Promised Land" of the North, but was able to accept and tolerate it, however reluctantly, as a peculiar feature of southern life. In the spring of 1956, as the civil rights movement confronted the evils of segregation and white racism in Jim Crow's own backyard, it was hardly surprising that Cole's moderation and pragmatism were interpreted as cowardice by many of those involved.

Black disillusionment with Cole's position quickly spread beyond a hostile press and the civil rights leadership. "Overnight, he has practically lost his Negro audience," claimed Abner Berry. The *New York Post* also observed the mounting black hostility to Cole, quoting an editorial in the *Baltimore Afro-American* that complained that he had "stabbed in the back" those fighting for civil rights and announced, "We don't want him in the South."[106] The *Amsterdam News* noted that, "thousands of Harlem blacks who have worshipped at the shrine of singer Nat King Cole turned their backs on him this week as the noted crooner turned his back on the NAACP and said he will continue to sing to Jim Crow audiences." Several Harlem establishments pledged to boycott Cole's records, removing them from their jukeboxes until the singer abandoned Jim Crow dates.[107]

Faced by this rising tide of economic and moral pressure from his own core black audience and stirred by the dictates of his own conscience, Cole capitulated. On 28 April 1956, the *Amsterdam News* reported the success of one of the less publicized black direct action campaigns of 1956 and announced that Nat King Cole had become a life member of the NAACP.[108]

106. *Daily Worker*, 29 April 1956 (SC-File: "Cole"); *New York Post*, 19 April 1956 (SC-File: "Cole").

107. *Amsterdam News*, 21 April 1956.

108. *Amsterdam News*, 28 April 1956.

Notes on Contributors

William Beinart teaches at the University of Bristol where he is Reader in the Department of Historical Studies. His books include *Putting a Plough to the Ground*, 1986, edited with Peter Delius and Stanley Trapido, and, with Colin Bundy, *Hidden Struggles in Rural South Africa*, 1987. His *Twentieth Century South Africa* is to be published by Oxford University Press in 1994. He has edited the *Journal of Southern African Studies*, including an issue on the politics of conservation.

Martin Crawford teaches American History at the University of Keele. His publications include *The Anglo-American Crisis of the Mid-Nineteenth Century*, 1987, and (ed.) *William Howard Russell's Civil War: Private Diary and Letters, 1861–1862*, 1992. He has contributed essays to the *Journal of Southern History*, *Civil War History*, *Slavery and Abolition*, and other journals. He is currently engaged on a study of a southern mountain community in the Civil War era.

Pete Daniel's publications include *The Shadow of Slavery: Peonage in the South, 1901–1969*, 1972; *Deep'n as it Come: the 1927 Mississippi River Flood*, 1977; *Breaking the Land: The Transformation of Cotton, Tobacco, and Rice Cultures since 1880*, 1985; and *Standing at the Crossroads: Southern Life in the Twentieth Century*, 1986. He has been Curator/Supervisor of the Division of Agriculture and Natural Resources at the National Museum of American History at the Smithsonian Institution since 1982.

Rick Halpern is Lecturer in American History at University College London. He has published articles on race and labor and is the author of *Down on the Killing Floor: Black and White Workers in Chicago's Packinghouses, 1904–1954* (forthcoming, University of Illinois Press) He is currently working on a study of working-class culture and politics in Progressive era Chicago.

Richard King is the author of *The Party of Eros*, 1972; *A Southern Renaissance: The Cultural Awakening of the American South 1938–1955*, 1980; and *Civil Rights and the Idea of Freedom*, 1992. His interests include Southern politics and culture, political and social thought, and intellectual history generally. He is Chair of the British

Association for American Studies. He is currently Reader in American Studies at the University of Nottingham.

Valeria Gennaro Lerda's many interests in U.S. history include populism, progressivism, and women reformers in the South. Her publications include *American Populism*, 1981; (ed.) *City and Country in the Gilded Age: Utopia and Reform in the United States*, 1986; *From Arcady to Reform, Essays in Southern History*, 1992; *'The Sound of Our Voices': Southern Women as Social Reformers, 1877–1920*, 1992. She has co-edited *The United States South: Regionalism and Identity*, 1991, and *Re-Writing the South, History and Fiction*, 1993. She is currently Professor of North American History at the University of Genoa, Italy.

Alex Lichtenstein received his Ph.D. in American Civilization from the University of Pennsylvania in 1990. He is currently an assistant professor of history at Florida International University in Miami, and will be a National Endowment for the Humanities Research Fellow in 1994–95. His articles and essays have appeared in the *Journal of Social History*, *Journal of Southern History*, *Radical History Review*, and *Reviews in American History*.

Melvyn Stokes teaches American History at University College London, where he has been convenor of the Commonwealth Fund Conference since 1988. His published articles are on reform movements of the late nineteenth century, American progressivism and the European left, and differing treatments of the liberal tradition in the US. He is currently completing a book on progressive thought in America in the period up to the First World War and co-editing a collection of essays on the nineteenth century 'market revolution.'

David Turley is Senior Lecturer in History at the University of Kent at Canterbury. He has written about fugitive slaves and the attitude of American abolitionists to government. His book *The Culture of English Antislavery, 1780–1860* was published in 1991. He is completing a book on slavery and working both on the development of an African American intelligentsia 1890–1930 and on the role of religion in American society and culture.

Brian Ward is Lecturer in American History at the University of Newcastle upon Tyne and Director of that institution's Martin Luther King, Jr. Memorial Conference series. He is currently completing a book on the politics of African American popular music during the Civil Rights and Black Power eras.

Index

Index

Baker, Ella 164, 172
Baker, LaVern 183, 200
Baldwin, James 159
banks 122
Bearing the Cross (Garrow) 164, 172
Beinart, William xiii–xiv
Belknap, Michael 201
    Law and Southern Order 182
Benson, Ezra Taft 96
    Cross-fire 94
Berlin, Ira 163
Berry, Abner 206, 208
Berry, Chuck 194, 203
Billings, Dwight x
The Black Aesthetic (Addison) 160
Black History and the History Profession
    (Rudwick and
    Meier) 161
Black Panthers 161
Black Workers and the New Unions
    (Cayton and Mitchell) 61
Blease, Cole L. 154
Boas, Franz 145, 152
Bonacich, Edna 55
Book, A.B. 84
Boone, Pat 203
bourgeoise
    contrasted to white working class 155
Bowron, James 32
Boxill, Bernard 169
Brazilian slavery vii
Breaking the Land (Daniel) 103
Breckenridge, Madeline McDowell 122,
    130–2
Breckenridge, Sophonisba 131
Brier, Stephen 48
Brody, David 44–5
Bromfield, Louis 117
Brown, Edward 168, 170
Brown, Joseph 22
Brown, Roy 183
Brown v Board of Education xvi, 187–9,
    196
Brown, Judge John R. 90–1, 93, 95
Buber, Martin 173
Bureau of Agricultural Economics 80
Bureau of Labor 16
business 147–8
Byrd, Senator Harry F. xvi

Campbell, Harry H. 14
Camus, Albert 159
Canada
    bans convict imports 30
capitalism

agribusiness 79, 88, 91–7, 101–4
    bourgeoisification of South 6–10
    transition from slavery 41–2
Caribbean slavery vii
Carmichael, O.C. 192
carpetbaggers viii
Carson, Clayborne 159
Carter, Asa 182, 190, 191–4
    anti-music campaign 197–9
    background 187
    view of Cole 207
Cayton, Horace and George Mitchell
    Black Workers and the New Unions 61
Cell, John 111
Chase, William 135
children
    reforms 130
Christy, June 183, 198
churches *see also* religion
    civil rights movement 75
    DuBois on 146–7
    social injustice 177–8
    unions 68, 75
    women and social reform 136–7
CIO *see* Congress of Industrial
    Organizations
Citizens' Council, New Orleans 187
Citizens' Council of Alabama 192
civil disobedience 169–71
    non-violence 166, 177, 179
Civil Rights Act of 1964 162
civil rights movement vii, xiii, 79
    agriculture 97–8, 104
    identity 163, 168, 179
    lessons for elsewhere 179–80
    militancy 157
    modern movement xvi–xvii, 162
    non-violence 166
    Rosa Parks 166
    sharecroppers 94
    unions 65, 74
Civil War ix, 3, 6–7, 21 *see also*
    Reconstruction
class
    agricultural oligarchy 86–90, 95, 97–8,
    102, 106–7
    bourgeois entrepreneurs ix–x
    historians' focus viii
    imaginary construct 165
    planter elite ix–x
Clay, Laura 131
Cleaver, Eldridge 161
Clevenger, Orliss 185–6
coal mining *see also* mining
    convict labor 3–6, 16–39

Index

Index

Harris, Abram 47
Harris, William H. 44
Harrison, Shelby 15–16
Hayes, J. True 95
health xii
*Health and Physique of the Negro
    American* (Atlanta
    University Studies) 148
Heath, Ted 183, 184
Hegel, George W.F. 173, 176, 178
Hill, Herbert 48–51
Hill, T.J. 3–4, 5, 17–18, 31
Holmes, William F. 135
House, M.H. 185
Houston, Charles Hamilton 162
Howard University Law School 162
Howe, Mark DeWolfe 175
Hughes, Charles Evans 155
Humphrey, Eddie 66, 74

Illinois
    coal mining 17
Immigration Commission 20
Industrial Workers of the World 43
industry x, xii, 116
    convict labor develops 4–5
    Prussian Road to industrialization
        7–10
intellectual history
    abandonment of dualism 165
    concept of freedom 167–71
    culture 167
    grassroots support 162, 171
    King's influences 171–9
    new social history 163–5
    revitalized culture 161–2
    roots of civil rights movement 159–62
International Union of Mine, Mill and
    Smelter Workers 67–8
Inzer, H.B. 196
Irish workers 60
iron industry 21–2
    convict labor 4–5
    development 10–14
    need for reliable workers 15–16
Irvin, Helen Deiss 123, 131

Jackson, George 161
Jackson, M.E. 85, 106
Janiewski, Dolores 63, 65
Jenkins, W.R. 85, 106
Jim Crow laws *see* segregation
jobs *see* employment
Johnson, Oscar 83
Johnson, Robert 81

Jones, G.R. 186
Jones, LuAnn 100
Jones, Ruby D. 72

Kearney, Belle 121, 122, 124–5, 133–6
Kefauver, Senator Estes 202
Kelley, William 11–12
Kelly, Leigh 95
Kelly, T.R. 83
Kentucky
    mining 17, 55
    women 123, 130–1
Kentucky Equal Rights Association 131
King, B.B. 183
King Jr, Martin Luther xvi, 166
    accused of communism 196–7
    childhood 178
    concept of freedom 168
    education 159
    "Letter from Birmingham Jail" 173
    Montgomery bus boycott 189
    processing of influences 171–9
King Sr, Martin Luther 175–6
King, Richard xvi
Kloppenberg, James 164
Knights of Labor 32, 48
Knoxville Iron Co. 22
Ku Klux Klan 9, 191

Labor in the New South (Marshall) 61
landowners
    agricultural oligarchy 86–8, 95, 97–8
    county committees 81–2
    local oligarchy 102, 106–7
    relations with sharecroppers 85–7, 106
    South Africa 117
Law and Southern Order (Belknap) 182
laws *see also* segregation
    all-white 83
    civil disobedience 169–71
    destruction of Jim Crow 162
    mediates class tension 82
    South Africa 114, 116, 118
    status of women 122–3
    women 133
Lawson, J.O. 96
Lears, T.J. Jackson 163, 164
Lee, Don L. 160
LeGuin, Magnolia Wynn 123
Lerda, Valerie xiv–xv
"Letter from Birmingham Jail" (King Jr)
    173
Lewis, John L. 56, 68
Lewis, John (SNCC) 168
Lewis, Ronald 51–3

Index

Index

Index

Index

hostility from Alabama 189–90
Swank, James 13
Systematic Theology (Tillich) 174

Taft, Philip 53
TCI *see* Tennessee Coal, Iron and
    Railroad
technology
    agriculture 79, 80, 93, 96, 102, 117
    incompatible with sharecroppers
        114–15
temperance xv, 122
    breaking womens' silence 124–5
    Felton and 126–8
    link to suffrage 127–8
    women's security 126–7
tenancy vii, xi, 105
    laws 84, 107
    natural development 9
    South Africa 113, 116–17
Tennessee
    agriculture 84
    convict miners 3, 17, 36–7
    industrial development 11–13
    road gangs 40
Tennessee Coal, Iron and Railroad (TCI)
        22–6
    biracial unions 67
    hagiography 40, 42
    sells to U.S. Steel 40, 41
    union conflicts over convict labor
        32–40
    unions 69
Terrell, Mary Church xv
Texas
    agriculture 84
    meatpackers 62, 73–4
textile industry x
Thames, Roger 201
Thomas, Lawrence 169
Thomas, Patty 183
Thompson case 108
Thoreau, Henry David 159
Thornton, J. Mills 162
Thurman, Howard 174
Thweat, B.W. 88–9, 106
Tillich, Paul 173
    Systematic Theology 174
Tillman, Benjamin Ryan 154
tobacco xii, 44, 72, 80, 91, 107
    allotments 92, 95
    unions 61–6
Tom Watson (Woodward) ix
trade unions *see* unions
The Tradesman 38

Trotter, Joe W. 51, 54–5, 56
Turley, David xv–xvi
Turner, Joe 183

Uncle Tomism 205
unions xi–xiii *see also* individual unions
    African Americans lack shop-floor
        power 71
    biracial tradition 44–76
    conflict over convict labor 15–16,
        20–1, 31–40
    end of discriminatory practices 72–4
    food and tobacco workers 61–6
    informal 18
    limited social equality 71–2
    longshoreman 55–60
    social and political equality 45
    traditional view of white racism 43–4
    white strikes 47
United Automobile Workers (UAW) 45
United Mine Workers Journal
    on convicts 16, 31, 33, 35, 37
    racial tension 49
United Mine Workers of America
    (UMWA) xi
    conflicts over convict labor 15–16,
        33–40
    Debardeleben and 26–7
    Gutman-Hill controversy 47–51
    integration 46
    racial tension 49
    split elections 50
    strikes 51–3
United Packinghouse Workers (UPWA) 65
United States Steel Co 69
    buys Tennessee Coal, Iron and
        Railroads (TCI) 40, 41
Urban League 45

vagrancy laws 8, 42
Vardaman, James Kimble 135, 148–9, 154
Vinson, E.R. 184, 185–6
Vinson, Willis 184, 185–6
Virginia
    lien laws 82
voting rights viii, xiv, 104, 162 *see also*
    suffrage
    federal or state 131–3
    qualifications 134
    women against African Americans 128
Voting Rights Act of 1965 162

wages
    African American miners 52
    women 129

Index

Wallace, Henry A. 86–7, 96
Ward, Brian xvi
Ward, Julia 134
Washington, Booker T. xv, 116
    DuBois and 150–1, 153
    union policies 44
Weiner, Jonathan x, 6
Wells, Ida B. xv
Welter, Barbara 136
West Virginia
    biracial unions 51
    coal mining 17
Westfall, David 92
Whitely, Dr. John 191
Whites, Ann Lee 127
Wilhoit, Francis 188, 194
Wilkins, Roy 198, 206
Willard, Frances 134
Williams, Patricia J. 79
Williamson, Joel x–xi
Wilson, T.K. 99
Wilson, Woodrow 132, 154–5
women
    breaking the silence 124
    labor studies 46

    laws 133
    political careers 135–6
    rape and racism 121, 128–9, 195, 197
    reformers xv
    social reform 121–37
    southern ideal 127, 129, 132, 133,
    136–7
    tobacco workers 63–4, 64–5
Women's Christian Temperance Union
    124, 125
    Felton and 126–8
    suffrage 128, 134
Woodard, Henry 100, 104
Woodlawn Citizens' Council 198
Woodman, Harold 107, 109
Woodward, C. Vann vii, xiv
    destruction of class 6–8
    Origins of the New South 8
    Tom Watson ix
Work, Monroe 145, 149
Works Projects Administration (WPA)
    69–70
World War I
    shift in employment attitudes 65–6
Wright, Gavin 109